ALSO BY JEANE J. KIRKPATRICK

THE NEW PRESIDENTIAL ELITE

POLITICAL WOMAN

LEADER AND VANGUARD IN MASS SOCIETY

DICTATORSHIPS
AND
DOUBLE
STANDARDS

Rationalism and Reason in Politics

❧ BY ❧

JEANE J. KIRKPATRICK

A TOUCHSTONE BOOK

Published by The American Enterprise Institute
and
Simon & Schuster, Inc.
NEW YORK

Designed by Christine Aulicino

Manufactured in the United States of America

1 3 5 7 9 10 8 6 4 2
3 5 7 9 10 8 6 4   Pbk.

Library of Congress Cataloging in Publication Data

Kirkpatrick, Jeane J.
Dictatorships and double standards.
Includes bibliographical references and index.
1. Dictators—Addresses, essays, lectures.
2. Totalitarianism—Addresses, essays, lectures.
3. Rationalism—Addresses, essays, lectures.
4. Democracy—Addresses, essays, lectures.
5. United States—Foreign relations—Addresses,
essays, lectures. 6. United States—Politics
and government—Addresses, essays, lectures.
I. Title
JC495.K57   321.9   82-5596
AACR2

ISBN 0-671-43836-0
ISBN 0-671-49266-7 Pbk.

For Douglas, John, Stuart
and Ricardo with love

Contents

Introduction

THEY CALLED IT PARTY REFORM and they based it on a theory of participatory democracy. Guided and inspired by that theory, a commission on party structure overhauled the Democratic party's nominating process, replacing party leaders with issue activists, organization men with zealots, Richard Daley with Jerry Rubin.

More than a decade has passed in which to observe the largely unintended consequences of the reform rules: it is, as the Marxists like to say, no accident that the two chairmen of the reform commission, George McGovern and Donald Fraser, have been retired from Congress by the voters of their states; no accident that the White House has been occupied by two outsiders in their own national parties, Jimmy Carter and Ronald Reagan; no accident that party leadership in Congress and the country is even weaker than a decade ago. The unintended consequences of the McGovern-Fraser reforms spread from the Democratic to the Republican party, from the presidential contest to the Congress, from the state parties to the rank and file, undermining leadership, exacerbating divisions, dissolving the ties that bind individuals into the groups we call political parties.

Today there is general if not universal agreement that the reform rules worked out badly. It will of course be less difficult to rewrite the rules than to undo their negative effects on this country's majority party and political system. The whole experience constitutes one more example of what, with due apologies to Whitehead, might be called the fallacy of misplaced malleability:

7

treating institutions as though they can be structured on demand to fit a master plan.

Examples abound. In Iran and Nicaragua the Carter administration and the State Department withheld economic aid, weapons, ammunition, and moral support and urged the departure of the Shah and Somoza because the administration had a theory that these acts would promote human rights and build democracy in those countries. It is not necessary to believe that the United States "lost" Iran and Nicaragua to understand that our policies failed to produce the expected consequences. Policymakers acted on the belief, widely held in enlightened circles, that there existed in Iran and Nicaragua moderate democratic groups which represented a progressive alternative to traditional and revolutionary extremes, and that the moderate groups had a good chance of achieving power. Get rid of rightist dictators, support the democratic Left, promote reform, preempt the radicals, build democracy and development: thus went the theory that gave us the Ayatollah Khomeini and the Ortega brothers. The Ayatollah's policies mocked Western expectations that this anti-American holy man was some kind of (moderate) saint, as Nicaragua's continuing militarization, Cubanization, and repression mock the expectations of the FSLN's democratic supporters. Once again, good intentions and a mistaken theory produced results as destructive as they were unintended.

Ideas have consequences, bad ideas have bad consequences.

This book is about the impact of ideas on politics. The essays collected here, written over two decades, have in common a concern with freedom and unfreedom. What kinds of ideas encourage and support democracy or tyranny? How are they institutionalized? Why and how do so many liberating revolutions go wrong? Why did the American Revolution produce constitutional democracy, while its eighteenth-century counterpart bred a reign of terror? Several of the essays deal with the impact of bad ideas on our political life and institutions.

"Dictatorships and Double Standards" describes how mistaken theories about development and democracy led U.S. policymakers astray. "U.S. Security and Latin America" examines the negative consequences for the United States, Central and South America of some other bad ideas concerning history, geography, development, and U.S. foreign policy; how a misconceived globalism left the nations of the hemisphere vulnerable to the "hegemonic presumptions" of Soviet rulers, how misconceived arms sales policies failed to "demilitarize" the hemisphere and succeeded only in diminishing U.S. influence. The two essays on totalitarianism describe the tragic consequences of mixing bad ideas and power in a coercive effort to transform man and society. "Dismantling the Parties" describes the unanticipated consequences of the Democratic party's efforts to reform itself on the basis of some unworkable ideas about representation.

"Sources of Stability in the American Tradition" takes a different perspective and discusses what went *right* when the Founding Fathers undertook to write a constitution for this country. It analyzes how the mixture of principles—similar to that advocated for a "mixed constitution"—can, just as Aristotle thought, produce a stable, constitutional system and framework for the good life. It is not self-evident that so sensible and creative a document could have been written today.

All times and places have their share of mistaken ideas and practices. Like violence and pestilence, old age and taxes, error and silliness are always with us because, while knowledge in fields like mathematics and science is cumulative, ideas about society and history change without getting better.

Our times seem especially hospitable to bad ideas, probably because, in throwing off the shackles of tradition, we have left ourselves especially vulnerable to untried nostrums and untested theories.

Tradition, to be sure, does not filter out bestial conceptions any more than it eliminates brutal practices. Human sacrifice, slavery, inquisitions, caste systems, have all been justified and preserved by a tradition. But traditional ideas have at least the merit of being integrally related to actual societies and social practices. However, in times of rapid change and mass communication, culture can become detached from its foundation in society and character. When a disjunction develops between ideas and experience, theories about human nature and history proliferate and flourish, become objects of fashion and faith, to be changed with changing styles, like hemlines, regardless of the evidence.

Ideas may be cut loose from experience in two senses: either they have no roots in experience, or they are not submitted to the test of experience. Either way, they are free to be foolish. They may postulate the most farfetched phenomena—unicorns, witches, universal disarmament, world government—without being regarded as impractical, especially among those who value change and innovation. But the most serious problem with theories ungrounded in experience is that they can never be tested: unless experience is the proof of the pudding, there is no proof. Thus, the fact no one has ever seen a unicorn will be taken to imply nothing about the existence of unicorns: tomorrow a whole herd may be spotted. The fact that no socialist system has proved effective at producing economic development does not prove that next year Tanzania, say, will not achieve a higher rate of growth and productivity than Singapore or Hong Kong. The fact that no political system has achieved perfect equality will not be taken to prove that no such society will be constructed. And the fact that there has never been in human history a society of purely altruistic people or one governed by all-wise rulers will not be interpreted to mean such societies are impossible. Once experience is eliminated, anything appears possible.

Thought set free from experience is unlimited by the constraints of experience or of probability. If history is not relevant, then the future is free from the past. Therefore, theories cut loose from experience are usually blindly optimistic. They begin not from how things are but how they ought to be, and regularly underestimate the complexities and difficulties concerning how you get there from here. They tend also to be abstract and unembarrassed by the need for empirical indicators of their major assumptions.

Failure to distinguish between the domains of thought and experience, of rhetoric and politics, is, of course, the very essence of rationalism. Rationalism encourages us to believe that anything that can be conceived can be brought into being. The rationalist perversion in modern politics consists in the determined effort to understand and shape people and societies on the basis of inadequate, oversimplified theories of human behavior. Not all theory is rationalist, not all reform suffers from rationalist fallacies. Rationalist theories are speculative rather than empirical and historical; rationalist reforms seek to conform human behavior to oversimplified, unrealistic models.

Rationalism not only encourages utopianism, but utopianism is a form of rationalism. Utopianism shares the characteristic features of rationalism: both are concerned more with the abstract than the concrete, with the possible than the probable, both are less concerned with people as they are than as they might be (at least as rationalists think they might be).

Confusing the domains of rhetoric and experience is the very essence of rationalism as I understand it. The rationalist approach to social thought fails to distinguish between ideas and institutions, between form and substance, between conceiving and realizing. Plato's *Republic* is a prototype of rationalist political philosophy. What is the just state? asks Socrates in the *Republic*. How can we construct one? A just society, he tells us, would be very different than Athens, its people would feel and think very differently than the people of Athens. In a just society, people would be assigned (by some all-wise ruler) a place in society on the basis of intelligence and talents, and would remain all their lives in their assigned roles, doing that for which they were (thought to be) fit by nature. A great myth about how God made some men of gold, some of silver, some of brass, would give divine sanction to the whole. A key assumption was that in planning a just society Socrates could start from scratch, moving people about at will—as if the subjects of his ideal state did not already exist in families, professions, economic classes; did not already have loves, hates, habits, temperaments, and ideas of their own that would cause them to resist being shuffled into new roles like so many cards being dealt into various piles. It is characteristic of the rationalist approach that Plato starts not from what is, not even from a sober consideration of what might be, but from a conception of perfection—what the really good society would look like—and never once doubted that he knew better than the people of Athens how they should live their lives.

In that assumption—that the architect of the scheme knows best—lies the affinity between rationalism and tyranny. There is not a perfect correlation, but there is a powerful tendency to move from the conviction that one *knows* the public good to the use of power to impose that good. Two problems are regularly associated with the rationalist assumption concerning the public good: one is the awful arrogance of assuming that one knows better what is good for the people than the people themselves; the other is that, because he is unconstrained by experience, the rationalist may identify public goods that are incapable of achievement.

When an unrealizable goal becomes the operational aim of an elite endowed with coercive power and a sense of righteousness, tragedy becomes more probable than progress. Historians may contemplate the irony of liberating revolutions that enslave, of brotherhood that ends at the guillotine, of equality enforced by a maximum ruler; the people, on the other hand, are left to suffer.

In the years since World War II, evidence has accumulated on the existence and operation of the Nazi death camps, on Soviet slave labor, on Pol Pot's murderous utopia—evidence that small bands of men who possessed the instruments of government could wreak mayhem and murder on large populations. Survivors provided the personal witness, subsequent decades the corroborative evidence of mass murder in our times.

Various morals leap out of these tales and archives: that man's capacity for brutality has resisted the civilizing influences of education, of democracy; that instead of taming man's capacity for evil, modern science has extended its reach; and that government and politics are desperately important activities worthy of our closest attention. Most important of all: *the defining quality of these twentieth-century tragedies is their roots in the deliberate decisions of persons who gained control over the instruments of government.*

"Licensed mass murder," someone called the extermination camps, emphasizing thereby their essential elements. A licensed act is sanctioned through authoritative processes; it is institutionalized and, within a given institutional structure, public and legitimate. The distinctive characteristic of the misery wreaked by Nazi and Soviet regimes on millions was precisely that it represented deliberate policy. The torturing, enslaving, freezing, starving, gassing, shooting, were not the acts of furtive madmen, but the purposive, collaborative action of thousands who had achieved in their societies a role of authority and access to the coercive power that is a defining characteristic of government. These authorities justified their policies—as authorities always do—by reference to a *public* purpose: a vision (however diabolic) of a public good that grants permission to torture, murder, and otherwise indulge aggressive instincts.

The fact that such evil can be carried out through politics or, conversely, that political acts can wreak such evil, suggests an affinity between politics and evil which has occurred to more than one observer: Rousseau, in the *Discourse on Inequality*, for example, presaged Marx's argument that the state is an instrument of repression whose purpose is to institutionalize exploitation and theft. In *Jonathan Wild*, Henry Fielding offered a parallel argument in fictional form: that politics is a process whereby private crime is transformed into public policy.

If we do precisely what the rationalist declines to do—look at experience with politics and evil—it becomes clear that, at least in the modern period, when great political evil occurred, coercion was employed in the service of a particular kind of rationalist political theory. I am not suggesting that rationalism *causes* totalitarianism but that the totalitarian impulse is grounded in the search—through power—for virtue, solidarity and perfect unity: the end of conflict, the end of the exploitation of man by man.

THOUGH THIS IS OFTEN DESCRIBED as a secular age characterized by the loss of faith, our times are remarkable above all for their credulity. Literate people, educated in science and experimental method, steeped in the assumptions of empiricism, not only hold beliefs which are not supported by evidence, but cling to views which vast accumulations of evidence have proven mistaken. There is, however, a significant difference between faith in our times and that in earlier centuries.

The core doctrines of traditional Christianity have lost their power to compel belief and order societies. In their place one finds political doctrines motivating men and policies. The most extraordinary fact about our times is the tenacity with which persons who pride themselves on being rational and scientific hold to a mystical faith in political propositions which are demonstrably false and unreasonable. A good example among the beliefs which have been repeatedly demonstrated to be false but which nonetheless continue to command the assent and faith of educated men of goodwill is the belief in absolute equality as an operational social good.

One of the most widespread notions of our age is that justice requires egalitarian allocations of wealth, opportunity, and other social goods. But although equality is the dominant passion of the age, no nation achieves it, no nation ever has. Not the Soviet Union, not China, not Cuba. None. The experience of this century's socialist revolutionary regimes suggests that equality is unachievable at any price and, moreover, that in regimes that try to achieve it, less wealth is produced, fewer comforts are available, and ordinary people are less free than in many other societies.

The reason doubtless is that so many of the inequalities among humans are rooted in nature and accident that it is quixotic to imagine they can be eliminated by government policy. It might be possible (though certainly very difficult) for government to equalize incomes, but not equality of opportunity, for that would require eliminating inequalities of beauty, strength, health, intelligence, size, and talent. A child with average intelligence and a clubfoot does not have the same chance as a strong boy with an IQ of 140. The society can provide good doctors to correct the clubfoot, but how can government protect against the psychic scars of early incompetence and pain? Against unloving mothers, allergies, bullies, slow wits, or sloth? The fact is that government cannot produce equality, and any serious effort to do so can destroy liberty and other social goods.

Equality is easy to conceive, literally impossible to realize. An even more striking example of the failure of political belief to yield to experience (that is, to empirical testing) is the belief that Marxist-Leninist revolutions will enhance the freedom and well-being of the people who endure them, will permit freedom and power-sharing among the people they govern.

The persistence of these beliefs is a different order of phenomenon than the persistence of basic tenets of Christian dogma in the two thousand years since the birth of Christ, different than the doctrines of any transcendental religion, because there is never definitive empirical evidence about supernatural events and relations (such as that Jesus Christ is the Son of God, that he ascended into heaven, or that whoever believes in him will not perish but have everlasting life). There is therefore no question of maintaining belief in the face of massive empirical evidence to the contrary.

But the political, social, and economic events that occur where Marxist-Leninists rule are matters of fact, facts which are, moreover, readily available, and have been replicated in every country which has had the misfortune to experience a liberating Communist revolution. The list of such countries is now long: the Soviet Union, Latvia, Lithuania, Estonia, Poland, Czechoslovakia, Albania, East Germany, Yugoslavia, Cuba, Vietnam, Korea, Cambodia, China, Laos, Yemen, Ethiopia, Angola, Mozambique, Guinea-Bissau, Benin, Nicaragua, Grenada. And in not one country where a Communist revolution has occurred have the citizens been permitted free elections, a free press, trade unions, free speech, and freedom to emigrate without official obstacles. In not one country where Communists have come to power have the "objective" conditions ever been judged such that the "vanguard" could safely turn over to the "toiling masses" control of their government, economy, society—control, that is, over their lives. Not all Communist governments feature slave labor, forced migrations, engineered famines, and forced separation of families of the sort that have at some time characterized the Soviet Union, Cambodia, Afghanistan. Not all have, after the fashion of Stalin or Castro, imprisoned tens of thousands of political prisoners. But none has produced either freedom or development. Not one has evolved into a democracy. Not one.

Despite the various iron curtains—electronic, political, physical—with which Communist rulers try to keep information in (and information out), knowledge of political repression, social regimentation, and economic failure is widely, easily available everywhere. But the faith that Communism is progressive—a good thing—and the hope that each new Marxist-Leninist triumph will turn out well persist. Many liberals who had great expectations for the humane "nationalists" and "agrarian reformers" of China, Cuba, Vietnam, Cambodia, and the Sandinistas now pin their hopes on Salvador's guerrilla coalition. And already we are beginning to hear marvelous accounts of Guatemala's "indigenous agrarian reformers."

"Is it then possible or impossible to transmit the experience of those who have suffered to those who have yet to suffer?" Solzhenitsyn asked.

Can one part of humanity learn from the bitter experience of another or can it not? Is it possible or impossible to warn someone of danger?

How many witnesses have been sent to the West in the last 60 years? . . . How many immigrants? How many millions of persons? They are all here. You meet them every day. You know what they are: if not by their spiritual disorientation, their grief, their melancholy, then you can distinguish them by their accents, by their external appearance. Coming from different countries and without consulting with one another, they have brought you exactly the same experience; they tell you exactly the same thing, they warn you of what is already happening, what has happened in the past.

How can it be that persons so deeply committed to the liberation of South Vietnam and Cambodia from Generals Thieu and Lon Nol were so little affected by the enslavement that followed their liberation? Why was there so little anguish among the American accomplices who helped Pol Pot to power? Why was there so little consternation when Viet Cong victory led not to liberation and development in the South but to mass deportations, slave labor, and chaotic privation?

Why are Western liberals—who often are such smart people —such slow learners about Communism?

Since the evidence is overwhelming that Marxist-Leninists everywhere impose economic systems that do not produce goods and political systems that do not produce loyalty, the continuing appeal of each new variant to men and women of goodwill can be explained only by fundamental cultural predispositions that condition the response to the political world.

Those predispositions lie, I believe, in the rationalist spirit of the age, that spirit that assumes that human nature in the future may be qualitatively different than in the past, that views non-rational factors such as sentiment, habit, and custom as obstacles that should and can be overcome, the spirit that views each situation as a *tabula rasa* on which a plan can be imposed and therefore sees experience in other times and places as having no relevance. Intention becomes more important than experience, intelligence more important than custom. The rationalist spirit takes no note of the fact that institutions are patterned human behavior that exist and function through the people of a society, and that radically changing institutions means radically changing the lives of people who may not want their lives changed. Because it assumes that man and society can be brought to conform to a preferred plan, the rationalist orientation tends powerfully to see everything as possible and prospects for progress as unlimited. When we forget, or willfully choose to ignore, the intractability of human behavior, the complexity of human institutions, and the probability of unanticipated consequences, we do so at great risk, and often immense human cost. In its various manifestations, that is the theme of this volume.

DICTATORSHIPS
AND
DOUBLE
STANDARDS

❦ I ❧
RATIONALISM
IN
FOREIGN
AFFAIRS

Dictatorships and Double Standards

THE FAILURE OF the Carter administration's foreign policy is now clear to everyone except its architects, and even they must entertain private doubts from time to time about a policy whose crowning achievement was to lay the groundwork for a transfer of the Panama Canal from the United States to a swaggering Latin dictator of Castroite bent. While Carter was President there occurred a dramatic Soviet military buildup, matched by the stagnation of American armed forces, and a dramatic extension of Soviet influence in the Horn of Africa, Afghanistan, southern Africa, and the Caribbean, matched by a declining American position in all these areas. The United States never tried so hard and failed so utterly to make and keep friends in the Third World.

As if this were not bad enough, in one year, 1979, the United States suffered two other major blows—in Iran and Nicaragua—of large and strategic significance. In each country, the Carter administration not only failed to prevent the undesired outcome, but actively collaborated in the replacement of moderate autocrats friendly to American interests with less friendly autocrats of extremist persuasion. It is too soon to be certain about what kind of regime will ultimately emerge in either Iran or Nicaragua, but accumulating evidence suggests that in both countries things are as

23

likely to get worse as to get better. The Sandinistas in Nicaragua appear to be as skillful in consolidating power as the Ayatollah Khomeini is inept, and leaders of both revolutions display an intolerance and arrogance that do not bode well for the peaceful sharing of power or the establishment of constitutional governments, especially since those leaders have made clear that they have no intention of seeking either.

There were, of course, significant differences in the relations between the United States and each of these countries during the past two or three decades. Oil, size, and proximity to the Soviet Union gave Iran greater economic and strategic import than any Central American "republic," and closer relations were cultivated with the Shah, his counselors, and family than with President Somoza, his advisers, and family. Relations with the Shah were probably also enhanced by our approval of his manifest determination to modernize Iran regardless of the effects of modernization on traditional social and cultural patterns (including those which enhanced his own authority and legitimacy). And, of course, the Shah was much better-looking and altogether more dashing than Somoza; his private life was much more romantic, more interesting to the media, popular and otherwise. Therefore, Americans were more aware of the Shah than of the equally tenacious Somoza.

But even though Iran was rich, blessed with a product the United States and its allies needed badly, and led by a handsome king, while Nicaragua was poor and rocked along under a long-tenure president of less striking aspect, there were many similarities between the two countries and our relations with them. Both these small nations were led by men who had not been selected by free elections, who recognized no duty to submit themselves to searching tests of popular acceptability. Both did tolerate limited opposition, including opposition newspapers and political parties, but both were also confronted by radical, violent opponents bent on social and political revolution. Both rulers, therefore, sometimes invoked martial law to arrest, imprison, exile, and occasionally, it was alleged, torture their opponents. Both relied for public order on police forces whose personnel were said to be too harsh, too arbitrary, and too powerful. Each had what the American press termed "private armies," which is to say, armies pledging their allegiance to the ruler rather than the "constitution" or the "nation" or some other impersonal entity.

In short, both Somoza and the Shah were, in central ways, traditional rulers of semitraditional societies. Although the Shah very badly wanted to create a technologically modern and powerful nation and Somoza tried hard to introduce modern agricultural methods, neither sought to reform his society in the light of any abstract idea of social justice or political virtue. Neither attempted to alter significantly the distribution of goods, status, or power (though the democratization of education and skills that accompanied modernization in Iran did result in some redistribution of money and power there).

Both Somoza and the Shah enjoyed long tenure, a large personal fortune (much of which was no doubt appropriated from general revenues), and good relations with the United States. The Shah and Somoza were not only anti-Communist, they were positively friendly to the United States, sending their sons and others to be educated in our universities, voting with us in the United Nations, and regularly supporting American interests and positions even when these entailed personal and political cost. The embassies of both governments were active in Washington social life, and were frequented by powerful Americans who occupied major roles in this nation's diplomatic, military, and political life. And the Shah and Somoza themselves were both welcome in Washington, and had many American friends.

Though each of the rulers was from time to time criticized by American officials for violating civil and human rights, the fact that the people of Iran and Nicaragua only intermittently enjoyed the rights accorded to citizens in the Western democracies did not prevent successive administrations from granting—with the necessary approval of successive Congresses—both military and economic aid. In the case of both Iran and Nicaragua, tangible and intangible tokens of American support continued until these regimes became the object of a major attack by forces explicitly hostile to the United States.

But once an attack was launched by opponents bent on destruction, everything changed. The rise of violent opposition in Iran and Nicaragua set in motion a succession of events which bore a suggestive resemblance to one another and a suggestive similarity to our behavior in China before the fall of Chiang Kai-shek, in Cuba before the triumph of Castro, in certain crucial periods of the Vietnam War, and more recently, in Angola. In each of these countries, the American effort to impose liberalization and democratization on a government confronted with violent internal opposition not only failed, but actually assisted the coming to power of new regimes in which ordinary people enjoy fewer freedoms and less personal security than under the previous autocracy—regimes, moreover, hostile to American interests and policies.

The pattern is familiar enough: an established autocracy with a record of friendship with the United States is attacked by insurgents, some of whose leaders have long ties to the Communist movement, and most of whose arms are of Soviet, Chinese, or Czechoslovak origin. The "Marxist" presence is ignored and/or minimized by American officials and by the elite media on the ground that U.S. support for the dictator gives the rebels little choice but to seek aid "elsewhere." Violence spreads and American officials wonder aloud about the viability of a regime that "lacks the support of its own people." The absence of an opposition party is deplored, and civil rights violations are reviewed. Liberal columnists question the morality of continuing aid to a "rightist dictatorship" and provide assurances concerning the essential moderation of some insurgent leaders who "hope" for some sign that the United States will remember its own revolutionary origins. Requests for help from the beleaguered autocrat go unheeded, and the argument is increasingly voiced that ties should be established with rebel leaders "before it is too late." The President, delaying U.S. aid, appoints a special emissary who confirms the deterioration of the government position and its diminished capacity to control the situation, and recommends various measures for "strengthening" and "liberalizing" the regime, all of which involve diluting its power.

The emissary's recommendations are presented in the context of a growing clamor for American disengagement on grounds that continued involvement confirms our status as an agent of imperialism, racism, and reaction; is inconsistent with support for human rights; alienates us from the "forces of democracy"; and threatens to put the United States once more on the side of history's "losers." This chorus is supplemented daily by interviews with returning missionaries and "reasonable" rebels.

As the situation worsens, the President assures the world that the United States desires only that the "people choose their own form of government"; he blocks delivery of all arms to the government and undertakes negotiations to establish a "broadly based" coalition headed by a "moderate" critic of the regime who, once elevated, will move quickly to seek a "political" settlement to the conflict. Should the incumbent autocrat prove resistant to American demands that he step aside, he will be readily overwhelmed by the military strength of his opponents, whose patrons will have continued to provide sophisticated arms and advisers at the same time the United States cuts off military sales. Should the incumbent be so demoralized as to agree to yield power, he will be replaced by a "moderate" of American selection. Only after the insurgents have refused the proffered political solution and anarchy has spread throughout the nation will it be noticed that the new head of government has no significant following, no experience at governing, and no talent for leadership. By then, military commanders, no longer bound by loyalty to the chief of state, will depose the faltering "moderate" in favor of a fanatic of their own choosing.

In either case, the United States will have been led by its own misunderstanding of the situation to assist actively in deposing an erstwhile friend and ally and installing a government hostile to American interests and policies in the world. At best we will have lost access to friendly territory. At worst the Soviets will have gained a new base. And everywhere our friends will have noted that the United States cannot be counted on in times of difficulty and our enemies will have observed that American support provides no security against the forward march of history.

No particular crisis conforms exactly with the sequence of events described above; there are always variations on the theme. In Iran, for example, the Carter administration—and the President himself—offered the ruler support for a longer time, though by December 1978 the President was acknowledging that he did not know if the Shah would survive, adding that the United States would not get "directly involved." Neither did the United States ever call publicly for the Shah's resignation. However, the President's special emissary, George Ball, "reportedly concluded that the Shah cannot hope to maintain total power and must now bargain with a moderate segment of the opposition" and was "known to have discussed various alternatives that would effectively ease the Shah out of total power" (*Washington Post*, December 15, 1978). There is, furthermore, not much doubt that the United States assisted the Shah's departure and helped arrange the succession of Bakhtiar. In Iran, the Carter administration's commitment to nonintervention proved stronger than strategic considerations or national pride. What the rest of the world regarded as a stinging American defeat, the U.S. government saw as a matter to be settled by Iranians. "We personally prefer that the Shah maintain a major role in the government," the President acknowledged, "but that is a decision for the Iranian people to make."[1]

Events in Nicaragua also departed from the scenario presented above, both because the Cuban and Soviet roles were clearer and because U.S. officials were more intensely and publicly working against Somoza. After the Somoza regime had defeated the first wave of Sandinista violence, the United States ceased aid, imposed sanctions, and took other steps which undermined the status and the credibility of the government in domestic and foreign affairs. Between the murder of ABC correspondent Bill Stewart by a National Guardsman in early June and the Sandinista

victory in late July 1979, the U.S. State Department assigned
new ambassador who refused to submit his credentials to Somoza
even though Somoza was still chief of state, and called for replacing the government with a "broadly based provisional government
that would include representatives of Sandinista guerrillas."[2]
Americans were assured by Assistant Secretary of State Viron
Vaky that "Nicaraguans and our democratic friends in Latin
America have no intention of seeing Nicaragua turned into a second Cuba,"[3] even though the State Department knew that the top
Sandinista leaders had close personal ties and were in continuing
contact with Havana, and, more specifically, that a Cuban secret-police official, Julian Lopez, was frequently present in the Sandinista headquarters and that Cuban military advisers were present
in Sandinista ranks.

In a manner uncharacteristic of the Carter administration,
which generally seemed willing to negotiate anything with anyone
anywhere, the U.S. government adopted an oddly uncompromising
posture in dealing with Somoza. "No end to the crisis is possible,"
said Vaky, "that does not start with the departure of Somoza from
power and the end of his regime. No negotiation, mediation, or
compromise can be achieved any longer with a Somoza government. The solution can only begin with a sharp break from the
past."[4] Trying hard, we not only banned all American arms sales
to the government of Nicaragua but pressured Israel, Guatemala,
and others to do likewise—all in the name of ensuring a "democratic" outcome. Finally, as the Sandinista leaders consolidated
control over weapons and communications, banned opposition,
and took off for Cuba, President Carter warned us against attributing this "evolutionary change" to "Cuban machinations" and
assured the world that the United States desired only to "let the
people of Nicaragua choose their own form of government."

Yet despite all the variations, the Carter administration
brought to the crises in Iran and Nicaragua several common assumptions each of which played a major role in hastening the
victory of even more repressive dictatorships than had been in
place before. These were, first, the belief that there existed at the

moment of crisis a democratic alternative to the incumbent government; second, the belief that the continuation of the status quo was not possible; third, the belief that any change, including the establishment of a government headed by self-styled Marxist revolutionaries, was preferable to the present government. Each of these beliefs was (and is) widely shared in the liberal community generally. Not one of them can withstand close scrutiny.

Although most governments in the world are, as they always have been, autocracies of one kind or another, no idea holds greater sway in the mind of educated Americans than the belief that it is possible to democratize governments, anytime, anywhere, under any circumstances. This notion is belied by an enormous body of evidence based on the experience of dozens of countries which have attempted with more or less (usually less) success to move from autocratic to democratic government. Many of the wisest political scientists of this and previous centuries agree that democratic institutions are especially difficult to establish and maintain—because they make heavy demands on all portions of a population and because they depend on complex social, cultural, and economic conditions.

Two or three decades ago, when Marxism enjoyed its greatest prestige among American intellectuals, it was the economic prerequisites of democracy that were emphasized by social scientists. Democracy, they argued, could function only in relatively rich societies with an advanced economy, a substantial middle class, and a literate population, but it could be expected to emerge more or less automatically whenever these conditions prevailed. Today, this picture seems grossly oversimplified. While it surely helps to have an economy strong enough to provide decent levels of well-being for all, and "open" enough to provide mobility and encourage achievement, a pluralistic society and the right kind of political culture—and time—are even more essential.

In his essay *Representative Government*, John Stuart Mill identified three fundamental conditions which the Carter administration would do well to ponder. These are: "One, that the people should be willing to receive it [representative government]; two, that they should be willing and able to do what is necessary for its preservation; three, that they should be willing and able to fulfill the duties and discharge the functions which it imposes on them."[5]

Fulfilling the duties and discharging the functions of representative government make heavy demands on leaders and citizens, demands for participation and restraint, for consensus and compromise. It is not necessary for all citizens to be avidly interested in politics or well informed about public affairs—although far more widespread interest and mobilization are needed than in autocracies. What *is* necessary is that a substantial number of citizens think of themselves as participants in society's decision-making and not simply as subjects bound by its laws. Moreover, leaders of all major sectors of the society must agree to pursue power only by legal means, must eschew (at least in principle) violence, theft, and fraud, and must accept defeat when necessary. They must also be skilled at finding and creating common ground among diverse points of view and interests, and correlatively willing to compromise on all but the most basic values.

In addition to an appropriate political culture, democratic government requires institutions strong enough to channel and contain conflict. Voluntary, nonofficial institutions are needed to articulate and aggregate diverse interests and opinions present in the society. Otherwise, the formal government institutions will not be able to translate popular demands into public policy.

In the relatively few places where they exist, democratic governments have come into being slowly, after extended prior experience with more limited forms of participation during which leaders have reluctantly grown accustomed to tolerating dissent and opposition, opponents have accepted the notion that they may defeat but not destroy incumbents, and people have become aware of government's effects on their lives and of their own possible effects on government. Decades, if not centuries, are normally required for people to acquire the necessary disciplines and habits. In Britain, the road from the Magna Carta to the Act of Settlement, to the great Reform Bills of 1832, 1867, and 1885, took seven centuries to traverse. American history gives no better grounds for believing that democracy comes easily, quickly, or for the asking. A war of independence, an unsuccessful constitution, a civil war, a long process of gradual enfranchisement, marked our progress toward constitutional democratic government. The French path was still more difficult. Terror, dictatorship, monarchy, instability, and incompetence followed on the revolution that was to usher in a millennium of brotherhood. Only in the twentieth century did the democratic principle finally gain wide acceptance in France, and not until after World War II were the principles of order and democracy, popular sovereignty and authority, finally reconciled in institutions strong enough to contain conflicting currents of public opinion.

Although there is no instance of a revolutionary "socialist" or Communist society being democratized, right-wing autocracies do sometimes evolve into democracies—given time, propitious economic, social, and political circumstances, talented leaders, and a strong indigenous demand for representative government. Something of the kind is in progress on the Iberian Peninsula, and the first steps have been taken in Brazil. Something similar could conceivably have also occurred in Iran and Nicaragua if contestation and participation had been more gradually expanded.

But it seems clear that the architects of Carter's foreign policy had little idea of how to go about encouraging the liberalization of an autocracy. In neither Nicaragua nor Iran did they realize that the only likely result of an effort to replace an incumbent autocrat with one of his moderate critics or a "broad-based coalition" would be to sap the foundations of the existing regime without moving the nation any closer to democracy. Yet this outcome was entirely predictable. Authority in traditional autocracies is transmitted through personal relations: from the ruler to his close associates (relatives, household members, personal friends), and from them to people to whom the associates are related by personal ties resembling their own relation to the ruler. The fabric of authority unravels quickly when the power and status of the men at the top are undermined or eliminated. The longer the autocrat has held power and the more pervasive his personal influence, the more dependent a nation's institutions will be on him. Without him, the organized life of the society will collapse, like an arch from which the keystone has been removed. The blend of qualities that bound the Iranian Army to the Shah or the National Guard to Somoza is typical of the relationships—personal, hierarchical, nontransferable—that support a traditional autocracy. The speed with which armies collapse, bureaucracies abdicate, and social structures dissolve once the autocrat is removed frequently surprises American policymakers and journalists accustomed to public institutions based on universalistic norms rather than particularistic relations.

The failure to understand these relations is one source of the failure of U.S. policy in recent administrations. There are others. In Iran and Nicaragua (as previously in Vietnam, Cuba, and China), Washington overestimated the political diversity of the opposition, especially the strength of "moderates" and "democrats" in the opposition movement; underestimated the strength and intransigence of radicals in the movement; and misestimated the nature and extent of American influence on both the government and the opposition.

Confusion concerning the character of the opposition, especially its intransigence and will to power, leads regularly to downplaying the amount of force required to counteract its violence. In neither Iran nor Nicaragua did the United States adequately appreciate the government's problem in maintaining order in a society confronted with an ideologically extreme opposition. Yet the presence of such groups was well known. The State Department's 1977 report on human rights described an Iran confronted

with a small number of extreme rightist and leftist terrorists operating within the country. There is evidence that they have received substantial foreign support and training . . . [and] have been responsible for the murder of Iranian government officials and Americans . . .[6]

The same report characterized Somoza's opponents in the following terms:

> A guerrilla organization known as the Sandinista National Liberation Front (FSLN) seeks the violent overthrow of the government, and has received limited support from Cuba. The FSLN carried out an operation in Managua in December 1974, killing four people, taking several officials hostage . . . since then, it continues to challenge civil authority in certain isolated regions.[7]

In 1978, the State Department's report said that Sandinista violence was continuing—after the state of siege had been lifted by the Somoza government.

When U.S. policymakers and large portions of the liberal press interpret insurgency as evidence of widespread popular discontent and a will to democracy, the scene is set for disaster. For if civil strife reflects a popular demand for democracy, it follows that a "liberalized" government will be more acceptable to "public opinion."

Thus, in the hope of strengthening a government, U.S. policymakers are led, mistake after mistake, to impose measures almost certain to weaken its authority. Hurried efforts to force complex and unfamiliar political practices on societies lacking the requisite political culture, tradition, and social structures not only fail to produce desired outcomes; if they are undertaken at a time when the traditional regime is under attack, they actually facilitate the job of the insurgents.

Vietnam presumably taught us that the United States could not serve as the world's policeman; it should also have taught us the dangers of trying to be the world's midwife to democracy when the birth is scheduled to take place under conditions of guerrilla war.

If the Carter administration's actions in Iran and Nicaragua reflect the pervasive and mistaken assumption that one can easily locate and impose democratic alternatives to incumbent autocracies, they also reflect the equally pervasive and equally flawed belief that change per se in such autocracies is inevitable, desirable, and in the American interest. It is this belief which induced the Carter administration to participate actively in the toppling of non-Communist autocracies while remaining passive in the face of Communist expansion.

At the time the Carter administration came into office it was widely reported that the President had assembled a team who shared a new approach to foreign policy and a new conception of the national interest. The principal elements of this new approach were said to be two: the conviction that the cold war was over, and the conviction that, this being the case, the United States should give priority to North-South problems and help less developed nations achieve their own destiny.

More is involved in these changes than meets the eye. For, unlikely as it may seem, the foreign policy of the Carter administration was guided by a relatively full-blown philosophy of history which includes, as philosophies of history always do, a theory of social change, or, as it is currently called, a doctrine of modernization. Like most other philosophies of history that have appeared in the West since the eighteenth century, the Carter administration's doctrine predicted progress (in the form of modernization for all societies) and a happy ending (in the form of a world community of developed, autonomous nations).

The administration's approach to foreign affairs was clearly foreshadowed in Zbigniew Brzezinski's 1970 book on the U.S. role in the "technetronic era," *Between Two Ages.* In that book, Brzezinski showed that he had the imagination to look beyond the cold war to a brave new world of global politics and interdependence. To deal with that new world a new approach was said to be "evolving," which Brzezinski designated "rational humanism." In the new approach, the "preoccupation" with "national supremacy" would give way to "global" perspectives, and international problems would be viewed as "human issues" rather than as "political confrontations." The traditional intellectual framework for dealing

with foreign policy would have to be scrapped: "Today, the old
framework of international politics . . . with their spheres of influence, military alliances between nation states, the fiction of sovereignty, doctrinal conflicts arising from 19th-century crises—is
clearly no longer compatible with reality."[8]

Only the "delayed development" of the Soviet Union, "an
archaic religious community that experiences modernity existentially but not quite yet normatively," prevented wider realization of
the fact that the end of ideology was already here. For the United
States, Brzezinski recommended "a great deal of patience," a more
detached attitude toward world revolutionary processes, and a less
anxious preoccupation with the Soviet Union. Instead of engaging
in ancient diplomatic pastimes, we should make "a broader effort
to contain the global tendencies toward chaos," while assisting the
processes of change that will move the world toward the "community of developed nations."

The central concern of Brzezinski's book, as of the Carter administration's foreign policy, is with the modernization of the
Third World. From the beginning, the administration has manifested a special, intense interest in the problems of the so-called
Third World. But instead of viewing international developments in
terms of the American national interest, as national interest is
historically conceived, the architects of administration policy have
viewed them in terms of a contemporary version of the same idea
of progress that has traumatized Western imaginations since the
Enlightenment.

In its current form, the concept of modernization involves
more than industrialization, more than "political development"
(whatever that is). It is used instead to designate "the process
through which a traditional or pre-technological society passes as
it is transformed into a society characterized by machine technology, rational and secular attitudes, and highly differentiated social
structures."[9] Condorcet, Comte, Hegel, Marx, and Weber are all
present in this view of history as the working-out of the idea of
modernity.

The crucial elements of the modernization concept have been

clearly explicated by Samuel P. Huntington (who, despite a period at the National Security Council, was assuredly not the architect of the administration's policy). The modernization paradigm, Huntington has observed, postulates an ongoing process of change: complex, because it involves all dimensions of human life in society; systemic, because its elements interact in predictable, necessary ways; global, because all societies will, necessarily, pass through the transition from traditional to modern; lengthy, because time is required to modernize economic and social organization, character, and culture; phased, because each modernizing society must pass through essentially the same stages; homogenizing, because it tends toward the convergence and interdependence of societies; irreversible, because the direction of change is "given" in the relation of the elements of the process; progressive, in the sense that it is desirable and in the long run provides significant benefits to the affiliated people.[10]

Although the modernization paradigm has proved a sometimes useful as well as influential tool in social science, it has become the object of searching critiques that have challenged one after another of its central assumptions. Its shortcomings as an analytical tool pale, however, when compared to its inadequacies as a framework for thinking about foreign policy, where its principal effects are to encourage the view that events are manifestations of deep historical forces which cannot be controlled and that the best any government can do is to serve as a "midwife" to history, helping events to move where they are already headed.

This perspective on contemporary events is optimistic in the sense that it foresees continuing human progress; deterministic in the sense that it perceives events as fixed by processes over which persons and policies can have but little influence; moralistic in the sense that it perceives history and U.S. policy as having moral ends; cosmopolitan in the sense that it attempts to view the world not from the perspective of American interests or intentions but from the perspective of the modernizing nation and the "end" of history. It identifies modernization with both revolution and morality, and U.S. policy with all three.

The idea that "forces" rather than people shape events recurs each time an administration spokesman articulates or explains policy. The President, for example, assured us in February 1979:

> The revolution in Iran is a product of deep social, political, religious, and economic factors growing out of the history of Iran itself.[11]

And of Asia he said:

> At this moment there is turmoil or change in various countries from one end of the Indian Ocean to the other; some turmoil as in Indochina is the product of age-old enmities, inflamed by rivalries for influence by conflicting forces. Stability in some other countries is being shaken by the process of modernization, the search for national significance, or the desire to fulfill legitimate human hopes and human aspirations.[12]

Harold Saunders, Assistant Secretary for Near Eastern and South Asian Affairs, commenting on "instability" in Iran and the Horn of Africa, stated:

> We, of course, recognize that fundamental changes are taking place across this area of western Asia and northeastern Africa— economic modernization, social change, a revival of religion, resurgent nationalism, demands for broader popular participation in the political process. These changes are generated by forces within each country.[13]

Or here was Anthony Lake, chief of the State Department's Policy Planning staff, on South Africa:

> Change will come in South Africa. The welfare of the people there, and American interests, will be profoundly affected by the way in which it comes. The question is whether it will be peaceful or not.[14]

Brzezinski made the point still clearer. Speaking as chief of the National Security Council, he assured us that the struggles for

power in Asia and Africa are really only incidents along the route
to modernization:

> . . . all the developing countries in the arc from northeast Asia to
> southern Africa continue to search for viable forms of government
> capable of managing the process of modernization.[15]

No matter that the invasions, coups, civil wars, and political
struggles of less violent kinds that one sees all around do not *seem*
to be incidents in a global personnel search for someone to manage
the modernization process. Neither Brzezinski nor anyone else
seemed bothered by the fact that the political participants in that
arc from northeast Asia to southern Africa do not *know* that they
are "searching for viable forms of government capable of managing the process of modernization." The motives and intentions of
real persons are no more relevant to the modernization paradigm
than they are to the Marxist view of history. Viewed from this
level of abstraction, it is the "forces" rather than the people that
count.

So what if the "deep historical forces" at work in such diverse
places as Iran, the Horn of Africa, Southeast Asia, Central America, and the United Nations look a lot like Russians or Cubans?
Having moved past what the President called our "inordinate fear
of Communism," identified by him with the cold war, we should,
we are told, now be capable of distinguishing Soviet and Cuban
"machinations," which anyway exist mainly in the minds of cold
warriors and others guilty of oversimplifying the world, from evolutionary changes, which seem to be the only kind that actually
occur.

What can a U.S. President faced with such complicated, inexorable, impersonal processes *do?* The answer, offered again and
again by the President and his top officials, was, Not much. Since
events are not caused by human decisions, they cannot be stopped
or altered by them. Brzezinski, for example, has said: "We recognize that the world is changing under the influence of forces no
government can control."[16] And Cyrus Vance has cautioned:

"The fact is that we can no more stop change than Canute could still the waters."[17]

The Carter administration's essentially deterministic and apolitical view of contemporary events discouraged an active American response and encouraged passivity. The American inability to influence events in Iran became the President's theme song:

> Those who argue that the U.S. should *or could* intervene directly to thwart [the revolution in Iran] are wrong about the realities of Iran. . . . We have encouraged *to the limited extent of our own ability* the public support for the Bakhtiar government. . . . How long [the Shah] will be out of Iran, we have no way to determine. Future events and his own desires will determine that. . . . It is impossible for anyone to anticipate all future political events. . . . Even if we had been able to anticipate events that were going to take place in Iran or in other countries, obviously our ability to determine those events is very limited. [Emphasis added.][18]

Vance made the same point:

> In Iran our policy throughout the current crisis has been based on the fact that only Iranians can resolve the fundamental political issues which they now confront.[19]

Where once upon a time a President might have sent marines to ensure the protection of American strategic interests, there is no room for force in this world of progress and self-determination. Force, the President told us at Notre Dame, does not work; that is the lesson he extracted from Vietnam. It offers only "superficial" solutions. Concerning Iran, he said:

> Certainly we have no desire or ability to intrude massive forces into Iran or any other country to determine the outcome of domestic political issues. This is something that we have no intention of ever doing in another country. We've tried this once in Vietnam. It didn't work, as you well know.[20]

There was nothing unique about Iran. In Nicaragua, the climate and language were different but the "historical forces" and the U.S. response were the same. Military intervention was out of the question. Assistant Secretary of State Viron Vaky described as "unthinkable" the "use of U.S. military power to intervene in the internal affairs of another American republic."[21] Vance provided parallel assurances for Africa, asserting that we would not try to match Cuban and Soviet activities there.

What *is* the function of foreign policy under these conditions? It is to understand the processes of change and then, like Marxists, to align ourselves with history, hoping to contribute a bit of stability along the way. And this, administration spokesmen assure us, is precisely what we are doing. The Carter administration defined the U.S. national interest in the Third World as identical with the putative end of the modernization process. Vance put this with characteristic candor when he explained that U.S. policy vis-à-vis the Third World is "grounded in the conviction that we best serve our interest there by supporting the efforts of developing nations to advance their economic well-being and preserve their political independence." Our "commitment to the promotion of constructive change world-wide" (Brzezinski's words) has been vouchsafed in every conceivable context.

But there is a problem. The conceivable contexts turn out to be mainly those in which non-Communist autocracies are under pressure from revolutionary guerrillas. Since Moscow is the aggressive, expansionist power today, it is more often than not insurgents, encouraged and armed by the Soviet Union, who challenge the status quo. The American commitment to "change" in the abstract ends up by aligning us tacitly with Soviet clients and irresponsible extremists like the Ayatollah Khomeini or, in the end, Yasir Arafat.

Assisting "change" did not lead the Carter administration to undertake the destabilization of a *Communist* country. The principles of self-determination and nonintervention are thus both selectively applied. We accepted the status quo in Communist nations (in the name of "diversity" and national autonomy), but not in nations ruled by "right wing" dictators or white oligarchies. Concerning China, for example, Brzezinski observed: "We recognize that the PRC and we have different ideologies and economic and political systems. . . . We harbor neither the hope nor the desire that through extensive contacts with China we can remake that nation into the American image. Indeed, we accept our differences."[22] Of Southeast Asia, the President noted in February 1979:

> Our interest is to promote peace and the withdrawal of outside forces and not to become embroiled in the conflict among Asian nations. And, in general, our interest is to promote the health and the development of individual societies, not to a pattern cut exactly like ours in the United States but tailored rather to the hopes and the needs and desires of the peoples involved.[23]

But the Carter administration's position shifted sharply when South Africa was discussed. For example, Anthony Lake asserted in late 1978:

> We have indicated to South Africa the fact that if it does not make significant progress toward racial equality, its relations with the international community, including the United States, are bound to deteriorate.
>
> Over the years, we have tried through a series of progressive steps to demonstrate that the U.S. cannot and will not be associated with the continued practice of apartheid.[24]

As to Nicaragua, Hodding Carter III said in February 1979:

> The unwillingness of the Nicaraguan government to accept the [OAS] group's proposal, the resulting prospects for renewal and polarization, and the human rights situation in Nicaragua . . . unavoidably affect the kind of relationships we can maintain with that government.[25]

And on Latin American autocracies President Carter commented:

My government will not be deterred from protecting human rights, including economic and social rights, in whatever ways we can. We prefer to take actions that are positive, but where nations persist in serious violations of human rights, we will continue to demonstrate that there are costs to the flagrant disregard of international standards.[26]

Something very odd was going on. How did an administration that desired to let people work out their own destinies get involved in determined efforts at reform in South Africa, Zaire, Nicaragua, El Salvador, and elsewhere? How did an administration committed to nonintervention in Cambodia and Vietnam announce that it "will not be deterred" from righting wrongs in South Africa? What should be made of an administration that saw the U.S. interest as identical with economic modernization and political independence and yet heedlessly endangered the political independence of Taiwan, a country whose success in economic modernization and egalitarian distribution of wealth is unequaled in Asia? The contrast is as striking as that between the Carter administration's frenzied speed in recognizing the new dictatorship in Nicaragua and its refusal to recognize the Muzarewa government of Zimbabwe, or its refusal to maintain any presence in Zimbabwe while staffing a U.S. Information Office in Cuba. Not only were there ideology and a double standard at work here, the ideology neither fit nor explained reality, and the double standard involved the Carter administration in the wholesale contradiction of its own principles.

Inconsistencies are a familiar part of politics in most societies. Usually, however, governments behave hypocritically when their principles conflict with the national interest. What made the inconsistencies of the Carter administration noteworthy were, first, the administration's moralism, which rendered it especially vulnerable to charges of hypocrisy; and, second, the administration's predilection for policies that violated the strategic and economic interests of the United States. The Carter administration's conception of national interest bordered on doublethink: it found friendly powers to be guilty representatives of the status quo and viewed the triumph of unfriendly groups as beneficial to America's "true interests."

This logic was quite obviously reinforced by the prejudices and preferences of many Carter administration officials. Traditional autocracies are, in general and in their very nature, deeply offensive to modern American sensibilities. The notion that public affairs should be ordered on the basis of kinship, friendship, and other personal relations rather than on the basis of objective, "rational" standards violates our conception of justice and efficiency. The preference for stability rather than change is also disturbing to Americans, whose whole national experience rests on the principles of change, growth, and progress. The extremes of wealth and poverty characteristic of traditional societies also offend us, the more so since the poor are usually *very* poor and bound to their squalor by a hereditary allocation of role. Moreover, the relative lack of concern of rich, comfortable rulers for the poverty, ignorance, and disease of "their" people is likely to be interpreted by Americans as moral dereliction pure and simple. The truth is that Americans can hardly bear such societies and such rulers. Confronted with them, our vaunted cultural relativism evaporates and we become as censorious as Cotton Mather confronting sin in New England.

But if the politics of traditional and semitraditional autocracy is nearly antithetical to our own—at both the symbolic and the operational level—the rhetoric of progressive revolutionaries sounds much better to us; their symbols are much more acceptable. One reason that some modern Americans prefer "socialist" to traditional autocracies is that the former have embraced modernity and have adopted modern modes and perspectives, including an instrumental, manipulative, functional orientation toward most social, cultural, and personal affairs; a profession of universalistic norms; an emphasis on reason, science, education, and progress; a deemphasis of the sacred; and "rational," bureaucratic organizations. They speak our language.

Because socialism of the Soviet/Chinese/Cuban variety is an

ideology rooted in a version of the same values that sparked the Enlightenment and the democratic revolutions of the eighteenth century; because it is modern and not traditional; because it postulates goals that appeal to Christian as well as to secular values (brotherhood of man, elimination of power as a mode of human relations), it is highly congenial to many Americans at the symbolic level. Marxist revolutionaries speak the language of a hopeful future, while traditional autocrats speak the language of an unattractive past. Because left-wing revolutionaries invoke the symbols and values of democracy—emphasizing egalitarianism rather than hierarchy and privilege, liberty rather than order, activity rather than passivity—they are again and again accepted as partisans in the cause of freedom and democracy.

Nowhere is the affinity of liberalism, Christianity, and Marxist socialism more apparent than among liberals who are "duped" time after time into supporting "liberators" who turn out to be totalitarians, and among Left-leaning clerics whose attraction to a secular style of "redemptive community" is stronger than their outrage at the hostility of socialist regimes to religion. In Jimmy Carter—egalitarian, optimist, liberal, Christian—the tendency to be repelled by frankly nondemocratic rulers and hierarchical societies was almost as strong as the tendency to be attracted to the idea of popular revolution, liberation, and progress. Carter was, *par excellence*, the kind of liberal most likely to confound revolution with idealism, change with progress, optimism with virtue.

Where concern about "socialist encirclement," Soviet expansion, and traditional conceptions of the national interest inoculated his predecessors against such easy equations, Carter's doctrine of national interest and modernization encouraged support for all change that takes place in the name of "the people," regardless of its "superficial" Marxist or anti-American content. Any lingering doubt about whether the United States should, in case of conflict, support a "tested friend" such as the Shah or a friendly power such as Zimbabwe against an opponent who despises us is resolved by reference to our "true," our "long-range" interests.

Stephen Rosenfeld of *The Washington Post* described the

commitment of the Carter administration to this sort of "progressive liberalism":

> The Carter administration came to power, after all, committed precisely to reducing the centrality of strategic competition with Moscow in American foreign policy, and to extending the United States' association with what it was prepared to accept as legitimate wave-of-the-future popular movements around the world—first of all with the victorious movement in Vietnam.
>
> . . . Indochina was supposed to be the state on which Americans could demonstrate their "post-Vietnam" intent to come to terms with the progressive, popular element that Kissinger, the villain, had denied.[27]

In other words, the Carter administration, Rosenfeld tells us, came to power resolved not to assess international developments in the light of "cold war" perspectives but to accept at face value the claim of revolutionary groups to represent "popular" aspirations and "progressive" forces—regardless of the ties of these revolutionaries to the Soviet Union. To this end, overtures were made looking to the "normalization" of relations with Vietnam, Cuba, and the People's Republic of China, and steps were taken to cool relations with South Korea, South Africa, Nicaragua, the Philippines, and others. These moves followed naturally from the conviction that the United States had, as our enemies said, been on the wrong side of history in supporting the status quo and opposing revolution.

One might have thought that this perspective would have been undermined by events in Southeast Asia since the triumph of "progressive" forces there over the "agents of reaction." To quote Rosenfeld again:

> In this administration's line, Vietnam has been transformed for much of American public opinion, from a country wronged by the U.S. to one revealing a brutal essence of its own.
>
> This has been a quiet but major trauma to the Carter people

(as to all liberals), scarring their self-confidence and their claim on public trust alike.[28]

Presumably, however, the barbarity of the "progressive" governments in Cambodia and Vietnam was less traumatic for the President and his chief advisers than for Rosenfeld, since there was little evidence of changed predispositions at crucial levels of the White House and the State Department. The President continued to behave as before—not like a man who abhors autocrats but like one who abhors only right-wing autocrats.

In fact, high officials in the Carter administration understood better than they seemed to the aggressive, expansionist character of contemporary Soviet behavior in Africa, the Middle East, Southeast Asia, the Indian Ocean, Central America, and the Caribbean. But although the Soviet/Cuban role in Grenada, Nicaragua, and El Salvador (plus the transfer of MiG-23s to Cuba) had already prompted resumption of surveillance of Cuba (which in turn confirmed the presence of a Soviet combat brigade), the President's eagerness not to "heat up" the climate of public opinion remained stronger than his commitment to speak the truth to the American people. His statement on Nicaragua clearly reflected this priority:

> It's a mistake for Americans to assume or to claim that every time an evolutionary change takes place in this hemisphere that somehow it's a result of secret, massive Cuban intervention. The fact in Nicaragua is that the Somoza regime lost the confidence of the people. To bring about an orderly transition there, our effort was to let the people of Nicaragua ultimately make the decision on who would be their leader—what form of government they should have.[29]

This statement, which presumably represented the President's best thinking on the matter, is illuminating. Carter's effort to dismiss concern about military events in this specific country as a

manifestation of a national proclivity for seeing "Cuban machinations" under every bed constitutes a shocking effort to falsify reality. There was no question in Nicaragua of "evolutionary change"
or of attributing such change to Castro's agents. There was only a
question about the appropriate U.S. response to a military struggle
in a country whose location gives it strategic importance out of
proportion to its size or strength.

But that is not all. The rest of the President's statement
graphically illustrated the blinding power of ideology on his interpretation of events. When he said that "the Somoza regime lost the
confidence of the people," the President implied that the regime
had previously rested on the confidence of "the people" but that
the situation had now changed. In fact, the Somoza regime had
never rested on popular will (but instead on manipulation, force,
and habit), and was not being ousted by it. It was instead suc-
cumbing to arms and soldiers. However, the assumption that the
armed conflict of Sandinistas and Somozistas was the military
equivalent of a national referendum enabled the President to imagine that it could be, and should be, settled by the people of
Nicaragua. For this pious sentiment even to seem true, the President would have had to be unaware that insurgents were receiving
a great many arms from other non-Nicaraguans and that the
United States had played a significant role in disarming the
Somoza regime.

The President's mistakes and distortions were all fashionable
ones. His assumptions were those of people who want badly to be
on the progressive side in conflicts between "rightist" autocracy
and "leftist" challenges, and prefer the latter, almost regardless of
the probable consequences.

To be sure, neither the President nor Vance nor Brzezinski
desired the proliferation of Soviet-supported regimes. Each asserted his disapproval of Soviet "interference" in the modernization process. But each, nevertheless, remained willing to "destabilize" friendly or neutral autocracies without any assurance that they
would not be replaced by reactionary totalitarian theocracies, by

totalitarian Soviet client states, or worst of all, by murderous fanatics of the Pol Pot variety.

The foreign policy of the Carter administration failed not for lack of good intentions but for lack of realism about the nature of traditional versus revolutionary autocracies and the relation of each to the American national interest. Only intellectual fashion and the tyranny of Right/Left thinking prevent intelligent men of goodwill from perceiving the *facts* that traditional authoritarian governments are less repressive than revolutionary autocracies, that they are more susceptible of liberalization, and that they are more compatible with U.S. interests. The evidence on all these points is clear enough.

Surely it is now beyond reasonable doubt that the present governments of Vietnam, Cambodia, and Laos are much more repressive than those of the despised previous rulers; that the government of the People's Republic of China is more repressive than that of Taiwan, that North Korea is more repressive than South Korea, and so forth. This is the most important lesson of Vietnam and Cambodia. It is not new, but it is a gruesome reminder of harsh facts.

From time to time a truly bestial ruler can come to power in either type of autocracy—Idi Amin, Papa Doc Duvalier, Joseph Stalin, Pol Pot are examples—but neither type regularly produces such moral monsters (though democracy regularly prevents their accession to power). There are, however, *systemic* differences between traditional and revolutionary autocracies that have a predictable effect on their degree of repressiveness. Generally speaking, traditional autocrats tolerate social inequities, brutality, and poverty, whereas revolutionary autocracies create them.

Traditional autocrats leave in place existing allocations of wealth, power, status, and other resources, which in most traditional societies favor an affluent few and maintain masses in poverty. But they worship traditional gods and observe traditional taboos. They do not disturb the habitual rhythms of work and leisure, habitual places of residence, habitual patterns of family and personal relations. Because the miseries of traditional life are familiar, they are bearable to ordinary people who, growing up in the society, learn to cope, as children born to untouchables in India acquire the skills and attitudes necessary for survival in the miserable roles they are destined to fill. Such societies create no refugees.

Precisely the opposite is true of revolutionary Communist regimes. They create refugees by the millions because they claim jurisdiction over the whole life of the society and make demands for change that so violate internalized values and habits that inhabitants flee in the remarkable expectation that their attitudes, values, and goals will "fit" better in a foreign country than in their native land.

The former deputy chairman of Vietnam's National Assembly from 1976 to his defection early in August 1979, Hoang Van Hoan, described the impact of Vietnam's ongoing revolution on that country's more than one million Chinese inhabitants:

> They have been expelled from places they have lived in for generations. They have been dispossessed of virtually all possessions—their lands, their houses. They have been driven into areas called new economic zones, but they have not been given any aid.
>
> How can they eke out a living in such conditions reclaiming new land? They gradually die for a number of reasons—diseases, the hard life. They also die of humiliation.[30]

It is not only the Chinese who have suffered in Southeast Asia since the "liberation," and it is not only in Vietnam that the Chinese suffer. By the end of 1978 more than six million refugees had fled countries ruled by Marxist governments. In spite of walls, fences, guns, and sharks, the steady stream of people fleeing revolutionary utopias continues.

There is a damning contrast between the number of refugees created by Marxist regimes and those created by other autocracies: more than a million Cubans have left their homeland since

Castro's rise (one refugee for every nine inhabitants), as compared to about 35,000 each from Argentina, Brazil, and Chile. In Africa more than five times as many refugees fled Guinea and Guinea-Bissau as left Zimbabwe, suggesting that civil war and racial discrimination are easier for most people to bear than Marxist-style liberation.

Moreover, the history of this century provides no grounds for expecting that radical totalitarian regimes will transform themselves. At the moment there is a far greater likelihood of progressive liberalization and democratization in the governments of Brazil, Argentina, and Chile than in the government of Cuba; in Taiwan than in the People's Republic of China; in South Korea than in North Korea; in Zaire than in Angola; and so forth.

Since many traditional autocracies permit limited contestation and participation, it is not impossible that U.S. policy could effectively encourage this process of liberalization and democratization, provided that the effort is not made at a time when the incumbent government is fighting for its life against violent adversaries, and that proposed reforms are aimed at producing gradual change rather than perfect democracy overnight. To accomplish this, policymakers are needed who understand how actual democracies have come into being. History is a better guide than good intentions.

A realistic policy which aims at protecting our own interest and assisting the capacities for self-determination of less developed nations will need to face the unpleasant fact that, if victorious, violent insurgency headed by Marxist revolutionaries is unlikely to lead to anything but totalitarian tyranny. Armed intellectuals citing Marx and supported by Soviet-bloc arms and advisers will almost surely not turn out to be agrarian reformers, or simple nationalists, or democratic socialists. However incomprehensible it may be to some, Marxist revolutionaries are not contemporary embodiments of the Americans who wrote the Declaration of Independence, and they will not be content with establishing a broad-based coalition in which they have only one voice among many.

It may not always be easy to distinguish between democratic

and totalitarian agents of change, but it is also not too difficult. Authentic democratic revolutionaries aim at securing governments based on the consent of the governed and believe that ordinary men are capable of using freedom, of knowing their own interest, of choosing rulers. They do not, like the current leaders in Nicaragua, assume that it will be necessary to postpone elections for three to five years during which time they can "cure" the false consciousness of almost everyone.

If, moreover, revolutionary leaders describe the United States as the scourge of the twentieth century, the enemy of freedom-loving people, the perpetrator of imperialism, racism, colonialism, genocide, war, then they are not authentic democrats or, to put it mildly, friends. Groups which define themselves as enemies should be treated as enemies. The United States is not in fact a racist, colonial power, it does not practice genocide, it does not threaten world peace with expansionist activities. In the last decade especially we have practiced remarkable forbearance everywhere and undertaken the "unilateral restraints on defense spending" recommended by Brzezinski as appropriate for the technetronic era. We have also moved further, faster, in eliminating domestic racism than any multiracial society in the world or in history.

For these reasons and more, a posture of continuous self-abasement and apology vis-à-vis the Third World is neither morally necessary nor politically appropriate. Nor is it necessary or appropriate to support vocal enemies of the United States because they invoke the rhetoric of popular liberation. It is not even necessary or appropriate for our leaders to forswear unilaterally the use of military force to counter military force. Liberal idealism need not be identical with masochism, and need not be incompatible with the defense of freedom and the national interest.

U.S. Security and Latin America

WHILE AMERICAN ATTENTION in the past few years has been focused on other matters, developments of great potential importance in Central America and the Caribbean have passed almost unnoticed. The deterioration of the U.S. position in the hemisphere has already created serious vulnerabilities where none previously existed, and threatens now to confront this country with the unprecedented need to defend itself against a ring of Soviet bases on its southern flanks from Cuba to Central America.

In the past four years, the Soviet Union has become a major military power within the Western Hemisphere. In Cuba, the Soviets have full access to the naval facilities at Cienfuegos, nuclear submarines, airstrips that can accommodate Backfire bombers. From these, Soviet naval reconnaissance planes have on several occasions flown missions off the east coast of North America. Cuba also has electronic surveillance facilities that monitor American telephone and cable traffic and a network of intelligence activities under direct Soviet control. And, of course, a Soviet combat brigade.

During the same four-year period the Soviets have continued to finance, train, and staff a Cuban military establishment which has by now become a significant instrument of Soviet expansion in

Africa, the Middle East, and South Asia as well as throughout the
Caribbean and Central and South America. Today Cuba possesses
a small navy; a sizable number of supersonic aircraft—including
Il-14s and MiG-21s and -23s—that can be quickly armed with
nuclear weapons; modern transport planes capable of airlifting
Cuban troops anywhere in the area; a huge army; and an estimated
144 SAM-2 antiaircraft missile sites. The presence of more than
50,000 Cuban troops and military advisers in Africa and the Middle East provides one measure of the size and utility of Cuba's
armed forces. The Cuban role in training, supplying, and advising
revolutionary groups throughout the Caribbean and Central America illustrates the hemispheric implications of this buildup.

The first fruits of these efforts are the new governments of
Grenada and Nicaragua, whose commitments to Marxist-Leninist
principles and solidarity with Soviet/Cuban policies led Castro to
brag on returning from Managua, "Now there are three of us."
There may soon be four. El Salvador, having arrived now at the
edge of anarchy, is threatened by progressively well armed guerrillas whose fanaticism and violence remind some observers of Pol
Pot. Meanwhile, the terrorism relied on by contemporary Leninists
(and Castroites) to create a "revolutionary situation" has reap-
peared in Guatemala.

Slower but no less serious transformations are under way in
Guyana, where ties to Castro have become extensive, tight, and
complex, and in Martinique and Guadeloupe, where Castroite
groups threaten existing governments. (In Dominica and Jamaica,
the recent electoral victories of Eugenia Charles and Edward
Seaga have for the moment reversed the Castroite tides there.)
Fidel Castro is much clearer than we have been about his interests
and intentions in the area, and frequently declares, as at last year's
meeting of the nonaligned nations in Havana, "I will pursue to the
end the anti-imperialist struggles of the Caribbean peoples and
especially those of Puerto Rico, Belize, Guadeloupe, Martinique
and Guyana."

American policies have not only proved incapable of dealing

with the problems of Soviet/Cuban expansion in the area, they have positively contributed to them and to the alienation of major nations, the growth of neutralism, the destabilization of friendly governments, the spread of Cuban influence, and the decline of U.S. power in the region. Hence one of our most urgent tasks is to review and revise the U.S. approach to Latin America and the Caribbean.

Such a review should begin not just with the previous administration's policy in the hemisphere, but with the quiet process by which new theories of hemispheric relations came to preempt discussion within that somewhat amorphous but very real group known as the foreign-policy establishment. For to an extent unusual in government, Carter administration policies toward Latin America and the Caribbean (as in the world more broadly) were derived from an ideology rather than from tradition, habit, or improvisation.

Indeed, nothing is as important as understanding the relationship between the recent failures of American policy—in Latin America and elsewhere—and the philosophy of foreign affairs that inspired and informed that policy. Such an effort of understanding requires, first, that we disregard the notion that the failure of the Carter policy was the personal failure of a man unskilled in the ways of diplomacy; and, second, that we look beyond superficial day-to-day policy changes to the stable orientations that reasserted themselves after each discrete crisis in world affairs.

Those orientations had their roots in the Vietnam experience, less as it was fought in Southeast Asia than as it was interpreted in Washington and New York. President Carter, after all, was not the only political leader in America to have lost his "inordinate" fear of Communism, lost his appetite for East-West competition, grown embarrassed by the uses of American power, become ashamed of past U.S. policies, and grown determined to make a fresh start. By the time Richard Nixon had left office, a large portion of the political elite in America, including a majority of the Congress, had withdrawn not only from Vietnam but from what was more and more frequently called the cold war—the revisionists' preferred term for U.S. determination to resist the expansion of Soviet power.

From these feelings were inferred the famous "lessons" of Vietnam: that the cold war was over, that concern with Communism should no longer "overwhelm" other issues, that forceful intervention in the affairs of another nation is impractical and immoral, that we must never again put ourselves on the "wrong side of history" by supporting a foreign autocrat against a "popular movement," and that we must try to make amends for our deeply flawed national character by modesty and restraint in the arenas of power and the councils of the world. Underpinning these "lessons" was a new optimistic theory of historical development which came in the decade of the seventies to focus the discussion of the future within the dominant foreign-policy elite.

No one expressed the new spirit better than Zbigniew Brzezinski, whose book *Between Two Ages*[1] (sponsored by the Council on Foreign Relations) spelled out the implications of the new spirit for Latin American policy. Brzezinski argued that our Latin American policies were inappropriate to the new realities of declining ideological competition, declining nationalism, increased global interdependence, and rising Third World expectations. The United States should therefore give up its historic hemispheric posture, which had postulated a "special relationship" with Latin America and emphasized hemispheric security and, since World War II, anti-Communism. We should, instead, make an explicit move to abandon the Monroe Doctrine, "concede that in the new global age, geographic or hemispheric continuity no longer need be politically decisive,"[2] adopt a "more detached attitude toward revolutionary processes,"[3] demonstrate more "patience," and take an "increasingly depoliticized" approach to aid and trade.[4]

The views of hemispheric policy expressed in *Between Two Ages* were further elaborated in two other documents born in the bosom of the foreign-policy establishment: the reports issued in the name of the Commission on United States–Latin American

Relations headed by Sol Linowitz and composed of "an independent, bipartisan group of private citizens from different sectors of U.S. society" funded by the Ford, Rockefeller, and Clark foundations. The intellectual framework and most of the specific recommendations of the two Linowitz reports were identical. Both affirmed that economic and technological developments had created new international problems, and that interdependence had generated a pressing need for a new global approach to those problems. U.S. policy toward Latin America, "from the Monroe Doctrine through the Good Neighbor Policy to the Alliance for Progress and its successor, the Mature Partnership," was outmoded because it was based on assumptions which had been overtaken by history. Earmarked for the dustbin were the beliefs that the United States should have a special policy for Latin America; that Latin America constituted a "sphere of interest" in which the United States could or should intervene (overtly or covertly) to prevent the establishment of unpalatable governments; and that national security should be an important determinant of U.S. policy toward that area. Now, the first Linowitz report counseled: "It [U.S. policy] should be less concerned with security in the narrowly military sense than with shared interests and values that would be advanced by mutually satisfactory political relations."⁵ The new approach was to be free of paternalism, "respectful of sovereignty," tolerant of political and economic diversity. Above all, it was to be set in a consistent global framework.

Most of the specific recommendations of the two Linowitz reports—negotiating the Panama Canal Treaties, "normalizing" relations with Cuba, "liberalizing" trade and "internationalizing" aid, promoting human rights, and never, ever, intervening militarily—flowed from these new assumptions. Given detente, the United States should "keep local and regional conflicts outside the context of the superpower relationship" and no longer "automatically see revolutions in other countries and intraregional conflicts . . . as battlefields of the cold war." And given interdependence (manifested in global phenomena like inflation and multinational corporations), the United States should no longer hope for or seek "complete economic and political security" but instead participate in the new international agenda.

Despite the commission's determined globalism, it recognized that Cuba constituted a special case. Both reports recommended U.S. initiatives toward "normalization" of relations with Cuba and some acts (removing restrictions on travel, increasing scientific and cultural exchanges) regardless of overall progress on normalization. But the second report also noted Cuba's military involvement in Africa and its support for "militant" and violence-prone Puerto Rican *independistas*, and concluded that full normalization of relations, however desirable, could take place only if Cuba gave assurances that its troops were being withdrawn from Angola and that it had no intention of intervening elsewhere.[6]

The most striking characteristic of the Linowitz recommendations was their disinterested internationalist spirit. U.S. policy, it was assumed, should be based on an understanding of "changed realities" and guided by an enlightened confidence that what was good for the world was good for the United States. Power was to be used to advance moral goals, not strategic or economic ones. Thus sanctions could be employed to punish human rights violations, but not to aid American business; power could be used "to the full extent permitted by law" to prevent terrorist actions against Cuba, but not to protect U.S. corporations against expropriation. Nor was power to be a factor in designing or implementing economic aid or trade programs *except* where these were intended to promote human rights, disarmament, and nuclear nonproliferation.

Like Brzezinski's *Between Two Ages*, the Linowitz reports were, in the most fundamental sense, utopian. They assumed that technological change had so transformed human consciousness and behavior that it was no longer necessary for the United States to screen policies for their impact on national security. To be sure, neither argued that self-interest, conflict, or aggression had been entirely purged from the world. But Brzezinski asserted (and the Linowitz commission apparently believed) that only the Soviet

Union was still engaged in truly "anachronistic" political behavior against which it was necessary to defend ourselves. Since no Latin American nation directly threatened the position of the United States, relations with them could be safely conducted without regard for national security.

Adopting the Linowitz commission's recommendations thus required abandoning the strategic perspective which had shaped U.S. policy from the Monroe Doctrine down to the eve of the Carter administration, at the center of which was a conception of the national interest and a belief in the moral legitimacy of its defense. In the Brzezinski-Linowitz approach, morality was decoupled from the national interest, much as the future was divorced from the past. The goals recommended for U.S. policy were all abstract and supranational: "human rights," "development," "fairness."

Still, if the Linowitz reports redefined the national interest, they did not explicitly reject it as a guide to policy or name the United States as the enemy. This was left to the report of yet another self-appointed group whose recommendations bore an even closer resemblance to the actual policies of the Carter administration. This report, *The Southern Connection*, was issued by the Institute for Policy Studies Ad Hoc Working Group on Latin America. The group included key personnel of the Linowitz commission, and it endorsed most of the specific recommendations of the second Linowitz report: divestment of the Panama Canal, normalization of relations with Cuba, strict control of anti-Castro activists, aid through multilateral institutions, nuclear nonproliferation, and systematic linkage of human rights concerns to all other aspects of policy. But the IPS report went beyond these in various respects.

First, it not only proposed a break with the past, but contained a more sweeping indictment of past U.S. policy as reflecting an "unquestioned presumption of U.S. superiority" and an "official presumption of hegemony" which was not only outdated but also "morally unacceptable."[7]

Second, it went beyond the call for normalization of relations

with Cuba to a demand that the United States *"support* the ideologically diverse and experimental approaches to development"[8]
(emphasis added), recognizing that "both the need for change and
the forces propelling such change in the developing areas are powerful and urgent."[9] Latin America's "most challenging development experiments" were identified as Cuba, Jamaica, and Guyana.

Third, the IPS report located the ground of human rights
violations and "institutionalized repression" throughout Latin
America in U.S. interests, "virulent anti-Communism," and "national development based on free play of market forces."[10] The
remedy: "practical steps to reduce [socioeconomic] inequities are
. . . steps toward the mitigation of the broader human rights crisis
of our times."[11] That is, fight for human rights with socialism.

The ease with which the Linowitz recommendations were incorporated into the IPS analysis and report demonstrated how
strong had become the affinity between the views of the foreign-
policy establishment and the New Left, how readily the categories
of the new liberalism could be translated into those of revolutionary "socialism," and how short a step it was from utopian globalism and the expectation of change to anti-American perspectives
and revolutionary activism. And the impact of these ideas on the
Carter administration was enhanced by the appointment of members and associates of the IPS group (such as Robert Pastor, Mark
Schneider, and Guy Erb) to key Latin American policy positions.
In the administration these officials joined others with like-minded
approaches to the Third World, including U.N. Ambassador An-
drew Young and his deputy Brady Tyson.

This whole cluster of ideas—of facing painful truths, making
a fresh start, forswearing force, and pursuing universal moral goals
—was enormously attractive to Jimmy Carter. No sooner was he
elected than he set out to translate them into a new policy for
dealing with the nations of the hemisphere.

The repudiation of our hegemonic past was symbolized by the
Panama Canal Treaties, to which the Carter administration—from
the President on down—attached great importance and of which it
was inordinately proud. As Vice President Mondale put it in Pan-

ama City, the treaties symbolized "the commitment of the U.S. to the belief that fairness and not force should lie at the heart of our dealings with the nations of the world."[12]

Anastasio Somoza's Nicaragua had the bad luck to become the second demonstration area for the "fresh start" in Latin America. Just because the regime had been so close and so loyal to the United States, its elimination would, in exactly the same fashion as the Panama Canal Treaties, dramatize the passing of the old era of "hegemony" in Central America and the arrival of a new era of equity and justice. As the editor of *Foreign Affairs*, William Bundy, noted, "Somoza [was] as good a symbol as could have been found of past U.S. policies in Latin America."[13]

The "global" approach adopted by the Carter administration constituted another sharp break with past U.S. practice. The "special relationship" with Latin America was gone. In speech after speech, the President, the Vice President, Secretary of State Vance, and Assistant Secretaries for Inter-American Affairs Terrance Todman and Viron Vaky explained that henceforth there would not *be* a U.S. policy toward Latin America. Instead, hemispheric policy would be incorporated into a global framework and Latin America would be treated in the context of the "North-South" dialogue. "What we do in Latin America," Vaky asserted, "must be a consistent part of our global policies."[14]

Incorporating the nations of Latin America into a "global framework" meant deemphasizing U.S. relations with them. Especially, it meant reducing U.S. assistance to the area, since from the perspective of North-South relations, Latin America's claim to assistance was not nearly as impressive as that of most other nations of the so-called Third World. And, once the strategic perspective was abandoned, there was no reason at all for military assistance.

Not surprisingly, therefore, U.S. assistance to the countries of Latin America declined steadily during the Carter years. By 1980 the administration was requesting only half as much economic aid for Latin America as a decade earlier. Military assistance declined even more drastically—both quantitatively and qualitatively.

Fewer countries were slated to receive military assistance, and more strings were attached to how they could use the amounts received. No new weapons systems could be purchased; instead, everyone was to be encouraged to acquire nonlethal weapons. Assistance in military training (which had produced many personal and professional ties between U.S. and Latin American officers) was cut sharply.

The "global" approach also encouraged the imposition of unprecedented curbs on the sale of arms. By 1978 the United States, long the most important supplier to Latin America, accounted for only 10 percent of arms sales. President Carter bragged to the OAS, "We have a better record in this hemisphere than is generally recognized. Four other nations of the world sell more weapons to Latin America than does the United States."[15]

The impact of the global approach was felt beyond arms sales. Although the nations of Latin America are major trading partners of the United States, and in 1979 accounted for one-sixth of total U.S. exports and 80 percent of U.S. private investment in the developing world, the Carter administration's manifest unconcern for hemispheric economic ties (as recommended in the Linowitz and IPS reports) resulted in a steady loss of ground to European and Asian competitors, all of whom enjoyed heavy support from their governments.

The global approach involved deemphasizing Latin American relations, not destabilizing governments. But other aspects of the Carter doctrine committed the administration to promoting "change." "Change," indeed, was the favorite word of administration policymakers. In speeches with titles like "Currents of Change in Latin America," Carter, Vance, and their associates voiced their conviction that the world was in the grip of an extraordinary process of transformation which was deep, irresistible, systematic, and desirable. Administration spokesmen reiterated in the fashion of a credo that "our national interests align us naturally and inescapably with the forces of change, of democracy, of human rights, and of equitable development" (Philip Habib). And the belief that the whole world was caught up in a process of modernization moving it toward greater democracy and equality subtly trans- formed itself into an imperative: the United States should throw its power behind the "progressive" forces seeking change, even if they "seemed" anti-American or pro-Soviet.

If commitment to "change" was the rock on which Carter's Latin American policy was built, his human rights policy was the lever to implement change. Two aspects of the Carter approach to human rights are noteworthy. First, concern was limited to viola- tions of human rights by governments. By definition, activities of terrorists and guerrillas could not qualify as violations of human rights, whereas a government's efforts to repress terrorism would quickly run afoul of Carter's human rights standards.

Secondly, human rights were defined not in terms of personal and legal rights—freedom from torture, arbitrary imprisonment, and arrest, as in the usage of Amnesty International and the U.S. Foreign Assistance Acts of 1961 and 1975—but in accordance with a much broader conception which included the political "rights" available only in democracies and the economic "rights" promised by socialism (shelter, food, health, education). It may be that no country in the world meets these standards; certainly no country in the Third World does. The very broadness of the defini- tion invited an arbitrary and capricious policy of implementation. Panama, for instance, was rather mysteriously exempt from meet- ing the expansive criteria of the State Department's human rights office, while at the same time the other major nations of Central America were being censored (and undermined) for violations.

Why Panama, a dictatorship with a higher per capita income than Nicaragua, El Salvador, or Guatemala, did not qualify as a gross violator of human rights while the latter countries did; why and how an administration committed to nonintervention in the internal affairs of nations could try to replace an unacceptable government in Nicaragua with one more palatable to it; why such an administration should attempt not only to "normalize" relations with Cuba but also to destabilize the governments of El Salvador and Guatemala—to answer these questions required on the part of policymakers an intuitive understanding of which governments were outmoded and which reflected the wave of the future. What was *not* required was an ability to distinguish between which were Communist and which non-Communist. The President and other members of his administration apparently believed with Brzezinski that in most of the world ideological thinking had already given way to pragmatism and problem-solving, and that a concern with Communist ideology was therefore just another artifact of a past epoch, "the era of the cold war."

Ignoring the role of ideology had powerful effects on the administration's perception of conflicts and on its ability to make accurate predictions. Although Fidel Castro has loudly and repeatedly proclaimed his revolutionary mission, and backed his stated intentions by training insurgents and providing weapons and advisers, Carter's Assistant Secretary for Inter-American Affairs, William Bowdler, described Cuba as "an inefficient and shabby dictatorship"[16]—a description more appropriate to, say, Paraguay, than to an expansionist Soviet client state with troops scattered throughout the world. The refusal to take seriously, or even to take into account, the commitment of Fidel Castro or Nicaragua's Sandinista leadership to Marxist-Leninist goals and expansionist policies made it impossible to distinguish them either from traditional authoritarians or from democratic reformers, impossible to predict their likely attitudes toward the United States and the Soviet Union, impossible to understand why in their view Costa Rica and Mexico as well as Guatemala and Honduras constituted inviting targets. Ignoring the force of ideology—and its powerful contemporary embodiments—fatally distorted the Carter administration's view of politics in Central America and elsewhere.

The policies which grew out of these expectations have had a large impact on U.S. relations with most nations of South America. In Central America in particular, the direction of administration policy interacted with the presence there of weak regimes and Cuban-supported insurgents to transform the region into a battleground in an ideological war that the administration did not understand and could not acknowledge.

Except for Mexico, the nations of Central America are quite

small and, by North American standards, quite poor. There are significant social and economic differences among them. Guatemala's large traditionalist Indian population and multiple linguistic groups are unique in the region, and bring with them special problems of economic, social, and political integration. El Salvador's overcrowding places especially heavy strains on its institutions. Revenues from the Canal and the Canal Zone give Panama a higher per capita income than any of its neighbors except Costa Rica and about twice that of the sparse, scattered people of Honduras.

Despite their differences, these countries also share a good many social and economic characteristics. All are "modernizing" nations in the sense that in each of them urban, industrial, mobile, "modern" sectors coexist with traditional patterns of life. In each, a large portion of the population is still engaged in agriculture—most often employed as landless laborers on large estates and plantations that have long since made the transition to commercial agriculture. Economic growth rates in Central America have been above the Latin American average, and per capita income is high enough to rank these nations among the "middle income" countries of the world. But in all of them, wealth is heavily concentrated in a small upper class and a thin but growing middle class, and large numbers live as they have always lived—in deep poverty, ill-nourished, ill-housed, illiterate.

Things have been getting better for the people of Central America—infant mortality rates have dropped, years in school have increased—but they have been getting better slowly. It has been easier to break down the myths justifying the old distribution of wealth in society than to improve access to education, medical care, decent housing, good food, respect, and political power.

There are also political differences among the small nations of Central America. Costa Rica has managed to develop and maintain (since 1948) a genuine democracy. Honduran politics has been especially violent, while Nicaragua (under the Somozas) was the most stable political regime. But again, despite differences, Guatemala, Honduras, El Salvador, Nicaragua, and Panama (like

Costa Rica before 1948) share several characteristics with one
another and with most of the nations of Latin America. These
include a continuing disagreement about the legitimate ends and
means of government, a pervasive distrust of authority, a broad
ideological spectrum, a low level of participation in voluntary associations, a preference for hierarchical modes of association
(church, bureaucracy, army), a history of military participation in
politics, and a tradition of *personalismo.*

The boundaries between the political system, the economy,
the military establishment, and the Church are often unclear and
unreliable. Weak governments confront strong social groups, and
no institution is able to establish its authority over the whole.
Economic, ecclesiastical, and social groups influence but do not
control the government; the government influences but does not
control the economy, the military, the Church, and so on.

A democratic façade—elections, political parties, and fairly
broad participation—is a feature of these systems. But the impact
of democratic forms is modified by varying degrees of fraud, intimidation, and restrictions on who may participate. Corruption
(the appropriation of public resources for private use) is endemic.
Political institutions are not strong enough to channel and contain
the claims of various groups to use public power to enforce preferred policies. No procedure is recognized as *the* legitimate route
to power. Competition for influence proceeds by whatever means
are at hand: the Church manipulates symbols of rectitude; workers
resort to strikes; businessmen use bribery; political parties use
campaigns and votes; politicians employ persuasion, organization,
and demagoguery; military officers use force. Lack of consensus
permits political competition of various kinds in various arenas,
and gives the last word to those who have at their disposal the
greatest force. That usually turns out to be the leaders of the
armed forces; most rulers in the area are generals.

Violence or the threat of violence is an integral, regular, predictable part of these political systems—a fact which is obscured
by our way of describing military "interventions" in Latin American political systems as if the systems were normally peaceable.

Coups, demonstrations, political strikes, plots, and counterplots are, in fact, the norm.

Traditionally, however, actual violence has been limited by the need to draw support from diverse sectors of the society and by the fact that politics has not been viewed as involving ultimate stakes. The various competitors for power have sought control of government to increase their wealth and prestige, not to achieve the "higher" and more dangerous purpose of restructuring society. In traditional Latin American politics, competitors do not normally destroy each other. They suffer limited defeats and win limited victories. The habit of permitting opponents to survive to fight another day is reflected in the tendency of the regimes to instability. In such a system a government normally lasts as long as it is able to prevent a coalition from forming among its opponents. Because there is no consensus on what makes government itself legitimate, successive regimes remain vulnerable to attacks on their legitimacy. They are also especially vulnerable to attacks on public order, which tends to be tenuous and to lack a firm base in tradition, habit, and affection.

To these patterns of political interaction there has been added in recent years the unfamiliar guerrilla violence of revolutionaries linked to Cuba by ideology, training, and the need for support, and through Cuba to the Soviet Union. Such groups rely on terrorism to destroy public order, to disrupt the economy and make normal life impossible, to demoralize the police, and to mortally wound the government by demonstrating its inability to protect personal security and maintain public authority. As Robert Chapman has emphasized, with the advent of terrorism as a *form* of revolution, a revolutionary situation can be created in any country whose government is weak or whose economy is vulnerable or dependent, with or without the participation of the masses.

Other new participants in the traditional pattern of political competition include the Socialist International and the Catholic Left. A number of socialist leaders (Willy Brandt, Olf Palme, Michael Manley), unable to win popular support for peaceful revolution in their own countries, have grown progressively enthusiastic about revolution elsewhere and less fastidious about the company they keep and the methods utilized. As for the Catholic Left, its interest in revolution on this earth has waxed as its concern with salvation in heaven has waned.

Traditionally, the ideological content of Latin American politics has been low, but since both the Socialist International and the radical Catholics conceive of themselves as specialists in rectitude, their participation has enhanced its moral intensity at the same time that Cubans have increased their violence.

The United States is by no means a new participant in Central America's politics, having played an important if intermittent role in its political struggles throughout much of the century. The United States has been important as a source of aid and has also exercised a veto power over governments in the area and reinforced with its tacit approval acceptable governments. Therefore, the objective economic and political dependency of nations in the area has been reinforced by a widespread sense of psychological dependency. Under the Carter administration the character of U.S. participation changed. Formerly, American representatives had been content to press the cause of U.S. economic or strategic interest. They now ask for something more problematic: internal reform, democracy, social justice—goods which even strong governments find it difficult to produce.

The nations of Central America (including Mexico) and the Caribbean all suffer from some form of institutional weakness because significant portions of the population have not been incorporated into the political system, and/or because political action is not fully institutionalized, and/or because the legitimacy of the government is in doubt, and/or because there is no consensus concerning legitimacy within the political elite, and/or because the economy is vulnerable to shifts in the international market, and/or because regular infusions of aid are required, and/or because rising expectations have outstripped capacities. All are vulnerable to disruption, and must rely on force to put down challenges to authority.

It is at this point that the roles of Cuba on the one hand, and the United States on the other hand, become crucial. Cuba stands ready to succor, bolster, train, equip, and advise revolutionaries produced within these societies and to supply weapons for a general insurgency when that is created. If customary aid and comfort from the United States in the form of money, arms, logistical support, and the services of counterinsurgency experts are no longer available, governments like those of Nicaragua, El Salvador, and Guatemala are weakened. And when it finally sinks in that the United States desires their elimination and prefers insurgents to incumbents, the blow to the morale and confidence of such weak traditional regimes is devastating.

The case of Nicaragua illustrates to perfection what happens when "affirmative pressures for change" on the part of the United States interact with Cuban-backed insurgency and a government especially vulnerable to shifts in U.S. policy.

The Nicaraguan political tradition combined participatory and autocratic elements in a characteristic Latin American mix. *Personalismo*, popular sovereignty, and brute force were present in the politics of Nicaragua from its founding as a separate nation in 1938 to the Sandinista triumph in July 1979. Throughout the nineteenth century and the first three decades of the twentieth, geographically based political factions representing a single, small ruling class competed under a symbolic two-party system in elections in which neither contender was willing to accept an unfavorable outcome. Frequently victory was obtained by enlisting the help of foreign governments and/or financial interests.

The United States was repeatedly called on by incumbent governments for assistance in maintaining peace. In 1910 it was the Conservatives who requested financial assistance and advice, and in 1912, again at their request, the United States posted a 100-man legation guard to Nicaragua. From then until 1933 an American military presence was a regular feature of the Nicaraguan political system. These U.S. troops (who at their height numbered about 2,700) supervised presidential elections and organized the National Guard, which was conceived as a professional national police force that would remain aloof from politics. In 1936, less than three years after American military forces had withdrawn, the leader of this "nonpolitical army," Colonel Anastasio Somoza García, ousted the Liberal president, Juan B. Sacasa. In this manner began the more than four decades of Nicaraguan politics dominated by the Somoza family.

Somocismo was based in the first instance on the military power of the National Guard. Its durability, however, also owed much to the political skills of the successive Somozas who ruled the country and headed its armed forces. These skills were reflected in the construction of an organizational base to support their personal power, long-standing success in exploiting divisions among their opponents, and the ability to retain U.S. support. The organizational basis of the Somozas' power is the most interesting factor because, like that of Juan Perón, it was largely created rather than captured.

The Somoza organization rested on four pillars: a hierarchically structured national party forged on the base of the traditional Liberal party; an expanded bureaucracy whose members also served as party workers; a national federation of trade unions created by the Somozas; and the National Guard. The whole operated rather like an efficient urban political machine, oiled by jobs, pensions, profits, status, and perquisites of various kinds. Most urban machines, however, do not have a private army. The loyalty of the National Guard was the most powerful testimony to the Somozas' political skill, for in Latin America armed forces are more easily won than retained. Nicaragua's National Guard remained loyal until after the last Somoza had fled.

Nicaraguan politics in the Somoza period featured limited repression and limited opposition. Criticism was permitted and, in fact, carried on day after day in the pages of *La Prensa* (whose editor was an opposition leader). Although the Somozas had large landholdings, the government enjoyed no monopoly of economic power, and made no serious effort to absorb or control the Church, education, or the culture. The government was moderately competent in encouraging economic development, moderately oppressive, and moderately corrupt. It was also an utter failure at delivering those social services that Americans and Europeans have come since the Depression to regard as the responsibility of government.

Anastasio Somoza Debayle, a West Point graduate with an American wife and an expansive appetite for women and alcohol, had accommodated successive American administrations and received aid from successive Congresses. He had every reason to suppose that his regime would continue to enjoy U.S. favor, and no reason to suppose that his power could be brought down by the small group of Cuban-backed terrorists who periodically disturbed the peace with their violence.

Three things seem to have upset these calculations. One was the progressive alienation of certain members of the country's *oligarquía* and business class when after the earthquake of 1973 Somozistas raked off too large a share of the international relief; a second factor was Somoza's heart attack; the third and most important factor was the election of Jimmy Carter and the adoption of an all-new Latin American policy.

At the time the Carter administration was inaugurated in January 1977, three groups of unequal strength competed for power in Nicaragua: the President and his loyal lieutenants, who enjoyed the advantages of incumbency, a degree of legitimacy, a nationwide organization, and the unwavering support of the National Guard; the legal opposition parties, which had been gathered into a loose coalition headed by Joaquin Chamorro, editor of *La Prensa*; and several small revolutionary groups, whose Cuban-trained leaders had finally forged a loose alliance, the FSLN (Sandinist National Liberation Front).

From the moment the FSLN adopted the tactics of a broad alliance, the offensive against Somoza was carried out on a variety of fronts. There was violence in the form of assassinations and assaults on army barracks. When the government reacted, the United States condemned it for violations of human rights. The legal opposition put forward demands for greater democracy which had the endorsement of the FSLN, thus making it appear that democracy was the goal of the insurgency.

Violence and counterviolence weakened the regime by demonstrating that it could not maintain order. The combination of impotence and repression in turn emboldened opponents in and out of the country, provoking more reprisals and more hostility in a vicious circle that culminated finally in the departure of Somoza and the collapse of the National Guard.

What did the Carter administration do in Nicaragua? *It brought down the Somoza regime.* The Carter administration did not "lose" Nicaragua in the sense in which it was once charged Harry Truman had "lost" China, or Eisenhower Cuba, by failing to prevent a given outcome. In the case of Nicaragua, the State Department *acted* repeatedly and at critical junctures to weaken the government of Anastasio Somoza and to strengthen his opponents.

First, it declared "open season" on the Somoza regime. When in the spring of 1977 the State Department announced that shipments of U.S. arms would be halted because of human rights violations, and followed this with announcements in June and October that economic aid would be withheld, it not only deprived the Somoza regime of needed economic and military support but served notice that the regime no longer enjoyed the approval of the United States and could no longer count on its protection. This impression was strongly reinforced when after February 1978 Jimmy Carter treated the two sides in the conflict as more or less equally legitimate contenders—offering repeatedly to help "both sides" find a "peaceful solution."

Second, the Carter administration's policies inhibited the Somoza regime in dealing with its opponents while they were weak enough to be dealt with. Fearful of U.S. reproaches and reprisals, Somoza fluctuated between repression and indulgence in his response to FSLN violence. The rules of the Carter human rights policy made it impossible for Somoza to resist his opponents effectively. As Viron Vaky remarked about the breakdown in negotiations between Somoza and the armed opposition: ". . . when the mediation was suspended we announced that the failure of the mediation had created a situation in which it was clear violence was going to continue, that it would result in repressive measures and therefore our relationships could not continue on the same basis as in the past."[17] When the National Palace was attacked and hostages were taken, Somoza's capitulation to FSLN demands enhanced the impression that he could not control the situation and almost certainly stimulated the spread of resistance.

Third, by its "mediation" efforts and its initiatives in the Organization of American States (OAS), the Carter administration encouraged the internationalization of the opposition. Further, it demoralized Somoza and his supporters by insisting that Somoza's continuation in power was the principal obstacle to a viable, centrist, democratic government. Finally, the State Department deprived the Somoza regime of legitimacy not only by repeated condemnations for human rights violations but also by publishing a demand for Somoza's resignation and by negotiating with the opposition.

Without these "affirmative pressures," William Bundy concluded in *Foreign Affairs*: "It seems a safe bet that Tacho Somoza would still be in charge in Nicaragua and his amiable brother-in-law still extending abrazzos to all and sundry in Washington as dean of the diplomatic corps."[18]

Why did the Carter administration do these things? Because it thought the fall of Somoza would bring progress to Nicaragua. Viron Vaky put it this way: "Nicaragua's tragedy stems from dynastic rule. Times have changed. Nicaragua has changed, but the government of Nicaragua has not."[19]

History was against Somoza. He was an obstacle to progress. He should relinquish power to make room for "change." When he declined to do so, the Carter administration accused him of "polarizing" the situation. When the National Guard responded to FSLN violence with violence, the State Department said that the National Guard had "radicalized the opposition."

On the other hand, the fact that Cubans were supplying arms to the FSLN was not regarded as being of much importance. Brandon Grove, Jr., Deputy Assistant Secretary for Inter-American Affairs, explained to the Foreign Affairs Committee of the House (June 7, 1979):

> The flow of such supplies is a symptom of the deeper problem in Nicaragua: polarization and its attendant violence that day by day are contributing to the growing alienation of the Nicaraguan government from its people. . . . The real cause for concern today should be the breakdown . . . of trust between government and people essential for the democratic process to function.[20]

Since the "real" problem was not Cuban arms but Somoza, obviously the United States should not act to reinforce a regime that had proved its political and moral failure by becoming the object of attack. Because the State Department desired not to "add to the partisan factionalism," it declined to supply arms to the regime. "The supplying of arms in a war situation we feel only adds to the suffering. We have urged others not to do that."

In the event, the Carter administration did a good deal more than "urge." In June 1979, after the United States and the OAS had called for Somoza's resignation, and U.S. representatives William Bowdler and Lawrence Pezzulo had met with the FSLN, the State Department undertook to apply the final squeeze to the Somoza regime—putting pressure on Israel to end arms sales, and working out an oil embargo to speed the capitulation of Somoza's forces. They were so successful that for the second time in a decade an American ally ran out of gas and ammunition while confronting an opponent well armed by the Soviet bloc.

The FSLN was not the State Department's preferred replacement for Somoza. Nevertheless, from the spring of 1977, when the State Department announced that it was halting a promised arms shipment to Somoza's government, through the summer of 1980, when the administration secured congressional approval of a $75 million aid package for Nicaragua, U.S. policy under Jimmy Carter was vastly more supportive of the Sandinistas than it was of the Somoza regime, despite the fact that Somoza and his government were as doggedly friendly and responsive to U.S. interests and desires as the Sandinistas were hostile and nonresponsive.

The Carter administration expected that democracy would emerge in Nicaragua. Their scenario prescribed that the winds of change would blow the outmoded dictator out of office and replace him with a popular government. Even after it had become clear that the FSLN, which was known to harbor powerful antidemocratic tendencies, was the dominant force in the new regime, U.S. spokesmen continued to speak of the events in Nicaragua as a democratic revolution. In December 1979, for example, Deputy Secretary of State Warren Christopher attempted to reassure doubting members of the Senate Foreign Relations Committee that "the driving consensus among Nicaraguans" was "to build a new Nicaragua through popular participation that is capable of meeting basic human needs."[21]

The expectation that change would produce progress and that socialism would mean social justice made it difficult for Carter policymakers to assess Nicaragua's new rulers realistically, even though grounds for concern about their intentions, already numerous before their triumph, continued to multiply in its aftermath.

Revolution begins with destruction. The first fruit of the destabilization of Somoza's government and the reinforcement of his opponents was a civil war in which some 40,000 Nicaraguans lost their most basic human right (life), another 100,000 were left homeless, and some $2 billion worth of destruction was wrought. Nicaragua was left in a shambles.

Where did the expectations, the hopes, the intentions of the Carter administration then lead us, and the Nicaraguans who took the consequences? Although the FSLN had solemnly committed itself to hold free elections, its leaders have shown no disposition to share the power they seized in July 1979. To the contrary, the consolidation and centralization of power have moved steadily forward. Despite the strenuous opposition of the two non-FSLN junta members, the Sandinista directorate which has effectively ruled Nicaragua since the fall of Somoza moved in the spring of 1980 to institutionalize its control of Nicaragua's Council of State by expanding and "restructuring" it to ensure the Sandinistas a permanent majority. (Under the reform they would be assured of 24 of 47 seats where previously they had been entitled to only 13 of 33.)

Meanwhile, the election to which the FSLN had committed itself has been pushed further and further into a receding future, even though the new rulers, who need all the help they can get, have been under heavy pressure from the governments of Venezuela, Costa Rica, and the United States to set a date. Sandinista leaders have made no secret of their opinion that competitive elections are an unsatisfactory and unnecessary mechanism for choosing rulers. Junta members have asserted that the people spoke through the revolution—"with their blood and with the guns in their hands the people have cast their votes"[22] (as a junta member told the *Economist*)—and that anyway, having been brainwashed by forty years of Somoza rule, they are not capable of choosing among candidates—at least not until they have been "reeducated."

In the last days of August 1980, the restructured Council of State announced that elections will not be held before 1985. And those elections, declared Humberto Ortega Saavedra (Minister of Defense), "will serve to reinforce and improve the revolution and not to give just anyone more power, which belongs to the people." Meanwhile, no "proselytizing activities" on behalf of any candidate will be permitted before candidates are officially designated by an electoral agency which itself will be created in 1984 (and violations will be punished by terms of three months to three years in jail).

Decrees accompanying these decisions have underscored the junta's distaste for criticism. Henceforth, dissemination of news concerning scarcities of food and other consumer goods is prohibited on pain of imprisonment (from two months to two years), as is "unconfirmed" information concerning armed encounters or attacks on government personnel.

These restrictions constitute one more significant step in the Sandinistas' gradual campaign to control the climate of opinion. Television and radio have already been brought under control. Among opposition newspapers, only *La Prensa* remains; it has already come under pressures more harsh than those applied to the media during the Somoza era, and its continuation as an independent critical voice is at best uncertain. The requirement that all professional journalists join a new government-sponsored union as a condition of employment represents yet another move to bring the press under control. The literacy campaign has extended the junta's reach further into the minds of Nicaragua's people as well as into the countryside. Every lesson in the literacy textbooks instructs students (and teachers) in the prescribed interpretation of Nicaragua's past, present, and future.

Parallel efforts to organize and coordinate other traditionally nongovernmental entities reflect the characteristic totalitarian desire to absorb the society into the state, to transform social groups into agencies and instruments of the government. This has required taking over some existing institutions (banking, industries, television and radio, trade unions), co-opting and/or intimidating others (the private sector, trade unions, the educational establishment, portions of the press), and forcibly eliminating still others (such as the National Guard, whose members have either fled into exile or remain in prison with little prospect of ever being tried, much less released).

When, in early November 1980, representatives of the private sector (COSEP) and the labor federation (CUS) withdrew from the State Council to protest the Sandinistas' ever-tightening grip on all aspects of the economy, no concessions were forthcoming. Instead, the offices of the leading opposition party, the social-democratic MND, were sacked, and an unarmed leader of the private sector, Jorge Salazar, was gunned down by Sandinista police.

Among the traditional pillars of Nicaraguan society only the Church remains relatively intact. While the presence of priests in prominent roles in the Sandinista directorate has facilitated communications between the two groups, this has not been translated into political domination of the Church hierarchy.

But the Sandinistas do not rely on control of these agencies or rules to preserve their power. To accomplish that task new institutions have been forged, the most important of which are an enormous, all-new revolutionary army whose training (military and political) and equipment have been provided by Cubans, and a

new internal police force which is already more extensive and
effective than Somoza's.

Other institutions developed to support the new government
include the "block" committees, which were found to be so useful
in Cuba (and in Nazi Germany), and the revolutionary brigades,
initially assigned to the literacy campaign.

The most telling indicator of the Sandinistas' intentions and
commitments is their unambiguous identification of Nicaragua
with the foreign policy and perspectives of the Soviet Union. The
first step was somewhat tentative: Nicaragua merely abstained on
the U.N. resolution condemning the Soviet invasion of Afghanistan. Subsequent moves have left less room for doubt. At the
Havana conference of the nonaligned nations, Nicaragua became
one of the few countries in the world to recognize Kampuchea (the
regime imposed by North Vietnam on Cambodia), an act which
Foreign Minister Miguel d'Escoto explained as "a consequence of
our revolutionary responsibility as Sandinistas to recognize the
right of the peoples of Kampuchea to be free." In Pyongyang,
another Sandinista leader, Tomas Borge, assured the North
Koreans of Nicaraguan solidarity and promised, "The Nicaraguan
revolution will not be content until the imperialists have been over-
thrown in all parts of the world."

In March 1980 the Sandinista directorate offered a public
demonstration that its ties extended beyond Cuba to the Socialist
Fatherland itself when four top leaders—Moises Morales Hassan,
Tomas Borge, Henry Hernández Ruiz, and Humberto Ortega
Saavedra—paid an official visit to the Soviet Union. A joint com-
muniqué formalized the attachment of Nicaragua to Soviet global
policy. In addition to signing multiple agreements concerning trade
and cooperation, condemning South Africa and Chile, and ap-
plauding Zimbabwe, Khomeini's Iran, and the "legitimate national
rights of the Arab people of Palestine," the "two sides" strongly
attacked the NATO decision to deploy medium-range nuclear
missile weapons and condemned the "mounting international tension in connection with the events in Afghanistan, which has been
launched by the imperialist and reactionary forces aimed at sub-

verting the inalienable rights of the people of the Democratic Republic of Afghanistan and of other peoples . . . to follow a path of progressive transformation."

Since "Zionism's loss of a bastion in Nicaragua" (Moises Hassan), the ties with the "Palestinian people" have become not closer, but more public. The PLO and the Sandinistas had long enjoyed a relationship of mutual support, we are now told. Sandinistas trained in Palestinian camps and participated in PLO raids; the PLO reciprocated by ferrying arms to the Sandinistas in their hour of need. Yasir Arafat received high honors when in July 1980 he opened a PLO embassy in Managua, where he assured the "workers" that "the triumph of the Nicaraguans is the PLO's triumph."

"We have emerged from one dictatorship and entered another," asserted MND leader Alfonso Robelo recently. "Nicaragua has become a satellite of a satellite of the Soviet Union."

Nothing that happened in Nicaragua seemed able to dampen the Carter people's enthusiasm for "change" in Central America. In El Salvador, Guatemala, Bolivia, and wherever else the opportunity presented itself, the administration aligned the United States with the "forces of change." "The fundamental problem we share with our neighbors," Warren Christopher explained, "is not that of defending stability in the face of revolution. Rather, it is to build a more stable, equitable, and pluralistic order. That is the challenge of Nicaragua in the present day and that is the challenge of the whole region."

To meet the challenge, the administration welcomed with enthusiasm a military coup in El Salvador which, in October 1979, overthrew President Carlos Humberto Romero, an event the State Department described as a "watershed date" on which "young officers broke with the old repressive order" and along with "progressive civilians" formed a government committed to "profound social and economic reforms, respect for human rights and democracy." Carter policymakers, had they taken more account of El Salvador's political culture and traditions, would have been less sanguine.

El Salvador is a prototype, almost a caricature, of a Central American republic. Its political history since it was established as an independent republic in 1838 has featured oligarchy, violence, revolution, militarism, and the slow evolution of the institutions of a modern polity.

To an extent unusual even in Latin America, El Salvador had been dominated by a relatively small, homogeneous economic and social aristocracy which controlled a large share of the arable land, much of the country's commerce, and a significant portion of its wealth. As elsewhere in the region, however, the social homogeneity of the elite did not lead to political harmony or stability. Factionalism, schism, low consensus prevailed. Elite factions operating under the symbolism of a two-party system competed for power by legal and nonlegal means. There were periods of peaceful alternation in power and periods when coups and counter-coups, uprisings and revolts, were common. At the beginning of the century there occurred a period of unusual stability. Gradually participation in El Salvador's political process was expanded, and after 1931 large numbers of Salvadorans participated in decision processes—now by legal means, such as the intermittent elections, now through strikes, demonstrations, and other forms of direct action. Through most of the last fifty years, politics in El Salvador was carried on through conventional political parties, occasional elections, military coups, student strikes, trade union actions—that is, by the multiple means and in the multiple arenas common in Latin American politics.

The fifteen-odd constitutions in El Salvador are perhaps the best indicator of its regime instability, and the periodic coups, the last of which occurred in October 1979, are perhaps the best indicator of the chronic institutional weakness that has made it impossible for any government to endure long. The important role of the military, the frequent recourse to force, the multiple constitutions, provide all the evidence required that El Salvador is a polity in which there is little agreement on who should rule, or on the means by which the question should be decided. This is, of course, another way of saying that El Salvador's governments and processes have a low level of legitimacy and authority. The absence of agreement about what makes government legitimate leaves all holders of power vulnerable to the charge that their power is *not* legitimate, gives a certain plausibility to *any* claim for power presented in the name of any conception of the public good, and ensures that there will be no generally accepted means for settling the dispute about who among the rival claimants for power should hold it. Moreover, the ubiquity of violence in the political tradition guarantees that resorting to violence will not be viewed as a disqualification for governing.

The fact of regime instability means that generalized loyalty to the "system" has no opportunity to develop. Under these circumstances, distinctions common in political science between "system" parties and "anti-system" parties become meaningless. There are only incumbents and their policies, and all those who are not with them are against them. Thus, to be anti-incumbent usually means to be anti-system. There is no constitutional means for resolving any dispute about the composition of a government or its policies, because there is, effectively speaking, no constitution, no generally accepted "arrangement of offices" (Aristotle's term). There are only those *persons* who hold power.

Yet serious students of politics agree that legitimacy is an irreducible element of a stable political regime. Max Weber emphasized this principle when he said: "Custom, personal advantage, pure affectual or ideal motives of solidarity do not form a sufficiently reliable basis for a given domination. In addition, there is normally a further element, the belief in *legitimacy*."[23] And Rousseau put it more succinctly at the beginning of Chapter III of his *Social Contract*: "The strongest is never strong enough to be always master, unless he transforms strength into right, and obedience into duty."[24]

Any government whose claim to obedience depends on the fact that it possesses power is vulnerable because any competitor who is able to seize power will then possess an identical claim to obedience. "Obey the powers that be," Rousseau commanded. "If this means yield to force, it is a good precept, but superfluous."[25]

El Salvador's political culture compounds the problem of legitimacy. Like the broader culture, its political culture emphasizes strength and *machismo* and all that implies about the nature of the world and the human traits necessary for survival and success. Competition, courage, honor, shrewdness, assertiveness, a capacity for risk and recklessness, and a certain "manly" disregard for safety are valued. There is a predictable congruity between the cultural traits and political patterns in El Salvador, a congruity expressed in the persistent tendency to schism and violence within the political class. Intermittent disruption and violence make order the highest value in such political systems.

Order, as John Stuart Mill emphasized, is the "preservation of all existing goods." It is also the precondition for all other public goods, as Mill understood better than is generally realized. And, as always, heroes are people who make a special contribution to highly valued goods.

In El Salvador, Hernández Martínez is viewed as such a hero by many. General Maximiliano Hernández Martínez, who governed El Salvador from 1931 to 1944, had been Minister of War in the cabinet of President Arturo Araujo when there occurred widespread uprisings said to be the work of Communist agitators. General Hernández Martínez then staged a coup and ruthlessly suppressed the disorders—wiping out all those who participated, hunting down their leaders. It is sometimes said that 30,000 persons lost their lives in the process. To many Salvadorans the violence of this repression seems less important than the fact of restored order and the thirteen years of civil peace that ensued. The traditionalist death squads that pursue revolutionary activists and leaders in contemporary El Salvador call themselves Hernández Martínez Brigades, seeking thereby to place themselves in El Salvador's political tradition and communicate their purposes.

There is, inevitably, an arbitrary quality about governments which can reform themselves only by force or intrigue. And there is an inevitable brittleness about a polity in which political loyalty means loyalty to particular individuals—not to individuals who have been institutionalized in the fashion that kings and presidents are institutionalized, but to individuals whose claim to power rests ultimately on the fact that they *have* it.

Where there is no legitimacy, there is also no authority. There is only power and the habit of obedience to whoever successfully claims the power of government. *Under these circumstances, a government's status depends, even more than usually, on its capacity to govern, to secure obedience, to punish those who disobey— in sum, to maintain order.* Such a government can command obedience only insofar as it can secure acquiescence in its policies, can rely on habits of obedience, or can impose its commands by force and fear. Such a government is, then, especially vulnerable to terrorist subversion, and for three reasons.

First, not having been chosen by the people, it has no persuasive claim to a popular mandate for its programs. Neither are there institutionalized means for securing such a mandate. Moreover, men who have gained power by force are rarely content to submit their programs for popular approval.

Second, the principal function of terrorism is to disrupt the ordinary life of the society, disturb the normal expectations of ordinary people, and destroy habit and order, which is the central value of a system that has no unique claim to a popular, legal, or moral mandate.

Third, where neither habit nor duty can be relied on to compel obedience, force will be necessary to maintain order. But force also disrupts order and feeds the impression that there is no important difference between rulers who govern by force and challengers who compete with force. *The ultimate weakness of a government that arrives in power by force and must govern by force is its defenselessness against the use of force by others.*

To secure order in El Salvador would either require that all participants (military, guerrillas) agree that they *should* obey the policies of the junta—agree, that is, that the government has a *legitimate* claim on their obedience—or require that the government be able to compel their obedience. But the traditional lack of consensus on the ends and means of government and the broad ideological differences among the parties make agreement on legitimacy unlikely. Like most of its predecessors, the present government probably lacks the necessary force, and moreover, has been inhibited in using the force at its disposal by our policymakers' powerful proclivity for believing that a government's using force is the equivalent of violating human rights.

Until the violent events of November-December 1980, which also saw the suspension of U.S. aid, the Carter administration backed the new Salvadoran junta in the only way it knew how: by helping it to bring about "profound social and economic reforms." In the effort to preempt the revolution and expedite the achievement of "social justice," the administration supplied experts who have planned the most thoroughgoing land reform in the Western Hemisphere. To encourage and finance these and related reforms, the U.S. embassy provided nearly $20 million in long-term loans at very low interest. Under the direction of the American Institute for Free Labor Development, and sponsored by the AFL-CIO, a plan was drafted to transfer to some 250,000 of El Salvador's 300,000 peasants ownership of the land they work.

So far, not all the land has been transferred, and titles have not been delivered for much of what has been transferred. Few of the former owners have yet received any significant compensation. In theory, the reforms will vaccinate the masses against Communism by giving them a stake in the society. In practice, as was made dramatically clear by the murder of three American nuns and a social worker in early December 1980, continuing violence from Communists, anti-Communists, and simple criminals has brought death and destruction to El Salvador. Under the pressure of that violence, the society has begun to come apart. "There is no name for what exists in my country," commented a Salvadoran, describing the random murder, intimidation, and looting. But there is a name; it is "anarchy."

The United States under Carter was more eager to impose land reform than elections in El Salvador. Although claims and counterclaims have been exchanged, there is no way of knowing whether the junta (in any of its manifestations) has enjoyed much popular support. It combines Christian Democrats committed to finding a middle way of "true democracy" between capitalism and Communism with representatives of various tendencies within the armed forces. It is chronically threatened with schism from within and coup from without. Though its civilian members and their State Department supporters have consistently emphasized the danger from the Right—that is, from authoritarian, intensely anti-Communist defenders of the status quo—El Salvador is more likely in the long run to fall to a coalition of revolutionaries trained, armed, and advised by Cuba and others. The cycle of escalating terror and repression is already far advanced. By failing to offer the junta the arms and advice required to turn back the well-equipped insurgency, the Carter administration undermined the junta's ability to survive and encouraged the insurgents in their conviction of ultimate victory.

More than nine thousand persons were slaughtered in El Salvador during the year since the new day dawned. The reforms that were counted on to provide social justice have been stalled by administrative inefficiency and sabotaged by both communitarians and defenders of the *status quo ante*. The harvests counted on to help El Salvador's acute balance-of-payments problems are being menaced and destroyed by revolutionaries for whose cause worse *is* better. Meanwhile, violence perpetrated by Communists, anti-Communists, and simple criminals continues.

WHAT IS TO BE DONE? It is not a problem to which the American temper is well suited. The problem confronting El Salvador is Thomas Hobbes's problem: How to establish order and authority in a society where there is none.

There are few grounds for thinking that Americans who have shaped U.S. policy toward El Salvador have been aware of the distinctive characteristics and problems of such political systems. Had they understood them, then some aspects of our policy would surely have been different. The administration would have been inclined to greet the coup of October 1979 which toppled President Carlos Humberto Romero with mixed feelings, instead of greeting it as Assistant Secretary of State William C. Bowdler did, as the dawn of a new era, a "watershed date," in which "young officers broke with the old repressive order" and along with "progressive civilians" formed a government committed to "profound social and economic reforms, respect for human rights and democracy."

A more prudent appraisal of politics in Central America would have left policymakers a little less enthusiastic about the destruction of any even semi-constitutional ruler, not because they approved the ruler but because they understood that authority in such systems is weak, stability fragile, and order much easier to destroy than reconstruct.

Second, a fuller understanding of the political system of El Salvador would have left U.S. policymakers a bit less sanguine about the short-range contributions of reform to political stability, not because reforms are not desirable but because political traditions and cultures change slowly, not rapidly.* Third, clear comprehension of the problem of order in El Salvador would have made U.S. policymakers more sympathetic to the inability of the government to control the situation, and less anxious to inhibit the use of force against violent challengers.

Armed with an optimistic, deterministic theory of social change, a profound distaste for existing governments in the area, a predilection for confusing revolution with progress, and a doctrine of human rights that makes illegitimate the use of force by governments, U.S. policymakers participated actively in the creation and control of a government and policies with which they are now profoundly unhappy.

One of the fictions widespread in our times is that a successful society can do without force, and that the resort to it is evidence of failure. We like to think that the "force" that decides political contests is *moral force* that derives from the loyalty and allegiance of the people. This was of course the premise of the U.S.

---

* There are, of course, other good reasons for undertaking reform, such as promoting well-being, alleviating poverty, and enhancing the quality of community.

campaign for the "hearts and minds" in Vietnam. It was (and is) also the grounds for the argument that land reform would reinforce the junta in El Salvador: Government would give land to landless peasants; peasants would give loyalty to the government. Revolution would wither away because peasants would be immune to its appeals.

The problem with this theory of course is that revolutions are not born out of the resentments of landless peasants but (as Plato understood) in the bosom of the ruling elite.[26] As Lasswell, Lerner, and associates showed[27] (and dozens of subsequent empirical studies confirmed), revolutions in our times are born in the middle class and carried out by sons of the middle class who have become skilled in the use of propaganda, organization, and violence. Modern tacticians of revolution seem to have understood as well as American policymakers have misunderstood the vulnerability of societies like El Salvador to challenges based on and pressed by force. They seem also to understand the special vulnerability of Western liberals to appeals that feature murder and morality.

Central America was not the only target of the Carter administration's restless search for "constructive change" in the hemisphere. Pressures were applied, and resisted, in Argentina, Brazil, Uruguay, and Bolivia. In Bolivia, the State Department withdrew our ambassador, "drew down" the embassy staff to approximately half its normal size, canceled U.S. aid, terminated the Drug Enforcement Agency's program that aimed at reducing the production of cocoa (and cocaine), and indicated in a dozen other ways its determination not to accept the military junta whose seizure of power prevented the inauguration of Hernan Siles Zuazo as President.

Why did the United States work so hard to undo a coup which had prevented the accession to power of a man whose Vice President had strong Castroite leanings and ties, whose coalition included the Communist party of Bolivia and the Castroite MIR, and whose elevation had been strongly supported by the Soviet Union? When Siles Zuazo polled 38 percent of the vote in a race against moderate socialist Victor Paz Estensorro and the more conservative Hugo Banzer Suarez, the selection of the President was left to the Congress. No legal or conventional niceties required that U.S. influence be exerted in behalf of the selection of Siles Zuazo rather than one of the other candidates. Yet Siles Zuazo became the "American candidate" even though the military had made clear that his selection would not be tolerated. After conversations with the U.S. ambassador that included both threats and promises of aid, Paz Estensorro withdrew and Siles's selection was ensured. The predictable coup occurred.

Even five years ago, the United States would have welcomed a coup that blocked a government with a significant Communist/Castroite component. Ten years ago the United States would have sponsored it, fifteen years ago we would have conducted it. This time, however, the U.S. ambassador to Bolivia and the State Department lobbied hard in Washington and with the press against the new military rulers, insisting that what had occurred was not a coup like the two hundred previous ones, but a singularly objectionable coup marked by unique violence, engineered by foreigners, and led by drug traffickers. The State Department's campaign coincided with a Soviet press offensive, resulting in a sustained international campaign bent on bringing Siles to power.

One understands the desire to see constitutional democracy replace authoritarian governments in Bolivia. Despite a good deal of recent mythmaking to the contrary, Americans have always believed that democracy is the best government for everyone. What was unusual about the Carter policy was the *intensity* of the expressed disapproval and of the administration's preference for a government that included in its leadership persons effectively attached to Soviet policies and hostile to the United States. The decision to throw its weight behind Siles reflected the characteristic predilections of the Carter administration in Latin America, including its indifference to strategic concerns and its tendency to believe that leftists were more likely than any other group to bring democracy and social justice to the area. Supporting Siles seemed to offer the Carter administration an opportunity to assume its preferred role: trying to "moderate," by its goodwill and friend-ship, the "extreme" elements in a governing coalition committed to "basic" social change.

Because it failed to take account of basic characteristics of Latin American political systems, the Carter administration under-estimated the fragility of order in these societies and overestimated the ease with which authority, once undermined, can be restored. Because it regarded revolutionaries as beneficent agents of change, it mistook their goals and motives and could not grasp the problem of governments which become the object of revolutionary violence. Because it misunderstood the relations between economics and politics, it wrongly assumed (as in El Salvador) that economic reforms would necessarily and promptly produce positive political results. Because it misunderstood the relations between "social justice" and authority, it assumed that only "just" governments can survive. Finally, because it misunderstood the relations be-tween justice and violence, the Carter administration fell (and pushed its allies) into an effort to fight howitzers with land reform and urban guerrillas with improved fertilizers.

Above all, the Carter administration failed to understand *pol-itics*. Politics is conducted by persons who by various means, in-cluding propaganda and violence, seek to realize some vision of the public good. Those visions may be beneficent or diabolic. But they constitute the real motives of real political actors. When men are treated like "forces" (or the agents of forces), their intentions, values, and world view tend to be ignored. But in Nicaragua the intentions and ideology of the Sandinistas have *already* shaped the outcome of the revolution, as in El Salvador the intentions and ideology of the leading revolutionaries create intransigence where there might have been willingness to cooperate and compromise, nihilism where there might have been reform.

The first step in the reconstruction of U.S. policy for Latin America is intellectual. It requires thinking more realistically about the politics of Latin America, about the alternatives to exist-ing governments, and about the amounts and kinds of aid and time that would be required to improve the lives and expand the liberties of the people of the area. The choices are frequently unattractive.

The second step toward a more adequate policy is to assess realistically the impact of various alternatives on the security of the United States and on the safety and autonomy of the other nations of the hemisphere.

The third step is to abandon the globalist approach which denies the realities of culture, character, geography, economics, and history in favor of a vague, abstract universalism "stripped," in Edmund Burke's words, "of every relation," standing "in all the nakedness and solitude of metaphysical abstraction." What must replace it is a foreign policy that builds (again Burke) on the "concrete circumstances" which "give . . . to every political principle its distinguishing color and discriminating effect."

Once the intellectual debris has been cleared away, it should become possible to construct a Latin American policy that will protect U.S. security interests and make the actual lives of actual people in Latin America somewhat better and somewhat freer.

On the Invocation of
Universal Values*

FORMER PRESIDENT CARTER'S EMPHASIS on human rights and his
assertion of its irreducible role in American foreign policy seem to
me a good thing, mainly because they remind us and the rest of the
world that this nation's identity and purposes are deeply involved
with the assertion of universal human rights. Totalitarian parties
and governments have so often tagged us the leading capitalist imperialist colonial power that we may, ourselves, find it hard to
remember that the first settlers, in fact, came seeking religious
freedom and espousing a political philosophy that linked legitimacy to consent. It may also be hard to remember that Americans
pioneered the development of government limited by law, popular
accountability, and natural rights.

Candidate Carter's emphasis on these themes was rewarding
to people sick to death of having their motives, characters, and
policies excoriated. For a long decade, the New Left seemed almost to have preempted the moral perspective on political events
—foreign and domestic—not because successive administrations
had embraced *Realpolitik* but because (for various reasons) our

* This essay was prepared in response to former President Carter's
major human rights policy address given at the University of Notre Dame,
May 22, 1977.

9 1

leaders preferred to explain their policies in cool rhetoric while critics delivered moral judgments in less measured, more excited voices. One important consequence of Carter's reemphasis of human rights was to break the anti-establishment monopoly on moral rhetoric. Another has been to reassure Americans and others that U.S. policy is guided by a vision of the public good. A third important effect of the human rights campaign was to affirm a moral principle which needs continuing reaffirmation: that there are universal moral rights that men as men (and women as women) are entitled to and that these ought to be respected by governments. Though aware of the pitfalls of conceiving of foreign policy as a crusade, I am convinced that people and governments cannot live on pragmatism and profits alone—however enlightened the former or abundant the latter. It seems likely that the decreasing frequency in a political system of appeals to conscience signals the erosion of moral consensus and also contributes to it. Since democracies have an especially great need for moral consensus, continuing appeals to conscience are both restorative and stabilizing. For having recalled Americans (and others) to historic moral imperatives and for having placed individual rights back on the international agenda, former President Carter wins my applause. This accomplishment seems to me more important than my misgivings about specific applications of the policy.

It should therefore be clear that my comments on Carter's Notre Dame speech do not reflect generalized disapproval of the administration's foreign policy. My comments are directed only to that speech, which seems to me a particularly poor one. My doubts and puzzlements can perhaps best be expressed by way of the following questions.

1. Why was the President "confident that democracies' examples will be compelling," when history so clearly establishes that democratic governments are both rare and difficult to establish? It is true that developments in Portugal, Spain, and Greece testify to the continuing power of the democratic idea and illustrate the possibilities of building democratic institutions on the ruins of traditional autocracies. But each of these happy cases also

demonstrates the perils and problems that confront efforts to construct governments limited by law, based on majority rule, and guaranteeing political competition and respect for minority rights. The less happy experiences of many nations in Latin America, Eastern Europe, and Africa illustrate how much easier it is to establish autocracies than viable democracies. One may *hope* that the example of freedom provided by the Western democracies will reinforce the human appetite for liberty, but there hardly seem to be adequate grounds for confidence that their example will prove compelling.

2. Why is the arms race "morally deplorable"? Did the President mean that it is intrinsically immoral to spend money on weapons—regardless of the context? Doesn't the moral quality of an arms race depend on the consequences for specified populations of arming or not arming?

3. Why did the President think that "a peaceful world cannot exist one third rich and two thirds hungry"? The implication is that the frustration of poor nations causes war. In fact, the notion that poverty causes war doesn't wash. Poverty causes hardship, suffering, and death among men, women, and children, but there is little evidence to support the notion that it causes war. The Second World War, to take a single example, was not caused by hungry peoples seeking food, but by a rich country seeking living room. Instead of attacking rich states, poor states fight with poor states, while rich states fight with each other. The fighting in Chad, Zaire, Ethiopia, the Sahara, Angola, and Uganda (to choose some conflicts almost at random) reminds us of the many noneconomic causes of war. Poverty does not make poor states indifferent to power and status, any more than wealth makes rich states indifferent to power and status. Poverty is abominable, not because it leads to war, but because it perpetuates human misery. We can approach problems of war and poverty more effectively if we are clear about the relationships between them.

4. A related question: Why did the President think that "we can no longer separate the traditional issues of war and peace from the new global questions of justice, equity, and human rights"?

As most wars are not caused by poverty or hunger, neither are they caused by breaches of "justice, equity, and human rights." Why did the President assert the contrary? Was he prepared to make observance of justice, equity, and human rights a condition of war and peace? Was he suggesting that this nation will or should go to war over such matters? Or that we can achieve peace only with states whose practices meet our standards of justice, equity, and human rights, or that the world will be at peace only if all states achieve justice, equity, and human rights, or what?

5. Why is it "important that we make progress toward normalizing relations with the People's Republic of China"? Is it because the President desires us to have full diplomatic relations with all countries or with all Communist countries? And if so, why? Is that more important than demonstrating the fidelity of our commitments? How would American economic and military interests be better served if we had an ambassador in Peking in place of a high-level representative without the title? Does the President believe that the future of the Sino-Soviet split depends on the title of the American emissary or that the "creative Chinese people" will cease to trade with the United States as long as we have goods and technology they desire?

6. Why, of all African states—or of all states in the world— did the President decide that southern Africa is *the* place in which the "time has come" for a political system based on majority rule and minority rights? I do not doubt Carter's sincerity in advocating a democratic system in Rhodesia, South-West Africa, and South Africa; I do not believe that he meant "black rule" when he said "majority rule" or that he covertly desired to replace white oligarchies with black dictators. But if a white oligarchy does not seem to him more obnoxious than a black dictatorship, on what principle did the President decide that it is more important to establish majority rule and minority rights in southern Africa than, say, in Uganda, or Tanzania, or Zaire, or Togo, or Ghana, or Nigeria, or Benin, or Kenya, or Guinea-Bissau, or Niger, Upper Volta, Chad, Ethiopia, Somalia, Senegal, Sierra Leone, Camaroons, Mozambique, or Angola? Or for that matter, how did he

decide that it is more important to have majority rule and minority rights in southern Africa than in, say, Cuba, Cambodia, North Korea, or the Soviet Union, or than in Chile, Paraguay, or Panama?

The very question testifies to the difficulties encountered when a government attempts to invoke universal moral rules as the justification for a policy which will necessarily be selectively applied. Obviously, President Carter and his advisers should have moved beyond the invocation of universal values and general principles to the knotty business of applying them in this notoriously imperfect, intractable world.

Reflections
on Totalitarianism

I. THE COUNTERCULTURE
OF TOTALITARIANISM

So, THE TOTALITARIANISM DEBATE has begun again and seems to inspire this time around more rage and even less reasoned discussion than before. Persons who doubt the power of ideas must be astonished that a concept can stimulate such fury—a concept that has no reference to a deity or duty, to faith or morals, but is purely analytical. The concept of totalitarianism names no persons, it only names a way of organizing political power, and suggests a way of thinking about the relation between government and society. The concept of totalitarianism names a type of government— one which uses its full power to orient the whole life of a society toward a particular public end. It suggests, thereby, a particular perspective on government that focuses on the relationship between what used to be called the state and society.

Most perspectives on government do not arouse such ire. It is possible to speak of autocracies and oligarchies, democracies and dictatorships, without finding oneself the target of hostile ideological attack. But a mention of totalitarianism stimulates rapid criticism: the word is said to be out of date, useless, tendentious. In our times no concept naming a form of government has been the object of so much obloquy. Indeed, the curious intensity of the critics alerts us that this concept and the perspective which it implies have ideological as well as analytic significance. What precisely is it that arouses these passions and instincts? The reason is that the notion of totalitarianism which was widely acceptable in thinking about the Nazi state suggests a way of thinking about government and society, about power and freedom, that is wholly incompatible with the claim of Marxist-Leninist leaders and movements to be instruments of human liberation. Totalitarianism is a concept that demystifies modern tyranny.

New tyrants prefer to focus attention on past frustrations and future perfections, carefully avoiding any note of who has the power to do what to whom in the actual present. But the concept of totalitarianism recalls one's attention to the specific question of how much power governments have over the lives and fortunes of subjects, or how subjects can protect themselves against the arbitrary use of power. This is precisely the dimension that modern tyrants most ardently desire to obfuscate.

Orwell, Solzhenitsyn, and others have noted that modern totalitarianism coats personal power in "sugary" euphemisms and abstruse Germanic abstractions which obscure the goals, interests, and preferences of real people in great collective nouns. The moral claims of modern tyrants depend entirely on all questions concerning power and freedom being directed to the past and future and *never* being permitted to focus on why this or that specific ruler is justified in depriving specific persons the freedom to read, write, paint, speak as they please, study what they choose, or criticize their own government.

That is not all. The concept of totalitarianism opens the way to comparing all governments on the extent to which government attempts to control the lives of citizens. This way of comparing governments is uniquely unfavorable to those that aim to control the whole lives of citizens.

Totalitarianism is an analytic concept which achieved widespread note during the 1940s and 1950s as a generation attempted to confront intellectually the horror of the Nazi and Soviet regimes —their slave labor and extermination camps, mutual surveillance, propaganda, and hostility to human liberty. Such scholars as Emil

Lederer, Hannah Arendt, J. L. Talmon, Alfred Cobban, and Carl J. Friedrich offered explanations of the Hitler and Stalin regimes—each of which was horrible in unique ways yet shared with the other some distinctive characteristics that distinguished them from previous dictatorships. Cobban emphasized the extent to which modern technology had expanded the reach and penetration of modern dictatorship and qualitatively altered its character. Arendt emphasized irrationality, organization, and terror. Talmon considered ideology, and Friedrich the institutional mechanisms of total power. All saw Nazi and Bolshevik governments as sharing the drive to establish comprehensive political control over the lives of individuals, obliterating in both theory and practice the distinction between public and private, between objective and subjective, claiming for the state the whole life of the whole people.

Today, four decades later, these thinkers remain our best guide to this extraordinary contemporary phenomenon. Yet much of the mystery remains: How can it be that in the contemporary world the many permit the few to deprive them of freedom, send them to slave camps, annihilate them? Why, it may be answered, this is accomplished by force. But how do some men gain control of the instruments of force? What are such men like? What do they think they are doing? This last question is especially interesting. Human beings are purposive, goal-seeking creatures who, as Harold Lasswell has emphasized, seek power in the name of some vision of a collective "good." It is particularly interesting to know how the elites of the great modern totalitarian states conceive their missions.

Understanding the modern totalitarian, however, is complicated by the fact that no one admits to the label. There is no body of doctrine which argues the case for totalitarianism as there are writings by anarchists that argue the case for anarchism, by democrats that argue the case for democracy, by nationalists that advocate nationalism. Totalitarianism, like tyranny, is a different kind of "ism," one without explicit defenders. It is, rather, a concept developed by political scientists, in the effort to understand some important and unfamiliar political systems of our times. Like most political terms, this one has developed affective political and moral connotations and has come under attack more for ideological than scientific reasons.[1]

Governments, it is well understood, may be classified according to various criteria. The most ancient and familiar taxonomy of regimes is, of course, based on the number of rulers: Herodotus, Plato, and their contemporaries classified governments according to this criterion, and arrived at such categories as monarchy, aristocracy, and democracy. Governments have also been classified according to their socioeconomic bases, their relationship to religious purposes, their relationship to law, their moral quality, the origins of their rulers, and so forth.[2] More recently, American political scientists have developed taxonomies classifying governments according to criteria that purport to measure their degree of political development.[3]

Systems of classification reflect characteristics of political life regarded as significant or interesting by the classifier. They are analytic tools, designed to help us think clearly about some dimensions of politics. A good system of classification produces categories which are exhaustive, mutually exclusive, and capable of being measured in some way. If it is successful, a taxonomy illuminates a slice of political reality of concern to the investigator and helps to distinguish it from other, somewhat similar phenomena.

The taxonomy which includes totalitarianism as a category focuses not on the number of rulers, nor on how they come to power, but on the operational goals of a regime. A totalitarian regime is distinguished by its rulers' determination to transform society, culture, and personality through the use of coercive state power. Nontotalitarian systems—whether autocracies or democracies—do not use power for such broad purposes.[4] The distinguishing characteristic of totalitarian goals is that they dramatically extend the scope of governmental activity. Since governments commit their power wherever they act, goals which expand the scope of government activity also expand the scope of coercion in a society.

All governments utilize coercive power to enforce their prescriptions, and, of course, the coercive power of government is but
one of various types of power present in any society. It differs in
certain crucial respects from the sanctions of other groups: the
coercive power of government is more comprehensive, its sanctions are more difficult to escape than the sanctions of such groups
as churches and voluntary associations, and the coercive power of
government may involve greater deprivations (e.g., imprisonment
or loss of life).[5] It is clear that action by governments does not
necessarily lead to a net increase of coercion in a society,[6] since
government action can—and sometimes does—eliminate other
types of social coercion, as when government acts to limit the
freedom of employers to punish workers who join unions or acts
against teachers who abuse pupils. But government involvement in
an aspect of life always alters the interaction in the affected area
by introducing new, potentially more severe deprivations. Some
critics of the concept of totalitarianism, such as Benjamin Barber,
have denied that there is a significant difference between law and
other forms of social control (that is, between the rules of government and the rules of other groups), suggesting that individual
freedom exists only in the absence of social pressure. This argument lacks persuasiveness, since it denies that however undesirable
it is to be fired or segregated or expelled, it is still more undesirable
(for almost all people, almost everywhere, under almost all circumstances) to be imprisoned or executed.

The rules of governments are authoritative not only because
they are regarded as legitimate by rulers and some portion of the
ruled, but also because, where necessary, obedience to them is
coerced and disobedience punished. Governments govern. When
their prescriptions (laws) are broadly or frequently ignored, governments do not govern. Neither do they long endure. Because of
the necessity of being obeyed (being regarded as authoritative),
wherever a government legislates, it commits its coercive power.
Therefore, the more areas in which a government legislates, the
more broadly it stands ready to coerce. It follows, then, that when

we speak of the scope of governments' activity (the scope of governments' commitment of coercive power) we are discussing a dimension of government especially significant for human freedom.

Totalitarian governments are those whose rulers see the whole of society, economy, culture, and personality as appropriate fields for governmental regulation. What one reads, writes, studies, publishes, works at, where one lives and works, what one is paid, and by whom, are all thought to be the business of government. The late Carl J. Friedrich identified totalitarian regimes as those which include:

(1) a totalist ideology; (2) a single party committed to this ideology and usually led by one man, the dictator; (3) a fully developed secret police, and three kinds of monopoly or, more precisely, monopolistic control: namely that of (a) mass communication; (b) operational weapons; (c) all organizations, including economic ones, thus involving a centrally planned economy.[7]

The definition I propose differs only in emphasis from Friedrich's. A totalitarian government is one prepared to use government's coercive power to transform economic and social relations, beliefs, values, and psychological predispositions. Totalitarianism obliterates the distinction between state and society and eliminates thereby those interstices of the law in which freedom thrives.

While there is no doctrine that advocates totalitarianism as such, totalitarian practices are closely related to a specific type of political doctrine. Totalitarianism is utopianism come to power.[8] Totalitarian practices derive from a variety of utopianism which (1) conceives the ultimate purposes of the individual as identical with those of the state (or race or class), and (2) conceives coercion as an instrument for the achievement of these ends. Totalitarian utopians attribute no independent or intrinsic value or reality to individuals. Persons matter only as examples and members of a collectivity.

Although the relationship between totalitarianism and utopianism is close, indeed crucial, the two are by no means identical.[9] The various kinds of political proposals and predictions commonly called utopian differ as to both ends and means. Not all have an affinity with totalitarianism. Some utopias are chiefly concerned with material aspects of life and seek to end want or work or pain. Others are mainly concerned with the achievement of moral perfection—with the good man and the good society. Some utopias are concerned with both moral and material goods. Some assume that the ends of the individual and the collectivity are identical, others do not. Some expect their goals must be achieved by education and persuasion, others are ready to use force.

The most influential utopian political philosophy of our times is Marxism, which, though it postulates economic determinism, has never been concerned chiefly with material goods. The moral impulse—to improve man's moral condition—has played a crucial role in the history of Marxism, as theory, political movement, and government. Karl Marx was missionary as well as revolutionary. His mission was the moral deliverance of man. To Marx, common ownership was not only a more just form of economic organization, it was also seen as a means to moral regeneration, a precondition to ending the exploitation of man by man. The redistribution of wealth was seen as the economic precondition to the elimination of power and exploitation in social relations, the elimination of greed and envy from the human soul.

All utopian political philosophies affirm the fundamental harmony of persons, otherwise utopia would be troubled with the same intractable conflicts as the existing world.[10] But the totalitarian variant also emphasizes the identity of individual and collective purposes, promising that the moral purposes of individuals will be fulfilled as the purposes of the race, class, species, or history are achieved. *The moral perfection of men is thus inextricably related to and made dependent on the perfection of society.* Since both individual and collective goals are teleological, morality lies in fulfilling the purposes and achieving the ends "intrinsic" to one's nature—as defined by the relevant ideology. Like medieval laws, individual purposes are found, not made. The individuals' goals are "given" in the structure of the universe, or history, or man, and are therefore always non-negotiable. Individuals cannot change them; they can only conform to them.

Not all utopians seek political power to accomplish their goals. Some—for example, the "utopian" socialists—eschew it. A distinguishing characteristic of totalitarian ideology is the choice of political power as the principal instrument for achieving the moral goals of man and society. Since the totalitarian ideologue knows what is moral, and since power should be used to serve morality, obviously power should rest in his hands. The utopian's moral goals are invoked to justify his use of power. The utopian's (imagined) monopoly of morality justifies his demand for a monopoly of power.

Totalitarianism is rooted in the variety of utopian political philosophy which seeks moral reform ends through political means. Totalitarians use power to remake men.

Totalitarian politics begins with a critique of the morality of existing persons and institutions and promises to reform them. The critique rejects as immoral existing patterns of social and economic relations (society); existing conceptions of reality and purpose (culture); existing modes of perceiving, wanting, and behaving (personality). To the putative immorality of existing social reality the totalitarian critique juxtaposes its own moral vision.

The totalitarian claim to power, then, rests on two pillars: distinctive goals and a distinctive critique of existing society which starts with a sweeping indictment of people as they actually exist and serves as a license for destroying existing institutions and people.

Because of its central importance to the ideological foundations of totalitarian movements, the radical critique deserves more attention than it gets. The essential elements of the critique are common to various utopian ideologies including Marxism, Communism, and some variants of Puritanism, and to such New Left thinkers as Herbert Marcuse and Frantz Fanon. The radical critique rejects existing culture, existing modal personality. It has four essential elements:

First, an attack on people as they actually exist as corrupt, greedy, envious, materialistic, egotistic, and so forth.

Second, an *assumption* that the moral failures of human beings (however these are defined) are a result of bad social organization and can be "cured": change the society, create "new" men.

Third, an attack on dominant conceptions of reality by way of a doctrine of "false consciousness" that invalidates the ideas and preferences of everyone except the revolutionary.

Fourth, the recommendation of a new epistemology which makes knowing a function of ideology: to know the workers' true wants or wishes, consult Marx or Marcuse.

From the perspective of the radical critique, existing societies are reprehensible not only because they are unjust but because they are responsible for the corruption, debasement, and dehumanization of almost everybody (except the totalitarian ideologue and his cohorts, who have—miraculously—escaped the general demoralization).

The assumption that people can be not merely different but better serves as the premise of the radical critique and associated ideologies. The gap between human degradation (or what is perceived as human degradation) and human potentiality (or what is perceived to be human potentiality) serves as both spur and moral mandate for revolution. Its theme admits of endless variations: once society is reordered on the basis of the new, true principles, men will be more heroic, more altruistic, more industrious, more creative, loving, reasonable, dedicated, integrated, "whole," and so forth. An important aspect of the rejection of existing persons is the charge that they are so alienated from reality and themselves that they do not even know their own wants and needs. Therefore they need not be consulted even about their own lives.

The doctrine of false consciousness is at least as old as Plato, in whose *Republic* it played essentially the same role as in subsequent doctrines of comprehensive revolution: to explain why most people do not see the world as the revolutionary does, and do not want what he wants.

Because it explains away alternative views as socially based illusions, the doctrine of false consciousness establishes an epistemological basis for the revolutionary's claim to be the arbiter of reality. Thus, the failure of British workers to desire revolution could be interpreted by Lenin not as an indication that Marx's theory had been mistaken, but as proof the workers did not know their own true interests and wants.

Epistemologies associated with doctrines of false consciousness settle questions about the nature of things by reference to their own doctrine. Since "evidence" is also defined with reference to doctrine and not to observation, it is never possible to disprove any portion of the revolutionary's ideology. Because they invalidate all perceptions and preferences inconsistent with prescribed doctrines, theories of false consciousness are necessarily antiempirical and antidemocratic. (The idea of false consciousness is closely associated with the sociology of knowledge and shares with such theories the problem of explaining how the critic managed to escape the social determinism that affects everyone else—how he manages to perceive reality while others share hallucinations.)

Although it suggests that almost everyone is confused about almost everything, the doctrine of false consciousness is often perceived as sympathetic to the masses—doubtless because it defines them as victims and "excuses" them at the same time it invalidates their views and preferences.

In our times, radical critiques of society have proliferated, and many versions have enjoyed—and in some circles continue to enjoy—great prestige. Versions of the radical critique have appeared in the writings of Laing, Marcuse, Fanon, and certain of the Women's Liberation spokespersons. The most influential version of a radical critique in this century is that of Karl Marx.

The Marxist version of the radical critique is well known: capitalism debases and dehumanizes workers at the same time that it exploits them, filling their heads with religion and other mystifications characteristic of the cultural "superstructure," the whole of which is an elaborate rationalization of exploitation. Only the dialectic can provide a true understanding of reality and history, and a guide to the future out of which a new noncompetitive, unconflicted, unaggressive man will emerge after the revolution has ended alienation and the economic exploitation of man by man.[11] It is less widely understood that in *Mein Kampf* Adolf Hitler also provided a classic version of the radical critique. In it are expressed Hitler's revulsion for the corrupt society of Weimar, an assumption that this corruption is caused by a maldistribution of power, an expectation that mankind can be "cured" of its moral imperfections, a doctrine of false consciousness, and a new racialist epistemology.

Hitler, for whom idealized Germans became the basis of a new religion, filled many pages with scornful descriptions of actual Germans. He describes the German masses as "no longer human beings,"[12] characterized by "moral and ethical coarseness . . . and low level . . . intellectual development."[13] He asks of the "gullible," "unreasoning" workers beside whom he labored, "are these people human, worthy to belong to a great nation?"[14] Hitler's contempt for real Germans knew no bounds of class. *Mein Kampf* is also studded with insults directed at the "bourgeois voting cattle" who helped create the alienation and degradation of the masses by their stupidity, cupidity, and egoism.

"I do not know which is more terrible," he wrote, "inattention to social misery such as we see every day among the majority of those who have been favored by fortune or who have risen by their own efforts, or else the snobbish or at times tactless and obtrusive condescension of certain women of fashion in skirts or trousers, who 'feel for the people.' In any event, these gentry sin far more than their minds, devoid of all instinct, are capable of realizing."[15]

Revolted by the depravity he perceived around him, Hitler concluded that "these people are the unfortunate victims of bad conditions." His explanation exculpated the masses at the same time that it depersonalized them, displaced his contempt and aggression, and integrated both into a political ideology.

"If I did not wish to despair of the men who constituted my environment at that time, I had to learn to distinguish between their external characters and lives and the foundations of their development. Then from all the misery and despair, from all the filth and outward degeneration, it was no longer human beings that emerged, but the deplorable results of deplorable laws . . ."[16]

Mein Kampf assigns German culture and institutions the responsibility for corrupting the "miserable wretches" who peopled Germany and Austria in the Weimar period. The process of political socialization through which bad institutions produced bad individuals is described in detail by Hitler: Leaving his native village for the city, attracted by the hope of less onerous work or a more glamorous life, "the peasant boy who goes to the big city" encounters unemployment, insecurity, urban poverty, and hardship.[17] Though not "made of poorer stuff than his brother who continues to make a living from the peasant sod,"[18] he eventually becomes demoralized, indolent, and irresponsible, an indifferent tool of the Marxist politicians, an improvident head of family, breeder of a new generation of cynical, half humans. The dingy, crowded apartment in which he lives helps destroy the family, for

in these circumstances, people do not live with one another, they press against one another. Every argument, even the most trifling, which in a spacious apartment can be reconciled by mild segregation, thus solving itself, here leads to loathsome wrangling without end. . . . Morally poisoned, physically undernourished, his poor little head full of lice, the young citizen goes to school, [where he learns little, and has little incentive to learn since his parents continually undermine the teacher, the government, religion, morality.] When at the age of fourteen the young man is discharged from school, it is hard to decide what is stronger in him: his incredible stupidity as far as any real knowledge and ability are concerned, or the corrosive insolence of his behavior, combined with an immorality, even at this age, which would make your hair stand on end.[19]

"Trashy films, yellow press and such-like dung" finish his education. His depravity is complete.

The people whom Hitler hoped to save were misled and corrupted by vile and corrupt institutions. The schools were given to stuffing children's heads full of unnecessary sterile facts,[20] dress was foolish, perverse, and promoted the seduction of "hundreds of thousands of girls by bow-legged, repulsive Jewish bastards."[21] The political parties were guilty of treason,[22] politicians were characterized by "degeneracy,"[23] stupidity,[24] lying, and treachery.[25] Parliament was a charade filled with self-seeking "good-for-nothings and lounge-lizards"[26] who posed as representatives of the people—"a wild gesticulating mass screaming all at once in every different key." And worst of all was the press: "the brutal daily press, shunning no villainy, employing every means of slander, lying with a virtuosity that would bend the beams, all in the name of their gospel of a new humanity."[27] The press, Hitler believed, had a special role in creating a false culture and consciousness. It derided authentic values, subverted national identifications and honor, insidiously planted doubts concerning all aspects of traditional German life and, always, prepared the way for the triumph of Marxism.

Behind them all—the corrupt institutions, the perverse practices, the subversion of the people—stood the ultimate villain: world Jewry with its diabolical plot of world domination. The corrupt German people were not to blame, for "who, in view of the diabolic craftiness of the seducer, could damn the luckless victims?"[28]

As Adolf Hitler saw it, it was his duty to destroy this corrupt culture and society, to rescue the hapless victimized people and restore them to purposeful moral lives. The strategy which he developed foresaw the transformation of German culture. Hitler was an idealist in the sense that he conceived culture (ideas) as the foundation of both institutions and history.[29] Aryan supremacy was justified because "human culture and civilization on this continent are inseparably bound up with the presence of the Aryan. If he dies out or declines, the dark veils of an age without

culture will again descend on this globe."[30] German mastery of
the world would mean "putting the world into the service of a
higher culture."[31] Culture is also at the base of Germany's problems. Lack of will, that is, cultural subversion, defeated Germany
in World War I. The "deadly poison of Marxist ideas"[32] had
infected Germany, demoralizing her people, undermining her
strength and purpose. The first and crucial task of the new order
was the destruction of the rotten culture of a rotten era.

For Hitler, as for the other totalitarian leaders, *culture is
ideology.* Internalized, culture is false consciousness. Art, literature, dress, values, habitual ways of conceiving, valuing, relating,
and behaving are political because the existing culture embodies,
is, the corrupt ideology of the existent society. The revolutionary's
ideology is, then, a counterculture.

The revolutionary task is to transform the new redemptive
ideology from counterculture to culture. The sector of the population most useful in the transformation of culture is that least
affected by the poisons of the existing culture, namely the lowest
portions of the working class, the bohemians, and other marginal
persons—the lumpen proletariat. Hitler says of this group that it
"did not count the worst elements in its ranks, but on the contrary
definitely the most energetic elements. The over-refinements of so-
called culture had not yet exerted their disintegrating and destructive effects. The broad mass of the new class was not yet infected
with the poison of pacifist weakness; it was robust and, if necessary, even brutal."[33]

For Hitler as for all totalitarians the translation of ideology
into culture is to be achieved through political power. This route
is, clearly, not the only conceivable route to the broad transformation of society, culture, and personality. Some religions have advocated cultural revolution and moral redemption through individual conversions. Some reformers, such as the Fabians, have
advocated cultural and political change through education and
propaganda. Some contemporary cultural revolutionists advocate
or predict transformation through manipulation of media or
through drug-induced alteration of consciousness. Through history

many strategies for change have been proposed. *A distinguishing characteristic of the totalitarian ideologue is the choice of political power and coercion as the principal instrument for transforming man and society, for translating his ideology into the dominant culture. It is this choice of political means which distinguishes totalitarianism from other types of utopianism—this choice which ensures that the road to utopia will pass through Gulag.*

When totalitarian ideology is conceived as a counterculture, several aspects of totalitarian politics are illuminated. First, the comprehensive character of totalitarian ideology is clarified; while ideology often concerns only politics—narrowly conceived—culture includes the entire symbolic environment. Culture defines reality: what is, what should be, what can be. It provides focus and meaning. It selects out of the myriad of events and interactions in the world those we pay attention to. Culture tells us what is important; what causes what, how events beyond our lives relate to us. Culture gives us values and standards of value. What we may distinguish analytically (and at our peril) as fact, value, and goal is existentially integrated in culture—in the identifications, expectations, and demands of individual persons. When culture is viewed as ideology, as by Hitler, Marx, Fanon, or Marcuse, conceptions of reality, value, and purpose become objects of political action, and securing acceptance of new conceptions of reality, value, and purpose becomes the object of political revolution. That is why control of the symbolic environment has such high priority for totalitarian governments.

Since culture lives through people who have internalized it, suppression of a culture involves the suppression of its carriers. The effort to eradicate a culture by official policy necessarily involves governments in massive repression. Hitler explicitly discussed the use of political power to eradicate an opposing ideology. He asks himself, "Can spiritual ideas be exterminated by the sword? Can 'philosophies' be combatted by the use of brute force?" He answers, "Conceptions and ideas, as well as movements with a definite foundation, regardless whether the latter is false or true, can, after a certain point in their development, only be broken with technical instruments of power if these physical weapons are at the same time the support of a new kindling thought, idea, or philosophy."[34]

Because culture is internalized by almost all the members of any society, commitment to the use of force to effect cultural change leads to quite literally saturating a society with coercion, not necessarily terror, but at least coercion. In any society—whether Weimar Germany, czarist Russia, turn-of-the-century Britain, *ancien régime* France, or contemporary America—people are both consequences and carriers of the culture. Therefore, transforming culture and character requires (a) that people be changed through purposive social engineering, thought reform, and other types of reeducation, and (b) that they be prevented from spreading moral infection to the next generation. Therefore, youth must be protected from corruption by careful control of the socialization process, from which the bad old conceptions and habits will be purged, through which the good new ways of thinking and being will be communicated. This is why direct and broad involvement in the socialization process is a hallmark of totalitarian systems. It is the preferred strategy by which the ruling elite attempts to create new men modeled on the moral ideal provided by the ideology. State nurseries, Young Pioneers, Hitler Youth, the close control of schools and texts, are all familiar manifestations of totalitarian interest in socialization.

The totalitarian doctrine and leaders of the movement provide the character models toward which the new socialization process is oriented. Marxism offers not one but two character ideals: one for the revolutionary struggle, provided largely by the biography and writings of Lenin; one for the Communist utopia, provided largely by the writings of the young Marx. These two character ideals are related to each other by their detailed dialectical opposition. The character model for Communist society demands utterly renouncing power; the model revolutionary is ceaselessly concerned with power. The model Communist citizen will treat human beings only as ends; the revolutionary is expert in the ways of war, sabotage, riot, and revolt. The model Communist has delicate moral sensibilities; the revolutionary must be prepared to lie, cheat, steal, murder. The dissimilarity of the two models is the movement's principal source of tension and of disillusion. Still, the two models are related as means to ends: the revolutionary's claim to morality derives entirely from the moral regeneration promised for the end of the struggle. Acceptance of the presumably temporary negation in the self of the ideals which bind the revolutionary to the movement requires faith, reinforced by ambivalence. Love/hate, skepticism/faith, peace/war, truth/lies, appreciation/manipulation—the dialectic is applied to the psyche. The abstract positive goals—love, peace—justify the concrete negative actions. Their invocation sanctifies aggression. Whatever its merits as a critical tool for understanding history, in the psychological realm the dialectic is the most powerful instrument since the discovery of religious war for the liberation of moral restraint and the mobilization of aggression.

The two models—of the revolutionary and of the Communist citizen—share the same principle of legitimacy: justification of the individual in terms of a collective historical purpose. Individual morality derives from collective purposes to which the individual devotes and subordinates himself. (Note that this subordination of the individual to the group seems to many to add moral status to the movement, for the tendency remains strong to approve remote, collective, transcendental goals as opposed to personal ones. However humane, enlightened, and temperate the pursuit of self-interest, large numbers judge it selfish and mean as compared to dedication to some self-transcending goal—however irrational or destructive. The multiple contemporary critiques of liberalism and liberal society hark back eventually to liberalism's lack of moral goals, with "moral" defined as self-transcending. Indeed, it is problematic whether an ideology which offers no glorious [and aggressive] transcendent purposes can compete with one which permits all and promises salvation.)

Hitler's moral vision rested on the same foundation of ambivalence. Unlike Bolshevism, however, Nazism offered one character model, not two. Opposite trends were embodied simultaneously in the same individual: with positive feelings directed toward the Aryans, negative feelings toward their enemies. Because Marxism treats aggression, violence, and power as means whose utility will wither away, it is possible to regard these as less real because less permanent than in Nazism, where they were assumed to be permanent aspects of character and society. For this reason the Nazi character ideal was less attractive to idealists who desire to indulge aggression and hostility while denying their reality. Still, Nazism also provided opportunities for love and hate, destruction and regeneration, for solidarity and for submerging the self in transcendent collective purposes. A credible opportunity to dedicate oneself to communal purposes, to integrate the tensions of divided modern man in a comprehensive system of loving and hating, denying and indulging—such an opportunity for murder and morality does not come often in our time. Nazism somehow attained the credibility for hundreds of thousands of symbolically impoverished central Europeans that Marxism enjoys much more widely. The bases of this credibility are still not fully clear, in part because revulsion at the Nazi orgy of destruction has inhibited the "empathetic" inquiry necessary to probe the appeals of a movement, though it should be noted that the massive human destruction of the Soviet political system has not inhibited empathetic examination of Marxism-Leninism. (It may be that success and failure are as important as moral quality in determining who tries to understand whom.)

It seems clear, however, that any revolutionary or totalitarian character ideal, to be persuasive, must give broad scope to hostile feelings, especially to anti-authority trends, since the revolutionary's job is above all destruction, and it must provide a powerful balm to the conscience, since patricide is a fearsome crime. A distinctive mix of indulgence and renunciation is therefore always present in revolutionary character. But aggression is the passion whose indulgence is permitted; love the passion that must be renounced till after the revolution has been achieved.

Accustomed to equating asceticism with sexual abstinence, we sometimes fail to remark the distinctive characteristics of totalitarian demands for discipline. Subordination of the self to the demands of the movement means a willingness to subordinate the concrete attachments and obligations of personal life to the exigencies of political organizations. In Goebbels' didactic novel, the steel-jawed Aryan hero marches bravely to war while his proud Aryan sweetheart cheers him on. In proletarian art, the steel-jawed worker concentrates on his productive function with single-mindedness.

Like most disciplines freely chosen, this one also offers rewards as well as constraints. Persons attracted to ideologies that feature enemies, struggle, and multiple opportunities for aggression are not likely to have untroubled private lives. The opportunity to renounce a "lesser" concrete love for an approved collective hate is not unwelcome to those who prefer mankind to men.[35]

Conceiving culture as ideology—and the revolutionary ideology as counterculture—clarifies the cultural task of totalitarian ruling elites, namely, to implant as the dominant culture of the society the ideology which is espoused by the revolutionary elite. The success of a totalitarian revolution depends on whether it can do this. Some scholars have argued that totalitarian ideologies are in their nature incapable of taking root and becoming operative cultures. Clement Moore takes this position: "Totalitarian systems are inherently unstable in that they attempt the logically impossible tasks, in Brzezinski's words, 'institutionalizing revolutionary zeal.' Totalitarian ideology is inherently incompatible with bureaucratic routine or legal order, for it demands the perpetual movement of permanent revolution."[36]

It has also been argued that ubiquitous terror is a necessary characteristic of totalitarianism (as in Stalinist Russia, the Nazi regime, or the Chinese Cultural Revolution) and that the decline of terror signals the end of the totalitarian regime. But if a chief task of the totalitarian is to translate ideology into culture, then one would expect the role of coercion in the cultural sphere to decline with time as habit, socialization, and the succession of generations result in progressive internalization of the new ways of thinking and valuing and in progressive conformity to new modes of behavior. As new norms are internalized, new beliefs accepted, new habits established, the need to coerce conformity through crash "thought reform" programs and punishment of dissenters should decline.

To the extent that the revolutionary ideology is internalized, it also becomes the foundation of new institutions; its principles are embodied and reflected in the institutions of society. Schools, government offices, military forces, theaters, and industries will be comprised of persons acculturated to the new culture, acting in patterns appropriate to it. Conformity to the new patterns would then be based on the mix of habit, loyalty, and fear characteristic of political institutions generally. This is what would be meant, I presume, by the institutionalization of a totalitarian ideology. If so, then what is the problem with the idea of "institutionalizing revolution"? Why has the possibility of its being institutionalized been repeatedly doubted? The explanation lies, I think, in some special characteristics of totalitarian ideologies.

To raise the question of internalizing these ideologies is to ask, "What are the limits, if any, of the capacity of rulers to change beliefs and behavior, to secure acceptance of new norms and models?" Obviously, human credibility and variability are impressive. In our own century societies have held an arresting range of beliefs about themselves, their world, their purposes, morality, and politics. We have watched whole societies succumb to the notion that they constituted a superior race ordained by history to order the world, or a superior civilization bound by moral obligation to civilize others, or a more virile, basically stronger people justified in wreaking violence on others. Within this century whole societies have moved from belief that women, blacks, Indians, and others were inferior in intellectual, moral, or other capacities to belief in their equality. We have watched dominant opinion shift from laissez faire to welfare state to socialist assumptions, and back again, on what type of economic system promotes widest prosperity and progress. We have seen societies institutionalize standardized tests as accurate, unbiased measures of intelligence and skill, and then begin to discard them as merely measures of the testers' preferences. We have watched segregation denounced as racist and reintroduced by black-power advocates. We have seen enemies become allies, and allies become enemies. We have seen intolerance on the Right largely supplanted by intolerance on the Left.

With these changes in belief about the nature of reality have gone equally wide shifts in the choice and interpretation of values. Within our country in this century we have seen such traditional American values as thrift, hard work, and self-denial give way to "consumer" orientations. We have seen the redefinition of patriotism, of rectitude, of national goals. With the revolution of present beliefs has gone the reevaluation of the past—of white settlers, Indians, the frontier, and the American experience.[37]

The rate of cultural change has sensitized us, too, to the range of behavior models acceptable to people. As late as 1950, the Beatles or the Grateful Dead—their hair, dress, beat, lyrics, drugs, life-style—would have been quite simply incredible as behavior models. From Horatio Alger to the Midnight Cowboy, from the post-Puritan capitalism of the early twentieth century to the romantic anarchism of the sixties, our own cultural revolution has proceeded—creating cultural stereotypes, inspiring new modes of thinking, dressing, listening, loving, politicking, in short, new ways of being, and leaving in its wake the debris of past identifications and habits. Other societies in other times and places provide still more dramatic proof of the range of human adaptability, the variety of acceptable behavior models: the Hindu widows on funeral pyres, the mendicant orders, the flagellants, the sun kings, the slaves, the slave auctioneers, the Adolf Eichmanns, the hangmen, the pacifists, the feet binders, the Inquisitors, the confessed witches and their accusers. Obviously, human patterns of adaptation are many and varied. Given the myriad ways of perceiving reality, conceiving purposes, and modeling behavior, are we justified in arguing that there are limits to human malleability, that there are varieties of ideology that cannot be translated into culture and institutionalized? That is the question with which we are confronted by those who argue that totalitarian ideology defies institutionalization.

This question turns on the nature of totalitarian ideology, the ingenuity and determination of totalitarian ruling elites, and the limits of human malleability. The goals that totalitarian ideologies postulate have some interesting characteristics already alluded to.

First, the goals are *universal*. They deal not with concrete aspirations of concrete people, but with the presumed ends of collectivities or trans-empirical powers, e.g., classes, races, history.

Second, they are *teleological*. They are depersonalized in the sense that they do not derive from the aspirations of concrete persons (past, present, or future) but constitute the "destiny" of some collectivity or trans-empirical power. The ruling elite is, of course, merely the "midwife" or agent of these foreordained purposes. Since the purposes are grounded "in the nature of things" (e.g., the laws of history, the cultural creativity of the Aryan) they are not subject to negotiation, nor influenced by human preferences. Marx put it clearly when he said, "It is not a question of what this or that proletarian, or even the entire proletariat, at one time or another imagines to be its goal. It is a matter of what [the proletariat] is, and what in accordance with that being, it will historically be forced to do."[38]

Third, the goals are *final*. They involve replacing flux with stability: the permanent ordering of the world, the thousand-year Reich, the end of history. The totalitarian is not interested in tinkering, in piecemeal resolution of problems, but in final solutions. Final solutions resolve conflict, are the *end* of conflict. Order and harmony replace flux and conflict. Marx communicated this sense of ultimate ordering of man and society with such descriptions of Communism as: "It is the true resolution of the conflict between existence and essence, objectification and self-affirmation, freedom and necessity, individual and species."[39]

Fourth, the goals are *comprehensive*, involving everyone, involving all aspects of human life and society.

Fifth, the goals are *moral,* in the sense that they postulate the fulfillment of man's moral mission: the end of exploitation of man by man, the ordering of human life for the achievement of higher culture, the elimination of power as a principle of human relations. The vision of a totalitarian ideologist always includes a future in which the masses have been morally elevated by the revolution. Totalitarian ideologues abhor the pedestrian, the personal, the practical, the self-interested, the materialistic, the conflicted. They seek to replace conflict with unity, flux with stability, materialism with dedication to ideals, self-interest with altruism, "muddling through" with comprehensive planning, messiness with order, politics with utopia.[40]

Sixth, they promise *an end to alienation.* Because they identify individual with collective goals and purposes, totalitarian ideologies are not only anti-individualist, they promise an end to disharmony among individuals and *within* individuals. False consciousness, isolation, anomie, separation, loneliness, purposelessness—all are defined as *subjective consequences of objective social ills,* therefore as capable of being eradicated through social engineering. All twentieth-century radical critiques deplore the loss of individual identification with social roles and social purposes as a curse of modern society. All promise to "solve" man's isolation and to restore him to a full sense of social membership. Peter Berger has argued that the very "essence" of totalitarianism is "the intention of overcoming the modern dichotomy of private and public spheres."[41] Whether or not the dichotomy between self and society is a specifically "modern" phenomenon as Berger argues or a more persistent aspect of human experience as it seems to me, modern totalitarians share a commitment to its elimination.

The totalitarian's methods are as distinctive as his goals. He is, as we have seen, distinguished from other utopians by his willingness—no, his determination—to use state power to achieve these goals. "Scientific" socialists are those that organize and use power to achieve their goals. They understand, even if most of the rest of us do not, that revolutions are made by revolutionaries welded into tight, purposeful organizations of dedicated zealots.

Lenin's advocacy of the cadre party was determined and articulate. Hitler's was no less so.[42]

Organization, they agree, is the scientific instrument for the seizure of political power. Party is crucial.[43] Personal discipline is indispensable.

Doctrine, organization, power, redemption: this is the scientific recipe for revolution. Totalitarians are prepared to use violence to achieve the moral redemption of man and history. Hitler and Lenin were explicit about the need for violence. Both denigrated those unwilling to brandish the sword in implementation of the faith. Hitler wrote, "The lack of a great, creative, renewing idea means at all times a limitation of fighting force. Firm belief in the right to apply even the most brutal weapons is always bound up with the existence of a fanatical faith in the necessity of the victory of a revolutionary new order on this earth."[44]

In the speech that became famous as the "silver platter" speech, Lenin commented on the same subject: "Every time I speak on this subject of proletarian government someone . . . shouts dictator . . . You cannot expect . . . that socialism will be delivered on a silver platter . . . Not a single problem of the class struggle has ever been solved in history without violence. . . . Violence when committed by the toiling masses against the exploiters is the kind of violence of which we approve."[45]

Nonetheless, it is interesting to note that neither of these theoreticians and practitioners of totalitarian revolution discusses the uses of violence in the manner that each discusses many other subjects, including organization, relations with other parties and groups, or propaganda. Neither praises violence for its effect on the wielders in the manner of Frantz Fanon. Neither systematically outlines its use in the achievement of total revolution.[46] Both are relatively silent on the means to the desired ends.

Lenin's neglect of *how* political power can be used to transform society, culture, and personality is probably explained by his economic determinism. There is good reason to think that the old Bolsheviks literally believed that once the structure of ownership had been altered, the transformation of society, culture, and personality would follow promptly and automatically. The policies of the War Communism period, when men, women, and children were liberated from traditional institutional restraints—of family, school, prison, factory, office—suggest colossal misunderstanding of the power of habit and the persistence of culture, and a touching faith in their own interpretations. Like Marx, they had predicted the human and cultural revolution without planning for it. But as was his wont, when Lenin was confronted with the practical problem of the persistence of old patterns, he reacted with flexibility, ingenuity, and with few inhibitions about using force to accomplish with power what the automatic working of the laws of economic materialism failed to do.

Totalitarian ideologues share a general tendency to underestimate the difficulties of achieving social and cultural character change. The reason doubtless lies in their original assumption that the observed imperfections of man are the result of bad institutions. If, as Marx suggested, the economic system is the root of evil, then it is only necessary to reorder it to abolish evil. If, as Fanon suggested, the political order is the root of all evil, then it is only necessary to reorder it to abolish evil. Just a little violence will eradicate the accumulated resentments.

The possibility that institutions reflect people as much as people reflect institutions is never seriously entertained by the totalitarian ideologue. This possibility would cast doubt on his goals, plans, and prospects; it would endanger the moral status of the outrage which serves as psychological foundation for the whole ideology.

All totalitarian ideologies (and many reformers) underestimate the power of habit. It is no accident that appreciation of the role of habit in sustaining society, culture, and personality is characteristic of conservative political philosophers—of men like Hume, Burke, Bradley. The role of habit in human affairs carries with it a pervasive pessimism about the practicability of blueprints for broad reform. It breeds sensitivity to the possibility that revolution may increase the total of human misery without increasing man's moral, intellectual, or spiritual perfection—as rulers who underestimate human orneriness turn to terror when persuasion and automatic adjustment fail. Robespierre and his fellow zealots, Cromwell's fanatical lieutenants, the old Bolsheviks, and Adolf Hitler—all progressively widened the scope of coercion as it became clear that it was easier to destroy a ruling class than a dominant culture. For each, imprisonment, torture, execution, and terror became symbols of "liberation." That totalitarian ideologues should prove ruthless in their determination to force reform, merciless in use of force to accomplish their ends, should not surprise us. After all, their contempt for the corrupt, petty, materialistic slobs of the existing society has been, in each case, clearly stated. Their moral claim, it should be remembered, derived not from respect for actual men, but from their contemplation of the gap between what men are and what they might become.

But it seems clear that even when they possess the coercive power of government and wield it in the service of their "moral" vision, the odds are against the totalitarians achieving the desired revolution of society, culture, and personality. Totalitarian revolutionaries never start from scratch, but always from an existing society with its existing culture and human types. The revolutionaries themselves have passed through the old culture and are always in jeopardy of falling into the old ways of thinking and being. The big problem is with their goals. Because they affirm the abstract over the concrete, the universal over the particular, the ideal over the material, the social over the personal, unity over conflict, totalitarian goals require that ordinary people renounce the ways of thinking and being that have characterized people known to human history and achieve habitual levels of dedication associated till now with heroes and saints.

Can any revolution bring it off? Can any such ideology be transformed into culture? The question brings us face to face with "human nature"—the extent to which it is biologically or, in Freud's term, constitutionally determined. The question is as old as political philosophy. The terms of the debate on human malleability and politics have remained remarkably stable since Aristotle rejected Plato's blueprint for the ideal state on grounds that it could never work because it was based on an unrealistic conception of man (and woman). In rejecting Plato's scheme for abolition of the family, strict regulation of sexual unions, and absolute community of possessions, Aristotle stated with consummate clarity the basic attraction and weakness of proposals for revolutionizing human society:

> Legislation such as Plato proposes may appear to wear an attractive face and to argue benevolence. The hearer receives it gladly, thinking that everybody will feel towards everybody else some marvelous sense of fraternity—all the more as the evils now existing under ordinary forms of government (lawsuits about contracts, convictions for perjury, and obsequious flatteries of the rich) are denounced as due to the absence of a system of common property. None of these evils, however, is due to the absence of communism. They all arise from the wickedness of human nature.[47]

The debate about the malleability of human nature has achieved special practical importance in this century, when for the first time in human history successive groups of revolutionary leaders determined to alter and control society, culture, and personality through the purposeful use of political power have managed to achieve power and hold on to it long enough to influence the socialization of successive generations. The life span of the Nazi regime was too brief to provide a test. Hitler's impact was intense and devastating, yet the total time from his rise to fall was only twelve years (1933–45).

But the world has already celebrated the sixtieth anniversary of the Soviet Union. Its rulers have had more than half a century to employ formal education, habit, imitation, group pressure, mass media, terror, and other environmental controls to bring about internalization of new norms and new behavior patterns. During their six decades in power, Bolshevik leaders have succeeded in developing a strong government, a military technology and strength that is second to none, and an empire that stretches from the Berlin Wall to the Sea of Japan, from Mozambique to Mongolia.

But have they managed to reform human consciousness? Have they managed to educate Soviet citizens so that they would freely choose to behave according to the norms of Soviet culture *if the constraints of coercion were removed*? The answer, of course, is that we do not know. Nor is there much opportunity to investigate the question. We know that in Eastern Europe, Communist leaders found it necessary to build a wall and to fortify frontiers to keep their citizens from fleeing those nascent utopias. We know that even now there are thousands of Jews in the USSR who incur drastic penalties for expressing a desire to emigrate. We know that there is a steady trickle of Soviet defectors among the small privileged group of entertainers and scientists allowed outside the Communist bloc. We know that hundreds of thousands of Cubans have fled each time they have had a chance. From intermittent trials and sentences, *samizdat*, expulsions from writers' unions, and official denunciations, from Solzhenitsyn, Sakharov, Synavsky, and Amlarik, we know that till now the Soviet Union has continued to produce artists, writers, and intellectuals whose ways of seeing, thinking, and valuing are unsatisfactory to the overseers of revolution. And, of course, there is that most famous failure of socialization: Stalin's daughter Svetlana, whose predilections for religion and individual freedom must have constituted a special embarrassment to socialist psychological engineering. But we know almost nothing about the subjectivities of Soviet masses. Public opinion polls, competitive elections, free emigration, and other measures of individual attitudes are unavailable to the student of Soviet politics.

It can, in any case, be argued that despite its shorter life, Communist China rather than the Soviet Union is a better testing ground for the achievement of totalitarian goals. At least through the period of the Cultural Revolution, the Chinese worked harder at the thought reform of a whole population. They were, moreover, more innovative, more determined, more clear about the priority of this task for the achievement of their revolution.[48]

The Cultural Revolution had no Soviet equivalent. Its denigration and rejection of traditional culture—including master-pieces of traditional art—contrast starkly with the Soviet and Eastern European assimilation of traditional art; its massive campaign against intellectuals, scientists, managers, and experts and its proliferation of labor universities had no Soviet parallel. By preferring moral goals to industrial ones, purity to efficiency, by improvising new institutions for the tasks of cultural revolution, by the repeated and vigorous use of brutal overwhelming force against old ideas and habits, the rulers of Communist China attempted to succeed where other totalitarian rulers have failed. But the prime example of the "new" Chinese man was only that institutionalized zealot: the Red Guard. More recently, evidence has multiplied that like other revolutionaries the Chinese too may be abandoning the quest. The most experienced China-watchers are agreed that the crest of utopian revolution is past, that after the orgy of the Cul-tural Revolution, technology, modernization, order, and efficiency have again taken priority over the reform of culture, society, and personality.

It is always possible that improved technology, superior knowledge of social and psychological factors, and the sophisti-cated and uninhibited use of force will enable some ruling groups to succeed where all other totalitarian reformers have failed. The use of drugs to alter human consciousness presents interesting new possibilities for restructuring personality and culture. But history, pockmarked with the failure of utopian communities, suggests otherwise. Existing evidence suggests that doctrine turns out to be more malleable than human nature, that conformity to totalitarian behavior models is easier to secure than conversion, that the "new" morality turns out to be more effective in coercing than liberating, and that the "new" rulers bear a remarkable and dis-couraging resemblance to the old tyrants.

In considering whether it is possible that a totalitarian state can be stable and enduring, it is clear, as Carl Friedrich pointed out, that "totalitarian dictatorship, like other political phenomena, is a relative rather than an absolute category."[49] It is clear, too, that total rulers, "once they have seized power and commenced to build a totalitarian system, find themselves seriously troubled by the more utopian aspects of their ideology, as well as by the consequences of trying to put some of them into effect."[50] But it is also true that the lack of quick success has not led contemporary totalitarian rulers to cease trying to remold man and to construct and preserve a culture and institutions consistent with their ideology. The rulers of contemporary Communist nations may occasionally feel, like Lenin, that "the vital work we do is sinking in a dead sea of paperwork."[51] It is conceivable that some are revolted by their own violence. But they have not abandoned their efforts to stay in power and to exercise comprehensive control over society, culture, and personality. These efforts distinguish them from other autocrats and from democrats. Because they have not abandoned the effort, they remain monuments to the danger of mixing utopianism and power.

II. THE LANGUAGE OF DECEPTION

COMMUNIST PARTIES, which we carelessly call Communism, achieve political power through political contests. This fact, which appears almost to be a tautology, is repeatedly, and in some cases systematically, overlooked and obscured. Its implications are of extreme importance. To assert that Communists achieve power by competition at the political level implies, first, that they are not swept into power on the tides of historical inevitability; second, that except where they gain control through military occupation, the success of Communist parties is determined by the political skill of Communist leaders in exploiting their opportunities; and third, that when we discuss the expansion of Communist power, we are dealing not with an amorphous historical force but with the activities of identifiable men in specific situations.

Communists themselves long ago made the transition from historical determinism to political voluntarism on the *operational* level. Since this transition is of basic importance to understanding the Communist movement, it seems worthwhile to examine it briefly.

It is by now well known to historians and social scientists outside the circle of Communist orthodoxy that the class struggle described by Marx, and thought by him to be the motor of historical change, has failed to develop as predicted. In the most industrially advanced nations, the working classes have not been kept at a subsistence level, the middle classes have not been pauperized, the cycles of prosperity and depression have not become shorter or the depressions more severe. The "inevitably" catastrophic development of capitalism failed to occur. History succumbed to "economism." Powerful trade unions developed which proved able to extract concessions in wages and security from employers and the state. Instead of becoming progressively more miserable and desperate, the working classes of the highly industrialized nations enjoy a level of prosperity unprecedented in history and, incidentally, unequaled in Communist countries. The capitalists themselves refused the self-defeating roles assigned them by Marx and declined to fight to the last ditch for the last possible cent of profit, which, as embodiments of the capitalist ethic, they should have done. The state in the industrially advanced nations was not transformed into an instrument of fascist repression. Instead, it undertook to eliminate through regulation the most important abuses of the capitalist system and, in some countries—such as the U.K., the Scandinavian countries, and France—to eliminate important sectors of the system itself. Social legislation governing the terms and conditions of employment, collective bargaining, securities and trust regulation, graduated income taxes, and social security systems are but a few of the "reformist" devices with which history has confounded Marx's predictions.

Lenin's efforts to salvage Marx's doctrine of historical determinism and class struggle on the scientific level by stretching the conception of class to include whole nations was as unsuccessful as scientific theory as it was successful as propaganda. In fact, of course, the doctrine of inevitable class struggle as expounded by Marx was simply a mistaken prediction, which would have long since become only a datum of intellectual history had it not been embodied in the official ideology of a world power. Its failure on the level of science—as opposed to that of propaganda—deprives the notion of Communism's inevitable triumph of any scientific or historical basis, and converts into a purely mystical doctrine the Communists' claim to have penetrated the laws of history. All this is well known, but its implications are regularly ignored.

The failure of Marx's central hypothesis concerning the future of political systems did not inhibit the growth of the political movement acting in his name. Neither did the growth of that movement constitute any confirmation of the Marxist hypothesis. As early as the Bolshevik Revolution itself, Lenin emancipated Communists from the encumbrance of Marx's error. The first major step in the transition from economic determinism to political voluntarism was taken at the crucial moment in the Russian Revolution when it appeared possible for the Bolsheviks to seize power. At this moment, Lenin decided that Russia could "bypass" the capitalist stage of development. This action was the first clear-cut decision by a Communist leader that leadership and state power could circumvent or transcend the laws of history. Determinism was tacitly abandoned in favor of human intelligence, will, and power. Marx had suggested that Communists could assist history; Lenin proposed they outwit it.

A second major step in sloughing off dialectical materialism was taken in response to the fact that underdeveloped and colonial regions appeared to offer a promising area for Communist expansion. By encouraging the formation of Communist parties in colonial, largely pre-feudal societies, Lenin emancipated the Communist movement from Marx's laws of economic development. According to Marx, Communist movements were a specific, inevitable product of capitalism. Lenin proposed to create them by political decision. Lenin believed that he had integrated pre-feudal societies into the theoretical structure of Marxism through his highly revisionist doctrine of imperialism, which introduced the concept of seduction into dialectical materialism and transferred the class struggle from the national to the international level. In fact, he had merely politicized the doctrine of the class struggle. It is nonetheless true that Lenin's essay on imperialism was the last major effort of a Bolshevik leader to revise Marxist doctrines in the light of practice.

Once the movement had assimilated the crucial decision of Lenin that state power could be used to circumvent whole stages of historical development, that is, once the transition from historical determinism to political voluntarism was made on the operational level, the capture of state power everywhere became the actual goal of the Communist movement. The presence, or absence, of an industrial proletariat and a capitalist class became irrelevant to the class struggle after it had been operationally redefined to mean the struggle of a Communist party against any non-Communist government, or internationalized to mean the struggle of the Communist bloc against non-Communist nations.

Economic determinism was abandoned in response to concrete historical developments in which Communist leaders were confronted with the possibility of extending their power in situations which did not conform to the "laws of history" which should have brought Communism to power. In each such conflict, the requirements of presumably inflexible laws of historical development have been ignored and the opportunity to seize or maximize power has been grasped. Inside the Soviet Union, terror, propaganda, and bureaucracies have been relied on to produce changes that should have occurred inevitably once the structure of ownership had been altered. The decision to deny nationality groups and "autonomous" republics the right to secede, the decision to impose revolution by military occupation in Eastern Europe, to seize power by coup d'état in Czechoslovakia, are but a few examples. The aggressive pursuit of power in societies which lack capitalists and industrial workers as well as a class struggle is perhaps the most dramatic example of Communist leaders' indifference to Marx and Engels' doctrine of the historic role of Communism.

If human behavior conformed to the rationalist's model, the Bolsheviks' willingness to subordinate doctrine to the exigencies of the power struggle would constitute evidence that Communist leaders were pragmatic rather than dogmatic, that they had submitted basic items of Marxism to the test of history and revised them in the light of experience. Of course, no such thing has occurred. Practice has been adapted to actual historical developments and to the Communist leaders' desire to maximize their power; basic doctrine has been maintained intact. Communist leaders are *both* pragmatic and dogmatic. Adaptation to historical experience has been named "tactics," and a substantial literature on tactics has been developed to guide the actual operations of Communist parties. This literature on tactics constitutes the most impressive existing guide to the capture of political power in a wide range of contexts. It is eminently realistic, pragmatic, and cynical. Its analyses and prescriptions are ideologically neutral: the tactics it recommends could be utilized with equal success by any minority engaged in the uninhibited pursuit of state power. Much of this literature deals with the pursuit of goals which, according to classical Marxism, could not conceivably be achieved. Heresy for the sake of expanded power is called tactical flexibility.

In the name of tactical flexibility "socialism" is imposed on pre-feudal societies; Communist parties serve as a "vanguard of the proletariat" in nations with no proletariat, no capitalists, no industry; military conquest, subversion, and coups d'état are substituted for proletarian revolutions; tiny elites of intellectual freebooters are substituted for the working masses.

All the while, classical Marxism is invoked to surround the quest for power with an aura of morality and science. It is occasionally augmented, but for the most part, it is simply invoked: its basic postulates are examined neither in the light of history nor of Bolshevik practice. It is left intact: a body of propositions about the development of history which has been disproved by history. It nonetheless serves valuable functions for the Communist movement. (1) It provides the movement with ultimate goals which serve as moral justification of the movement. (2) It frees the Communist elite of moral inhibitions in the unhampered pursuit of power. (3) It justifies unceasing hostility against all persons and organizations outside the movement and sanctions aggression as moral and inevitable. (4) It provides grounds for believing in the ultimate and inevitable triumph of the movement.

Instead of there being the much vaunted "unity of theory and practice" in the Communist movement, there is an absolute split between theory and practice. Unlike the central doctrines of a supernatural religion, those of Marx and Engels concern historical facts and are testable in history and by history. As we have seen, many have already been contradicted by actual developments, and have been discredited by non-Communists as theory and by Communists as a guide to action. The effort to preserve them intact, to avoid relating them to concrete historical realities while permitting concrete historical realities to guide day-to-day political behavior, necessitates a colossal dissociation of theory and practice. Maintaining it requires a habit of irrationalism, and makes irrationalism a necessity to the Communist movement and Communist leaders. It is hardly necessary to point out that maintaining this type of dissociation leads to extreme defensiveness, rigidity, and hostility toward any threat to the valued doctrine. But it does not necessarily affect efficiency.

We are tempted to believe that the dogmatic, unscientific character of official Communist ideology is a potential source of weakness which will eventually render the Communist movement and Communist governments less sensitive to reality and less efficient in the long run than governments guided by a pragmatic philosophy. These latter, it is believed, draw strength from regularly submitting their policies to the test of experience. This view overlooks the fact that, at the level of political conflict, the Communists are consummate pragmatists and masters of *Realpolitik*, as unhampered by dogmatic ideological considerations as by ethical inhibitions. It also misjudges the function of official ideology.

It has proved exceedingly difficult for non-Communists to assimilate the fact and implications of the irrelevance of the Marxist philosophy of historical development to the conduct of the Communist movement. In *fact*, the Communist movement has no economic base, and no specified relationship to any economic class. In *fact*, Communist parties have no predictable, determinate, or integral ties to any particular social or economic group. Once Marx and Engels' doctrine of historical determinism had been abandoned, and the class struggle operationally defined to mean the struggle between Communist parties and non-Communists, Communists were free to look for support in any quarter and to declare as enemies all those who opposed their accession to power.

This they regularly do. In studies of Communism in India, Burma, France, Italy, Africa, and elsewhere, one finds instance after instance of the indeterminate relations between Communists and other groups. Tribal membership, regional interests, language, personal rivalries, nationalism, color, and other factors often serve as the basis for separating enemies from friends, not their relation to the means of production. In the underdeveloped areas, we see again and again the efforts of Westernized Communist leaders to find or create a social base for a tiny party. Their efforts are concentrated on whichever group is most alienated from existing authority, or least integrated into the existing structure of authority. In China, this proved to be intellectuals and peasants; in India, certain regional and caste groups; in the United States, certain portions of the middle class; in Britain, certain ethnic minorities; in France, industrial workers and the intelligentsia; in Africa, certain tribes. And so forth. Communist parties do not reliably draw their support from the poorest class or classes in any given nation. They may or may not, depending on the degree to which these classes are or may be politicized and alienated. In short, they seek supporters wherever they think supporters are to be found.

The extent to which economic categories have become irrelevant to the Communist struggle for power is obscured by Communist leaders' universal habit of describing the political conflicts in which they are involved in the language of classical Marxism. A tribal conflict may be billed as a struggle against the bourgeoisie.

Clarity about the relation of Communist parties to the class structure has important practical consequences. The fact that Communist parties represent no particular class, but are simply an elite competing for political power, seems very difficult to assimilate. The notion that Communists are somehow engaged in the struggle between rich and poor, haves and have-nots, workers and employers, oppressed and oppressors, leads to the persistent notion that Communism is somehow more democratic and progressive than its undemocratic rivals. And this notion in turn leads to a lingering, half-conscious inhibition among many democrats to judge the Communist party by the same criteria it judges competing undemocratic elites. The notion persists that Communists are somehow morally superior to other elites which use amoral means to gain power and impose repressive, minority dictatorships.

Alienation from existing authority—not economic role—is the principal determinant of a group's susceptibility to Communism. The most depressed classes in a society may or may not be the most alienated. In the noncapitalist countries of Asia, Africa, and the Middle East, educated minorities who have felt the full impact of Western industrial civilization and of Western colonialism are usually most alienated from traditional authority, values, and social organization. They are the carriers of the famous "revolution of rising expectations." They are bearers of social change. They are the groups most likely to be anti-Western as well as Westernized, to be most conscious and resentful of the colonial period. The poorest, least privileged classes in these countries are often profoundly traditionalist. Their expectations have been undisturbed for centuries. Their political worlds are dominated by traditional loyalties and traditional rivalries. Through skillful exploitation of traditional conflicts, and extravagant promises of good things to come, they can sometimes be involved in struggles at the national level of politics. But in spite of rhetoric to the contrary, Communism in the underdeveloped areas is not fed by the restless hopes and resentments of the masses. The relation of indigenous Communists to native masses is manipulative and exploitative.

There is no significant predictable difference between the supporters of Communist elites and other nondemocratic elites. There is also no difference in the way they come to power. In no nation ruled by the Communists have they been elected to head the government, or even swept into power by a mass revolt which was overtly Communist in character. Where they have won the support of large numbers of peasants, as in China, and the Philippines during the Hukbalahap uprising, they have done so by promising land to the peasants (which promises they betray as soon as their power has been consolidated), conducting guerrilla warfare against opponents and the government, and infiltrating the government. In countries with a tradition of national unity, an established sense of national identity, and a central government capable of administering its laws, the Communists have come to power only through military occupation (Poland, Rumania, Bulgaria, Albania, and East Germany) or by coup d'état (Russia and Czechoslovakia). In areas with no tradition of national unity and central government, they have relied on guerrilla war and terrorism to exploit the weaknesses of the government (China, Viet Minh). The means by which Communist parties have come to power do not suggest either democracy or progress.

The important difference between Communist elites and other antidemocratic elites is found in the way Communist elites use power once they have achieved it. Many antidemocratic elites are interested in maintaining the traditional social structure and culture. Franco, for example, did not attempt to undermine the social power of the Catholic Church in Spain, nor that of the large landowners. Like many military dictators in Latin America and elsewhere, he did not attempt to alter significantly the cultural, social, or economic status quo. This means, of course, that he did not undertake reforms to correct traditional inequities. But since the needs, expectations, values, and cognitive structures of most people in any society reflect traditional culture and roles, it is a fact that maintaining a culture requires less repression than does the effort to radically alter it by administrative decision. The traditional social structure may impose hardships and poverty, but its norms are internalized. Traditional autocrats and oligarchs can rely largely on subjective needs and habits to keep masses of people performing traditional roles. Typically, they utilize coercion only to protect their own power. For the traditional autocrat, the political sphere, that is, the arena relevant to the contest for control of government, is quite narrowly defined. Like the European or American liberal he does not see society as coterminous with the state.

In practice, Communist elites are more repressive than traditional dictatorships because they aim at revolutionizing society, culture, and personality. Therefore, they perceive the totality of social structure and culture as involved in the political struggle. Attachment to traditional culture is likely to be interpreted as political opposition. And political opposition is not tolerated.

The most important consequence of treating society and culture as parts of the political sphere is that it multiplies many times the number of potential points of conflict between citizens and political authority. It greatly increases the issues in which the authority and the coercive power of the state are involved. Norms established by the state must be enforced by state power if the authority of the state is to be maintained. Therefore, the larger the number of sectors in which a state acts, the larger the number of issues on which it must be prepared to coerce. In the "labor universities" and army barracks of Red China, people are politically liable for what they say in their sleep, because the government of Communist China has staked a claim to the subjective lives of its citizens as well as to their behavior. This is, of course, the reason for its massive efforts at thought reform. In the Soviet Union, literature, styles of painting, architecture, and music are still as in the Stalinist era—official concerns of the state. Linguistics, philosophy, psychology, biology, as well as social science and history are areas in which the authority and coercive power of the state are engaged.

To summarize, Communist leaders' determination to revolutionize society and culture leads them to attempt to control by regulation a very wide range of activities normally governed by custom and personal preference. Where the state regulates, it stands ready to coerce. Extension of regulation and coercion into all spheres of society is the meaning of totalitarianism. Since regulation in social and cultural areas is uniquely difficult to enforce, it requires more police, more surveillance, more terror. This is the reason that totalitarian regimes are uniquely repressive.

Despite the fact that Communist parties have no reliable relation to the masses, do not come to power through mass action (either legal or illegal), do not submit industry to the control of the masses or organize production for the benefit of the masses, and do not rule at the pleasure of the masses, a vast body of myth, misunderstanding, and confusion supports the notion that there is some sort of mystical affinity of Communism and "the people."

This confusion, which often exists only on the half-articulate level of assumptions, is extraordinarily durable. Its sources are several. One is the semantic confusion fostered by the Communists themselves through their systematically perverse use of language. By calling "autonomous" that which is powerless, "federated" that which is unitary, "democratic" that which is autocratic, "united" that which is schismatic, "popular" that which is imposed by terror, "peaceful" that which incites war—in brief, by systematically corrupting language to obscure reality—the Communists have made inroads into our sense of political reality. Language is, after all, the only medium in which we can think. It is exceedingly difficult to eliminate all the traditional connotations of words—to associate words like "For a Lasting Peace and a People's Democracy" with neither peace nor popular movements nor democracy.

A related form of semantic subversion, practiced by Communist parties everywhere, is the effort to capture prestigious symbols, slogans, and traditions. Communist parties in the under-

developed world attempt to identify themselves with the slogans of
nationalism and anticolonialism. Communists in France attempt to
identify themselves with the symbols of the Resistance, the French
Revolution, and the tradition of the Left. French Communists
have attempted to capture Victor Hugo, as American Communists
staked a claim to Tom Paine and Abraham Lincoln.

*Communism does not grow by disseminating and winning
support for its own values.* Neither members nor followers are
regularly recruited through the appeal of Communist values.
Communism grows by identifying itself with the prestige symbols
of competing movements and so blurring issues, stakes, and alignments. In his seminal work, *World Politics and Personal Insecurity,* Harold Lasswell pointed out that the spread of a revolution
is often checked when opposing groups adopt key symbols of the
revolution. This he termed "restriction by partial incorporation."
The carriers of Communist revolutions reverse this process, and
attempt to advance their revolution by tactical incorporation of the
symbols of opposing groups.

If Communist parties spoke of collectivization to peasants, of
internationalism to the new nations, of inexorable conflict to pacifists, of ideological conformity to intellectuals, of state capitalism
to the working classes, and of dictatorship to the middle classes—
in short, *if Communist parties attempted to recruit support
through the appeal of their own values, the lines of conflict would
be clearly drawn.* Communism, whose values have sharply limited
appeal, would be readily defeated. The Communist movement is a
Trojan horse because it systematically conceals its identity—in its
propaganda and organizational tactics.

Another barrier to clarity about the character and habits of
the Communist movement arises from internal inconsistencies of
the movement, rather than an effort to deceive. The dissociation of
theory and practice discussed earlier, and the effort to bring the
two into harmony on the verbal level, introduces confusion into
the Communists' self-conception which is communicated to the
non-Communist world. Surprisingly often, non-Communists accept
at face value the Communist's own formulation of his role, when

in fact there is about as much reason for accepting the Communist's conception of his identity and role as there was for accepting a "divine right" king's view of his credentials.

A third source of persistent confusion about the Communist movement and Communist parties results from projecting our own expectations, needs and values, and cognitive habits. The programs of democratic political parties are influenced to varying degrees by the aspirations and expected responses of voters outside the party. But their general orientation and basic programs are determined by the values of leaders and members. Tactical flexibility of democratic parties is sharply limited by commitments to values other than power. Honest projection of the party's identity is itself a value which prevents parties from adopting programs that falsify basic aspects of their identity. The tendency to project habits and values has repeatedly led the non-Communist world to mistake a Communist party's temporary tactical position for its identifying characteristics, and temporary lulls in the cold war for peace. A nationalist posture assumed to gain specific tactical ends is taken as evidence that a Communist party is basically nationalistic. An antiwar position taken in response to Soviet foreign-policy requirements is mistaken for genuine pacifism. When the Communists negotiate agreements to gain time or a respite we feel that we have achieved peace.

Still another of the reasons we attribute a class character to Communist parties throughout the world is our habit of thinking about political alignments in terms of economic classes. It is paradoxical that the officially voluntaristic Western nations attach greater importance to economic and social factors than do the officially deterministic Communists. In the underdeveloped countries Communist leaders often behave as if they regarded social and economic structure as irrelevant to the struggle for power, while representatives of the United States and Western Europe often behave as if the basic economy held the key to the outcome of the political struggle. There is a double irony in the fact that when we concentrate on the development of an economic infrastructure in an underdeveloped country *to halt the spread of*

Communism, we are projecting to the local Communist movement an economic character which it claims but does not have, because of beliefs we have but do not claim.

To these sources of confusion must be added another. Until the last decade or two the study of politics has been crippled by a kind of formalism which persistently mistook form for reality. It encouraged appraising the Soviet Union in terms of its written constitution, and the Communist movement in terms of classical Marxism. It reinforced the tendency to accept any given tactical posture of a Communist party as a definition of the aims of the party, and to mistake a Communist party for a garden-variety political party because it called itself one. Because the Communist movement is fundamentally different from political organizations to which we are accustomed, because it deals regularly in deception and obfuscation, because its representatives decline traditional roles and ignore traditional rules, sophisticated functional analysis is all the more necessary.

There is only one strategy that may reasonably be expected to successfully demystify the politics of Communist movements and states. It is a careful, detailed investigation of reality. Tyranny thrives only on deception, freedom only on reality. We must ask concrete questions and offer concrete answers to translate vague concepts like "the revolution" into the ideas, feelings, and activities of specific people in specific places; must research the actual composition of the "vanguard of the proletariat" and the actual relations between it and actual working classes; must reexamine how power is used, as well as whose name is invoked by those using it; and must observe what actually happens in the U.N. as well as what should happen.

❧ I I ❧

RATIONALISM

IN

DOMESTIC

AFFAIRS

Dismantling the Parties: Reflections on Party Reform and Party Decomposition

TO A GOOD MANY COMMENTATORS, 1976 appeared to be a return to politics as usual—because the candidate of the majority party won the election, because he carried the South and won a majority of labor votes, because he and his opponent each eschewed extreme positions, wooed all the voters, practiced traditional virtues, cultivated an ideologically ambiguous image, and attracted support from all portions of the political spectrum. Casual observers therefore concluded that after three deviant elections—1964 and 1972, when we were presented with a choice, not an echo; and 1968, when antiwar protests nearly drowned out both candidates—the 1976 presidential contest brought us back to the good old days of pragmatic politics, the Roosevelt coalition, and reliable Democratic victories.

Closer scrutiny, especially of the nominating process, suggests otherwise. There was, first, the extraordinary fact that an incumbent President—Gerald Ford—was very nearly denied the nomination of his party, even though he enjoyed the support of virtually all his party's governors, senators, and state chairmen, and most of its congressmen, including such leading conservative spokesmen as Senators Goldwater and Tower. And in the Democratic party, a true outsider moved past opponents who, collectively, enjoyed the support of virtually all party and pressure-group leaders and principal Democratic officeholders. The nearly successful campaign of Ronald Reagan utilized virtually the same tactics that had swept Senator McGovern's forces to victory in 1972: a sophisticated managerial team that understood the rules, a strategy that relied heavily on primary victories and on direct mail and the electronic media to mobilize an issue constituency that, in turn, provided money and volunteers. Candidate Carter's campaign was a striking manifestation of the new politics, one demonstrating that a candidate without standing as a national party leader could move through the nominating process to victory without either the support of the leadership or a powerful ideological appeal or an issue constituency. Both the Reagan and Carter feats dramatized what may be the single most important fact about contemporary party politics: the inability of either major American party to control the nominating process for the nation's most important political office.

These, of course, were not the only signs of change apparent in the presidential politics of 1976. There were also a continuing decline in confidence in the political parties as in all society's major institutions, a continuing decrease of the extent and strength of party identification, a continuing increase in split-ticket voting, and a continuing decline of voter turnout. There was fresh evidence of the parties' decreasing capacity to represent voters, mount campaigns, elicit resources, and recruit leaders who were devoted to the institution. There were new indications of significant changes in the social, political, and personal characteristics of the elite and mid-elite of national politics. And there was accumulating evidence that the functions of the parties were being progressively assumed by government, public relations firms, professional campaign consultants, and candidate organizations. Even the revival of the Roosevelt coalition turned out, on examination, to be largely chimerical. Blacks, who had played no role in the Roosevelt coalition, were a major component of the Carter success. White Southerners, who *had* been an important part of the Roosevelt coalition, gave slightly under half their votes to Carter —in spite of his regional and religious identifications. Despite massive efforts in his behalf by the union leadership, the white working class, which had voted overwhelmingly for Roosevelt, was much less unanimous in its support for Carter. Instead of being a return to normal, 1976 presidential politics reflected continuing changes in the leadership, composition, mass base, and functions of political parties.

In this essay I shall argue, first, that a trend toward party decomposition is still in process; second, that this trend has had and continues to have various sources—cultural, social, technological, demographic, political, and legal—but, third, that the most important sources of party decomposition are the *decisions* made by persons attempting to reform the parties. Some of these efforts at party reform have aimed to weaken one or both parties. (In the words of one McGovern-Fraser commission member, "You've got to get these party people out of the process, you've got to, or at least you've got to have a system which is so open that they get overwhelmed. I think most reformers now agree that you cannot allow these regular party people to have any control over anything, and still hope that you will have democracy in the parties.")[1] But beyond the reforms intended to weaken the parties, others undertaken to perfect the political process have had the *un*intended effect of hastening party deinstitutionalization. Again and again reforms undertaken by party leaders and legislators have hampered the capacity of the parties to carry out their historical tasks and have encouraged the development of alternative institutions which perform some activities of political parties but are less effective than parties as instruments of recruitment, representation, and accountability.

The reader may reasonably wonder at this point just what "parties" I am talking about: national parties? state parties? mass parties? formal organizations? or what? Distinctions among these levels and groups are conventional among political scientists and are valid and important for some analytical purposes, as, for example, in the study of party identification in an electorate or the investigation of political organization in a particular place. The late V. O. Key, among others, emphasized that "national" parties were ephemeral bodies which came into being every four years for the purpose of nominating a President and Vice President and making certain decisions relating to their election. At that time, 1956, state party organizations made their own rules, controlled their own membership, determined the composition of national decision-making bodies, and raised and spent their money. Since Key wrote, however, a nationalizing trend has set in which has made it progressively more difficult for a state party to operate autonomously, unaffected by the decisions of national bodies. As national decisions affect state organizations, so do leadership decisions affect the rank and file. Though unorganized, the party rank and file are affected by the decisions of organization leaders. The rise of Republicanism in the South and the border states since 1948 is a dramatic example of the cumulative impact on masses of the decisions of party leaders.

Thus, the "parties" involved in presidential politics include portions of state and local organizations and also the rank-and-file voters. The process of decomposition has affected both state and national parties, their organizations and their rank and file. I do not intend to imply that each and every state and local party has been affected by these changes—the Democratic party in, say, Plains, Georgia, may be as strong as it ever was—but Democratic parties in many states and many localities have been adversely affected by national trends.

In considering this subject, the reader as well as the author should bear in mind that recent comment on the parties' decline (including this essay) is part of a much larger literature lamenting the condition of American political parties. Some of this literature has measured American parties against someone's conception of what a party should be[2] (disciplined, cohesive, and so on), while other writers have measured parties against the parties' own previous capacities. V. O. Key, for example, denied that "there ever were any good old days,"[3] but nonetheless argued in his influential book on state politics published in 1956 that the vigor of party competition had declined in the first half of this century and that interparty competition was being progressively replaced by the rivalry of individuals within the parties.[4] The fluid, informal, unplanned, "organic" character of parties (discussed later in this essay) encourages such concern, I believe.

For the purposes of this discussion, it is not necessary to enter the debate about whether the high point of American party functioning has ever been very high. It is enough to identify the chief functions which the parties have performed and to determine whether these are still being performed.[5] Though experts do not wholly agree about the functions of parties, there is general consensus that parties are the crucial institution for organizing democratic competition for public office and holding leaders accountable, and that this requires that parties: (1) recruit, screen, and develop candidates and party leaders; (2) conduct campaigns; (3) "structure" the electorate; and (4) articulate and aggregate views and interests of large groups of voters. Through these activities parties perform their most important function, namely, serving as an intermediary, voluntary association linking society to government in such a way that rulers and governments are subordinated to the society.

RECRUITMENT, SCREENING, AND SOCIALIZATION OF POLITICAL LEADERS

Two types of political leadership are traditionally recruited, screened, and developed through the political parties: candidates for public office and persons who will staff the party. In other democratic nations, leadership recruitment and candidate nomination are the exclusive business of the party organization (that is, leaders) at national and local levels. American parties have always had less control over candidate selection than their European counterparts because that distinctive American institution, the direct primary, gives voters rather than party leaders the last word, and also because legislators and judges have claimed a uniquely large role in the nominating process—by regulating the conduct of primaries and by asserting jurisdiction over questions of the fairness of other party processes.[6] In the past decade changes have occurred that further decreased the parties' already limited control over the presidential nominating process. Most important among these has been the dramatic proliferation of presidential primaries.

As long as primaries were one among several equally or more important methods of choosing a presidential nominee, control over the ultimate decision could be retained by party leaders. However, as the number of primaries increased from seventeen in 1968 to twenty-two in 1972, to thirty in 1976, the impact of primaries grew more profound and pervasive. In 1972, for the first time ever, a majority of the delegates to the national conventions was chosen in primaries; in 1976 the proportion chosen by primaries was nearly three-fourths of all delegates. It is almost impossible to overstate the impact of primaries on the nominating process. They affect the character of delegates, candidates, campaigns, conventions, and parties. Convention delegates chosen in presidential primaries are selected because of their relationship to a presidential candidate instead of their relationship to the party. Since a national convention is the highest decision-making body for a party, choosing delegates without regard to their knowledge of or commitment to the party means vesting control over the party in persons who may have little concern for it.[7]

That is not all. Because candidates can go directly to the voters in search of the nomination, primaries permit candidates as well as delegates to be selected without having ever served an apprenticeship in the party, without ever being screened in or socialized by the party. In addition, the absence of any role for party organizations encourages a focus on personality and at the same time communicates to voters and activists alike a sense of the party's irrelevance to this most important decision process. Primaries force on candidates functions which have historically been party functions. To compete successfully in primaries, candidates need an elaborate personal organization capable of performing diverse tasks in diverse states. The existence of these organizations reduces a candidate's dependence on a party organization.

Primaries have other effects on the outcomes of nominating

contests. The capacity to appeal directly to voters makes it possible to bypass not only the party leadership but also the dominant political class, their standards, and their preferences. The 1976 campaigns of George Wallace and Ronald Reagan could not have gotten off the ground without primaries. Nor could the campaign of George McGovern. Most observers believe that primaries give extremist candidates a better chance than they would otherwise have, though it should be noted that McGovern did better in non-primary than in primary states and that Barry Goldwater won his party's nomination before primaries had achieved their contemporary importance.

Primaries also tend to personalize politics by focusing attention on disagreements within parties and on individuals who compete not as their parties' nominees but as persons with distinctive characteristics. Because the competing candidates often share most ideological orientations, personal attributes such as appearance, style, and wit attain new importance. (Presidents today must be fit and not fat, be amusing, not dull, and have cool, not hot, personalities.)

What caused the proliferation of primaries? Primaries are the institutional embodiment of the persistent American suspicion of organization. They reflect the conviction that in passing through the web of personal ambitions and structural complexities that compose a political party, the voice of the people is distorted beyond recognition. In the American tradition the populist instinct and the distrust of organization go hand in hand. Robert M. La-Follette and the early reformers advocated the direct primary as an antidote to bossism and corruption and as a mechanism for achieving greater democracy.

The proliferation of primaries since 1968 is also closely related to determined reform efforts to purify the political process by reforming those practices that inhibited expression of the people's will. Unlike the LaFollette Progressives, however, the reformers on the McGovern-Fraser commission did not believe that it was necessary (or desirable) to resort to primaries. Nonetheless, most observers agree that the recent proliferation of primaries occurred largely as a response to the McGovern-Fraser reforms, even though a majority of that commission's members did not desire the result and "preferred a reformed national convention to a national presidential primary or a major increase in the number of state presidential primaries."[8] Following the promulgation of the reform commission's report,[9] some states adopted primaries as a way around the complex demands of the new rules. Elsewhere, primaries were adopted because state party leaders preferred to let voters make decisions in primaries rather than compete with "new politics" activists in caucuses.

The spread of presidential primaries, then, has been stimulated by reformers who sought to break the control of bosses, by reformers who made the alternatives too unattractive, by advocates of direct democracy who believed that the most legitimate judgment is that which flows most directly from the people, and by boosters seeking to attract publicity, jobs, and money to their states.

In nonprimary states, candidate selection has traditionally been carried out by "the organization." Party regulars and bosses (whether a traditional machine, a courthouse gang, or a reform clique) met in caucuses and conventions to select candidates and make other important decisions. But at least in the Democratic party, new rules have fundamentally altered the character of caucuses and conventions and further weakened the role of the party in the nominating process. The McGovern-Fraser commission was determined to "open" party meetings to all interested persons; they adopted rules to achieve that purpose. New requirements governing public notice, slating, and "timeliness" effectively diminished organizational control over caucuses. Instead of being meetings of persons with experience in the party and demonstrated commitment to it, caucuses have become assemblages of persons interested in particular candidates or issues. Under the new rules anyone willing to state that he is a Democrat (at least for the evening) can join the small group making decisions about the party's presidential nominee. The dynamics of participation (about which a good deal is known) ensures that turnout at these meetings will be relatively low and made up mainly of persons whose interest in politics is much more intense than that of the ordinary voter, and whose views are probably also more extreme.

Opening the caucuses, in sum, has made them vulnerable to manipulation by candidate or issue enthusiasts who may or may not have a broad or long-term concern with the party. Opening the caucuses coincided with the emergence of ever stronger candidate organizations capable of turning out supporters. Because anyone can participate, open caucuses dilute the influence of party leaders. Though the easy manipulability of the caucus system has been overlooked by many academic observers, it was well understood and described by Senator McGovern's manager for the nonprimary states, Richard Stearns, in his Oxford thesis.[10] The caucus victories of McGovern in 1972 and of Carter in 1976, at a time when neither candidate had significant support from party leaders and regulars, were evidence of the changed character of caucuses and conventions.

Open caucuses are a clear-cut example of party reform drastically weakening a party. The transformation of caucuses was a direct consequence of rules changes that opened the Democratic party, transferring control over the composition and decisions of delegations from party leaders to ad hoc assemblages of candidate and issue enthusiasts. It illustrates the continuing tendency of many American reformers to find ad hoc groups less sinister than institutionalized ones, just as they find enthusiasm for a candidate, or better still, an issue, a more elevated motive for political activity than loyalty to an organized party—in spite of clear evidence of the crucial importance of party to democratic processes.

Not only have party leaders lost a large part of their influence over recruitment of presidential candidates, they are also less able to control the recruitment and socialization of the leaders and volunteers who work in the party's name. Association with a successful candidate's organization has become an acceptable substitute for organizational apprenticeship and service. After 1964, the Republican party was dominated in many areas by persons whose influence had grown with Goldwater's; the post-1968 and 1972

Democratic party included even larger numbers of "peace" Democrats who had entered politics with the McCarthy and McGovern movements.[11] And in 1976 everyone understood that the composition of both the Republican and Democratic National Committees would be determined by the outcome of the parties' nominating contests.

An important consequence of the inability of parties to control access to their organizations is that it becomes possible for persons with little concern about the organization to achieve influence over its policies. This is a matter of capital importance to the polity because a long-range concern for the American type of party breeds habits of compromise, inclusiveness, and moderation. My study of delegates to the 1972 Democratic convention confirmed the presence there of large numbers with weak, instrumental attachments to the party, who were opposed to many of the practices necessary to preserving an organization—such as compromising conflicts, building coalitions, and rewarding the faithful.[12] In the 1976 Democratic convention, there were fewer delegates than in 1972 without prior party experience, more who had held party and public office, fewer who were indifferent to winning, more who expressed generalized concern for the party.[13] But the cumulative evidence indicates that the new type of activists drawn to politics by candidate or issue enthusiasm had by no means disappeared from the national scene. In 1976, as in 1964, such activists were more numerous at the Republican than at the Democratic convention. In that year, "New Right" intellectuals encouraged conservative activists to abandon Republican loyalties,[14] and the behavior of a good many (but not all) disappointed Reagan supporters demonstrated lack of concern about their party's prospects with Ford as the nominee. Barry Sussman's survey (undertaken for *The Washington Post*) established that a majority of Ford's backers were pragmatic and party oriented, while 57 percent of Reagan's delegates preferred ideological agreement to electoral victory.[15]

In 1976, then, it was possible for the highest decision-making levels of either party to be penetrated by persons without seasoned, reliable ties to the party. The outcomes of the preconvention primaries and caucuses—which of course were beyond the control of party—determined the kind of people attracted into party roles. Both parties remained vulnerable to penetration by people without a strong, generalized attachment to the party. Such people, should they become influential, can be expected to adopt policies (concerning, for example, compromise, victory, and party structure) that leave already weak parties still weaker.

The inability of American parties to control the recruitment and socialization of their cadres is in part a result of the same efforts to reform political life that have stripped the parties of control over nominations. But there are also other sources. The fact that American parties are dependent on volunteers and that more volunteers are needed than are available makes parties more permeable than most organizations. Reliance on volunteers, for whom politics is a hobby and a leisure-time activity, causes rapid turnover of party officeholders and makes it easier for newcomers to achieve influence in a political party than in most other institutions. Therefore, brief apprenticeship and socialization prevail.

Primaries and candidate organizations contribute to the problem by providing activists an opportunity—outside the parties—to demonstrate skills and accumulate influence. Lack of prior experience and reputation in national politics mattered little to the future of Hamilton Jordan, Jody Powell, or Rick Hutchenson once their candidate had achieved the nomination and won the election. Commenting on this relationship, Leon Epstein noted that although direct primaries make it possible for a candidate to win control of a party label without gaining control of a statutory (or extralegal) party, "Generally control of the label and of the statutory party will go together since even an organizational shell is likely to be taken over by those who secure the party label (if they did not control the statutory party to begin with)."[16]

An interesting question, rarely raised, is *why* American parties depend so heavily on volunteers to conduct their most important ongoing activities. This question leads, I believe, back to the theory and practice of party reform. In this country material incentives to political participation are not well regarded.[17] An important reason for the disappearance of paid precinct captains, for example, was the widespread feeling that buying the service of precinct leaders is, if not exactly corrupt, somehow gross, and that the volunteer who donates his services as precinct leader is to be preferred—politically and probably morally—to one who can be "bought." This ethos, which conflicts sharply with the practices and moral codes of democratic politics elsewhere, becomes more curious in view of the range of services that *are* regularly bought and paid for by the most morally sensitive candidates. Instead of paying ward heelers "walking-around money," today's candidates pay much higher fees to consultants who are knowledgeable about mass media, public relations, and direct mail to get out the vote. Like the traditional "pol," professional campaign managers, political pollsters, and a host of media and direct-mail specialists make their living out of politics by mobilizing and delivering support.

There are some interesting differences between past and present types of persons who get paid for political activity, but these are not differences in function. The most important differences are in the skills and the social backgrounds of the different types of experts. Unlike the professionals of earlier times, those who receive lucrative fees in presidential politics today are usually highly educated specialists skilled in market research or communications technology. Could it be that the high fees of these paid professionals are more acceptable than the lower fees of traditional "pros" because the former closely resemble in background, skills, and style the educated, upper-income, high-status professionals who have come to dominate both national parties? Apparently, the reform spirit that deprived low-status, lower-middle-class pols of jobs abetted the incomes as well as the influence of persons much like the reformers. At the same time, it weakened party organization,[18] because, unlike the professional of yesterday, who was dependent on, and identified with, the party organization, the contemporary professional is fundamentally independent of party. His income depends less on the party than on his skills, which are useful to different kinds of organization.

The rise of the new professionals is paralleled by the ascendance to political power of the "new class," a development which also contributes to the growing weakness of the parties. In 1976 as in 1972, there were enormous, and apparently increasing, discrepancies between the social backgrounds of the delegates to the two conventions and those of the parties' rank and file. The elite and mid-elite of the national parties had much more education, much better jobs, much higher incomes than most people. As in 1972, delegates were heavily drawn from the professions, especially from law, teaching, and government employment. About half the Democratic delegates were highly educated professionals: nearly 90 percent had been to college and over 40 percent held graduate degrees; about a third had incomes of at least $30,000.[19] More important, there was a marked tendency for these socially privileged political influentials to have very different opinions from those of ordinary voters on many subjects.[20]

It was not always thus. The urban boss and his lieutenants and the county courthouse gangs often had financial interests that diverged from those of their constituents. Usually, however, they shared their constituents' religion, values, mores, and political preferences. The rise of the new class to political influence has brought with it a growing distance between party (and political) elite and mass. This trend, which is fraught with pitfalls for any party afflicted by it, and for the society more generally, has been accelerated by changes in the processes through which party leadership is recruited. Technological and social change produced a larger, educated middle class with the leisure and the inclination to participate in volunteer politics, and parallel cultural changes heightened the prestige of the communications skills this group possessed, but without the adoption of rules hospitable to its skills and proclivities the new class could not have achieved its current dominance of national politics.

There can be little reasonable doubt that the reform rules of the Democratic party, which stress persuasive skills, self-presentation, ideological motivation, and such nonpolitical characteristics as sex, race, and age, have greatly aided the rise to political influence of the new class and at the same time dramatically decreased the political value of such traditional assets as local ties, organizational skills, and team loyalty. Party reform, especially the Democratic variant, advanced the class interests of the reformers in the sense that it rewarded persons with the skills, styles, and values of the reformers at the expense of others. These reforms tended to weaken party organization because they gave power to "disinterested" persons whose careers were not tied to the future of the party and increased the gap between the elite and the rank and file. Reform has advanced the class interests of the reformers.

Conducting Campaigns

Electoral campaigns are structured competition, carried on in the name of parties, which links candidates to voters and relates government policies to the consent of the governed. Historically, presidential campaigns have relied heavily on national parties to plan strategy and on state and local party officials to extract such needed resources as money and services, to communicate with voters, to organize activities and mobilize support. The dependence of candidates on local party organizations has, however, been greatly reduced by new technology, new rules and laws, and new organizational practices. Access to television, especially, eliminates candidates' reliance on indirect "two-step" communication with voters, and the development of polling provides information on the electorate which is probably more accurate than that available through local leaders. Although in the past the pathway to big contributors passed through the county courthouse, the urban club, or the state organization, today computerized targeted direct-mail solicitation permits candidates to raise money independently of local leaders. The Goldwater, McCarthy, McGovern, and Wallace campaigns illustrated the potential for funding a presidential campaign with the contributions of like-minded donors. The federalization of campaign finances moved candidates and parties several giant steps farther down the road to candidate self-sufficiency. By severely limiting the amount which any individual or collective donor could contribute, the new rules have drastically reduced the capacity of party leaders to raise the funds necessary for a campaign. And by providing $20 million to the nominee of each major party, the latest campaign finance reform act emancipated candidates from the need to rely on party leaders to help finance a presidential election campaign. By reducing candidates' incentives to woo and win the active support of party and pressure-group leaders, this reform provided candidates new freedom from the party. Once again, the parties were clearly the victims of reform legislation which, in its concern with correcting abuses, ignored the damage it might do to the parties.

The capacity of party organizations to conduct campaigns has also been weakened by the emergence of nearly self-sufficient nationwide candidate organizations called into being by nomination procedures that require presidential hopefuls to mount long, far-flung campaigns. The modern candidate organization is an arsenal replete with all the skills and weapons of modern political combat: speechwriters, advance men, pollsters, public relations specialists, media consultants, fund raisers, computerized voter lists, and a general staff with lieutenants in every state.

It would hardly make sense for a candidate confronted with mounting a national election campaign to disband, disregard, or demote the staff with which he had just won the nomination, complete with its store of fresh information on field conditions, its skills honed in the primary contests, and its undivided loyalty to the candidate himself. So great is the appeal of a personal vehicle dedicated only to the victory of one man that Richard Nixon was stimulated to develop CREEP (Committee to Re-Elect the President) even though he faced no nominating contest.[21] And though in many discussions of Nixon's debacle personal campaign organizations were unfavorably compared with national parties, both Carter and Ford relied heavily on their own organizations to conduct their presidential campaigns.

The rise of multifaceted, multifunctional candidate organizations is a direct consequence of changes in the nominating process that make it necessary for a candidate to win primaries and capture "open" caucuses in many states and to do well in the opinion polls to qualify for matching funds. Nomination of presidential candidates by a congressional caucus or by a national convention made up of state and local party bosses neither required nor bred such organizations. U.S. history and that of other democracies suggest that the emergence of powerful candidate organizations is a necessary institutional byproduct of popular participation in the nominating process.

STRUCTURING THE ELECTORATE

Leon Epstein, a scholar who firmly rejects restrictive conceptions of political parties, nonetheless asserts that "structuring the vote is the minimum function of a political party in a modern democracy." But he adds, "All that is meant by the awkward word 'structuring' is the imposition of an order or pattern enabling voters to choose candidates according to their labels (whether or not their labels appear on that ballot)."[22]

Labels simplify choices, identify alliances, and almost always communicate something about orientations. In polities with far-flung mass electorates, party labels and party identification have served as the principal links between candidates and voters—at least until recently. The function and power of labels rest on party identification, the psychological mechanism by which people incorporate themselves into a party. Comparative research indicates that party identification is a powerful stabilizing factor in democratic political competition, one which inhibits the proliferation of parties and the rise of personalist factions and "surge" movements[23] and which reinforces existing party systems. The fact that most Americans have thought of themselves as Republicans or Democrats has therefore been one of the most important characteristics of the American political system. For this reason, the declining extent and strength of party identification in the United States are a significant indicator of change. Successive opinion studies have documented the growth of that group of Americans who identify with neither party—now about half the electorate.

The rise of split-ticket voting and sharp electoral swings—as from a Democratic landslide in 1964 to a Republican landslide in 1972 —are early indicators of some of the consequences. The Verba, Nie, and Petrocik study, *The Changing American Voter*, confirms and analyzes the declining scope and intensity of structured partisanship. It finds voters, especially young voters, less likely than ever before to identify with either major party, more likely to think of themselves as independents, less likely to think well of parties, less likely to relate their party identification to an evaluation of candidates or party positions, and all voters more ready to defect from their party.[24]

The causes of the parties' declining ability to structure the electorate are less clear than the fact of the decline. Verba, Nie, and Petrocik emphasize the generational aspects of the phenomenon, noting that the surge of independents—who now compose approximately two-fifths of eligible voters—comes more from younger voters entering the electorate than from older voters who once identified with a party, and also that the intensity of party identification among young voters is low as compared with that among older voters. They also document the rise of split-ticket voting among older voters. It seems clear that the declining extent and intensity of party identification are also associated with such phenomena as the increasing salience of issues and issue constituencies in the electorate. Not only do the new cultural and social issues—abortion, amnesty, welfare, busing—have a great capacity to engage the voters' attention, but the social and cultural upheavals associated with their rise have made voters more aware of the connections between questions of public policy and have left them much more disposed to see themselves as "liberal" or "conservative." American politics, then, is simultaneously becoming more ideological and less institutionalized.

This whole process of cultural-social-political polarization and deinstitutionalization was not caused simply by policies adopted to regulate nominations and elections. But the effects of formal processes on the structure of partisanship have been shaped by rules that favored persons with leisure, high education, highly developed persuasive skills, and extreme views on issues. The processes have thus affected the capacity of parties to represent voters. It is doubtless significant that party identification has declined precisely when the strength of party organization was diminishing, just as it was no accident that party organization developed and expanded alongside an expanding electorate. If there is a causal relation between strong organization and party identification, then policies which weaken the former should also tend to weaken the latter.

But the major causes of the declining extent and intensity of party identification probably lie beyond policies and rules—in the emergence of the new issues, the decreased confidence in social and political institutions,[25] the increased use of television, which enables candidates to establish a direct, personal relationship with voters unmediated by parties,[26] and, perhaps especially, in the progressive ineffectiveness of the family and other traditional agencies of socialization. Earlier research had established that in political systems such as those of Britain and the United States, party identification was largely hereditary, that it was acquired at an early age in the family and persisted through life, that it functioned to screen communications, focus attention, and structure responses, that it persisted in spite of disagreements on particular candidates and policies.[27] Because socialization into a party system normally occurs in the family, it is necessarily weakened by the weakening of the family structure, by the deemphasis on the transmission of explicit norms and identifications from one generation to the next, and by the increased role of peer groups and media in the socialization process.[28] Since familial socialization is the principal means for recruiting new party identifiers (and activists), any lessening of the extent or effectiveness of this intergenerational transmission would produce more independents who identify with neither party and more weak identifiers for whom party identification lacks the power to order the political world.

The declining capacity of the parties to attract and hold the loyalty of masses results from the interaction of broad social processes and deliberate decisions. It is quite clear that no one planned or intended it and that no one is quite sure how to reverse the trend.

THE LIMITS OF REFORM

It is well understood among historians and political scientists that political parties emerged as unplanned, unanticipated, unwanted institutions. Despite their undoubted importance, parties everywhere developed not in response to the plans of constitutional engineers (not even such remarkable constitution makers as the American Founding Fathers) but as informal extraconstitutional bodies more often deplored than welcomed by such astute students and practitioners of popular government as Tocqueville, Mill, Washington, and Madison. Because this process of unanticipated growth has occurred in every country that has democratized its decision-making process, it is clear that the emergence of political parties is closely related to the establishment of a legal right of opposition, the extension of the electorate, and the popular election of rulers. E. E. Schattschneider emphasizes this relation in his comment that a party is "a process formed about the election."[29]

The fact that political parties develop wherever there is popular participation in decision-making underscores their close relation to democratic institutions; and the fact that they develop in an informal, unplanned way underscores their extralegal character, which Schattschneider described as "one of their most notable qualities."[30] The extralegal character of parties points toward another basic characteristic: though they have an important influence on constitutions, democratic parties have everywhere been extraconstitutional bodies standing midway between the government on the one hand and, on the other, the myriad of individuals and groups which compose the society. Giovanni Sartori emphasized this aspect of parties in his assertion that "parties are *the* central intermediate and intermediary structures between society and government."[31] That parties emerged and function everywhere as unmandated institutions has significance for their responsiveness to changes in the environment in which they act, and also for their responsiveness to deliberate efforts to reform and restructure their composition and practices.

Like all institutions, political parties are enduring patterns of interaction based on the stable expectations of those who occupy roles in and around them. Expectations concern what those involved must do, should do, may and may not do in given contexts, and the rewards and penalties associated with various courses of action. To say that institutions depend on stable, reciprocal expectations is to say that political parties are rooted in the subjectivities of those who compose the party. This is true whether or not the institution is supported by legal restraints or formal rules. The chief difference between a legal and an informal institution lies in their incentive structures. All patterned interactions include a system of incentives, rewards for desired behavior and deprivations for unwelcome behavior. The institution whose interactions are underpinned by law will probably (though not necessarily) carry the threat of more severe sanctions.

Institutions such as political parties that rely on voluntary, cooperative behavior and on customary understandings necessarily reflect ends and means on which there is broad consensus in the community. Their practices constitute an expression of widely shared views about appropriate modes of behavior. By its very existence, a customary institution demonstrates its relevance to the life of the community and its acceptance by most of those affected by it. Legal constraints may be added to reinforce customary understandings and norms, but the presence of constraints does not in itself prove that severe sanctions are required to maintain the institutional practices. Severe sanctions and the threat of severe sanctions can, however, induce behavior that does not reflect agreed-upon community standards.

Because political parties are customary, permeable, and highly adaptive institutions formed about elections and *not* reinforced by law, there has characteristically been a very close fit between parties and the societies in which they exist. This fit between society, culture, modal personality, and party system means that parties change with social changes. French political parties and the party system underwent successive transformations in response to the adoption of de Gaulle's constitution. The composition, organization, and leadership styles of American parties have changed as the country was transformed from a society where transportation and communication were slow and difficult to a single media market, from a nation of immigrants and farmers to a postindustrial society in which the production and communication of knowledge and services have become major industries.[32]

There have been so many such changes in the United States since the stable 1950s that it is tempting to ascribe to them the growing incapacity of American parties—to explain the Republican party's weakness by the erosion of its traditional social base in small-town America and among self-employed businessmen and farmers; to ascribe the weak party attachment of many Democrats to Vietnam or Mayor Daley; to regard the dominance of professionals within both parties as a necessary consequence of mass education, mass communication, and the transformation of the occupational structure; and to interpret the growing personalism of presidential politics as an inevitable consequence of television and computer technology.

I have no inclination to write off these factors as sources of party transformation. But the weight of theory and experience indicates that the changes affecting American political parties in recent years have diverse sources. Some have been stimulated by events occurring outside the parties, in the environment in which they function, others have resulted from policies adopted by the parties; some have been desired, planned and deliberately undertaken, while others, willed by no one, have been the byproducts of social, cultural, or demographic developments or the unintended and often undesired consequences of reforms conceived with quite different intent. Of all these reasons for the continuing decline in the parties' ability to perform their traditional functions, I have stressed reform. Whether undertaken by the parties, the Congress, or the courts, reform, along with its intended and unintended consequences, is, I believe, the most important cause of this decline.

The impact of reform on American parties is illuminated by a comparison with the consequences of similar social and technological changes on parties in some other democratic systems. The growth of a new class of specialists in communication and symbol manipulation has occurred in all advanced industrial societies. So has the use of television and computer technology. But the social composition of the political class in other democratic countries has not been altered as dramatically as in the United States. Similarly, the experience of France, Britain, the German Federal Republic, and other democratic nations indicates that television, computers, and polling need not necessarily weaken political parties' control over the recruitment, development, and selection of candidates. It is the use of television in direct primaries and other open contests which enables would-be candidates to develop with voters relations that are not mediated by the parties.

It is technology, social structure, *and* a particular set of rules that render American parties unable to control their own organizations and functions. The interaction of rules, technology, and social structure produces effects none could produce alone. But the fact that rules shape consequences does not mean they can produce any desired outcome. Just as rules shape the impact on the parties of technological, social, and cultural change, these also affect the consequences of the rules and procedures. Advocates of the direct primary intended to wrest control from the bosses and return it to the people; presumably they did not intend to vest power in media moguls or to speed the development of a personalist politics with standards and practices more relevant to entertainment than to public affairs.

In fact, parties are quite resistant to planned manipulation. Although parties are loose, permeable institutions, they are not readily molded to fit any master plan. We know, for example, that single-member-district electoral systems discourage the growth of minor parties while proportional systems have opposite tendencies, and that the former favor local notables while the latter are more hospitable to centralized disciplined parties. Yet even very sophisticated efforts at electoral engineering to produce a two-party system featuring programmatic, cohesive parties usually fail. Instead of producing the desired results, they fall victim to the tendency of parties to reflect their society's deeply rooted patterns of cleavage and consensus, authority and organization. Democratic parties remain instruments of private persons for shaping and controlling government rather than agencies of the government whose function is to shape the society. The same "subsystem autonomy" (Gabriel Almond's term) that defines a democratic party also makes it resistant to manipulation. And the very responsiveness of parties to social currents makes them difficult to control and difficult to change according to plan. The fact that parties are never "closed systems" in which it is possible to hold all factors constant while changing one heightens the likelihood that any effort to alter a single aspect will have undesired and often unanticipated consequences.

Between the motive of the party reformer and the consequences of his reforms there lies ample room for surprise and error. The abolition of the two-thirds rule at Democratic conventions not only reduced the power of the South within the party but also eliminated the requirement for broad consensus on presidential candidates, laid the foundations for a regional third-party movement, permitted the national Democratic party to assume political leadership of the civil rights revolution, and created the preconditions of greater polarization on issues between the parties. Abolition of the unit rule, undertaken for the purpose of more accurately reflecting voter sentiment, also removed the capacity of state parties to act as units, and the requirement of proportional representation eliminated districts and states as action units in the presidential nominating process. When persons acting in the name of national parties claimed expanded jurisdiction over the composition of national committees and national conventions, the procedures by which slates are named and delegates chosen, and the racial, sexual, and age distribution of delegations, these claims were designed to secure fair and accurate representation and full participation, not to dismantle the parties. Neither, presumably, did the McGovern-Fraser commission intend to give a special advantage to articulate, well-educated activists or to handicap farmers and trade unionists or to widen the gap between the views and values of the party elite and the rank and file. It also seems unlikely that they desired to facilitate the nomination of complete outsiders such as Wallace or Carter (as opposed to relative outsiders like Mc-Govern) or to stimulate the rise of candidate organizations. The Federal Election Campaign Act intended to reduce the dependence of candidates on fat cats, vested interests, and big business, not to deprive parties of a major function and proliferate the number of candidates seeking the nomination, or to emancipate presidential nominees from the need to take account of a wide range of party and pressure groups, or to reduce the political influence of Jews or labor.

The capacity to persist and change in response to environmental change is an important indicator of institutional strength, and the persistence of the American party system through the last century of rapid, unprecedented social, cultural, and economic transformation testifies to the parties' strength. In the past decade, however, American parties have not only had to adapt to social, cultural, and technological change and to procedural reforms of the conventional type, but at the same time they have also had to conform to new rules whose goal is to make parties reflect the desired balance of power, not the actual strength of actual social groups. (Quotas, by any name, are good examples of such policies. Limits on financial and organizational contributions to campaigns are another clear-cut example of attempts to inhibit the parties' capacities to express social realities.)

The effort to make institutions conform to abstract principles is the very essence of the "rationalist" approach to politics, an approach which is potentially dangerous because it assumes that institutions and people are more malleable than they are and that the reformers are more prescient than they are. Not only does the rationalist approach to politics aim at replacing custom with purpose, but it almost always operates from an oversimplified conception of social process and fails to take adequate account of possible resistance to the desired goal and of the effects of interaction and of cumulative impact. In consequence, reforms inspired by the rationalist spirit are especially likely to produce utterly unintended consequences. Several such reforms are now pending which have an important, largely unexamined potential for further dismantling the parties. Among these are the abolition of the electoral college, the establishment of a direct national primary, public financing of congressional elections, and the reforms of the reforms of the reforms of the Democratic presidential nominating process.

REFORMS PENDING

Two related principles have inspired most political reforms in this century: the desire to end corruption in politics and the desire to achieve direct democracy with perfect equality for all citizens. In the American tradition the two are frequently perceived as related. The recurring desire to purify politics by sweeping away distorting obstacles between "the people and their government" is present in two proposals for reform currently under consideration: the abolition of the electoral college and the adoption of a national primary. Each of these proposals is motivated by a desire to make political institutions more fair, more orderly, and more perfect embodiments of direct popular rule.

The electoral college is conceived by the proponents of its abolition as an offense against the principle of one man, one vote, since, given certain assumptions and circumstances, some voters have more influence than others on the election of a President. (One widely cited analysis concludes that a New York voter has 3.312 times the influence of one in the District of Columbia.)[33] Its indirect procedures are said to be cumbersome and an affront to popular rule. The unit rule is said to deprive minorities of an opportunity to aggregate their strength and influence outcomes. Scenarios are offered in which faithless electors and improbable voting patterns result in the selection by the electoral college of a President who has lost the popular vote (an event which has not in fact occurred since 1888).

The arguments for adopting a national primary are very similar to those for abolishing the electoral college: existing procedures are said to be chaotic, to give voters in some places (such as New Hampshire) an unfair influence on outcomes, and to deny voters in other states (such as Iowa or Mississippi) the opportunity to exert equal influence with an equal expenditure of energy. Potential abuses of the existing system are plumbed, the most notable among these being the possibility that a candidate might be nominated who is not, in fact, the choice of a majority of voters.

Both the electoral college and the national primary reforms are inspired by the belief that democracy requires direct expression of the people's will under conditions of formal political equality. Both involve major changes in the manner of aggregating voter preferences: districts, states, conventions, electoral colleges, and other intermediate institutions are to be swept away. In a particularly lucid discussion of arguments against the abolition of the electoral college, Sayre and Parris emphasized that "the debate over the electoral college is not a debate over whether the President should be elected by the popular vote of the American people. The present system and all the seriously considered alternatives have long rested on a popular vote. Rather, the debate is over how the popular vote should be aggregated: whether by state subdivision (as in the district plan), or by state (as in the existing electoral college system and in the automatic plan), or by the nation as a whole (as in the direct vote plan)."[34]

Though they explore and emphasize even the most arcane possible abuses of the electoral college and the existing nominating system, the proponents of reform pay little attention to the probably effects of the proposed reforms on other aspects of the political system. But the method of aggregating votes affects the result. Aggregating votes in one national constituency would have major consequences for the structure and dynamics of American politics and for the parties through which they are conducted.

One set of consequences concerns the role of minorities in politics and parties. The smaller the electoral unit, the more important are all the people and groups which compose it. The Polish vote is more important in Milwaukee than in Wisconsin, and more important in Wisconsin than in the nation. Black, Jewish, and Latin votes in New York are much more important now than they would be if the state's votes were aggregated with those of a nationwide electorate.[35] As Bickel and some others have argued, the electoral college magnifies the importance of votes of minorities and urban dwellers because they are often relatively homogeneous groups in highly competitive states where every bloc has the chance of swinging the election.[36] More important, however, is the fact that the electoral college forces politicians to take account of *all* minorities—urban, rural, ethnic, religious. So do mixed, federally based nominating systems such as now exist.

Large electoral units, to the contrary, encourage candidates to concentrate on majorities. Bickel was correct in asserting that under conditions of group politics, "Majorities do not arise spontaneously and they are not found. They must be constructed and then maintained. They are conglomerates of minorities, each of which must have its share of power."[37] But making the nation a single constituency would dramatically alter the bases of group politics. The national majority most readily assembled is that racially, ideologically homogeneous collectivity variously termed the "real majority," the "silent majority," "middle America," the "forgotten Americans." This majority has a number of readily identifiable characteristics: it is white, Christian, middle class, and relatively conservative in its views. The power of this "natural" majority is enhanced in a national electorate.

A rational campaign strategy for a national electorate would probably eschew the support of controversial minorities. It would take account of the size and homogeneity of potential support groups (say, Jews, blacks, Mormons) and the compatibility of their perspectives with those of other groups needed to compose a majority. As Key emphasized, there is a "broad tendency" for candidates to pay less attention to those elements of the population which cannot contribute significantly to their victory and for parties to mold themselves in the image of those parts of the constituency that contribute most to their strength.[38] Candidates and parties operating in a national electorate could therefore reasonably be expected to take most account of large collectivities with uncontroversial demands and less account of minorities such as blacks, welfare recipients, Chicanos, or native Americans. The small size and controversial demands of such minorities would offset their homogeneity in realistic calculations of their potential contribution to a majority coalition. Low turnout, minority status, and special needs would probably make black support, for example, too costly for a presidential candidate.

Diminishing concern for minorities of all kinds[39] is only one of many probable unintended byproducts of abolishing the electoral college or establishing a national primary. States and state parties would almost surely be further weakened as state boundaries lost their relevance to outcomes; minor parties would be encouraged by the possibility of aggregating strength on a nationwide basis; and the parties would become even less relevant to the nominating process. Indeed it seems probable that the states, confronted with the myriad of federal rules that would inevitably accompany direct national election of the President, would simply separate the election of the President from state and local elections. This in turn would further personalize presidential politics.

The precise effects of adopting a national primary would, of course, depend on the rules governing the primary, but *any* national primary would accelerate the trend toward personalist politics, exacerbate intraparty divisions, increase the likelihood of selecting unrepresentative candidates and an unrepresentative President, render the parties still more irrelevant to the presidential contest, and enhance the importance of candidate organizations.[40]

A national primary which could be won by a simple plurality could be expected to intensify divisions within both parties and the electorate and to enhance ideological, class, and racial voting. It would give a large advantage to well-known national figures and diminish the chances of such long shots as McGovern and Carter. Depending on the number and kind of candidates, it might result in the selection of a nominee with a specialized appeal and no chance of winning a general election. Even in a national primary, turnout would probably remain significantly lower than in a general election, a fact that increases the prospects for the victory of a factional candidate unacceptable to a majority of voters.[41] A national primary with a runoff provision would be less likely to produce candidates with narrow appeal and more likely to produce voter fatigue and apathy.

In sum, abolition of the electoral college or establishment of a national primary would almost surely have important but largely unintended and unexamined consequences for both the parties and the states. Proponents of "nationalizing" presidential elections and nominations are aware of the concern about its potential impact on the federal system and the two-party system. But they are content, generally speaking, with denying the likelihood of such unintended consequences and affirming that altering the parties or the role of the states is not part of their purpose.

Because political systems consist of interrelated, interdependent parts, and because the resulting equilibrium of cultural, social, and political factors is complex, the consequences of any reform are never entirely clear. But it seems probable that the future of the parties—including their federal structure, their organization, and the size and stability of their mass base—will depend in significant degree on the extent to which they are permitted to function in habitual ways, as voluntary intermediate institutions, or are forced by the politics of abstract principles or short-range advantage to accept constraints with unknown consequences.

The moral of this essay is not that no effort should be made to correct abuses or to make practices conform to ideals. It is that reforms have unintended and cumulative effects which may be as remote from their authors' purposes as they are damaging to institutions. The problem with the reforms considered here—especially those undertaken in the past decade or so—is not only that their price has been high. It is that the full price has never been calculated. Inadequate consideration has been given to their context, to the suitability of proposed means to desired ends, to the claims of competing values, to available alternatives, and to the probable impact of the recommended measures on all parts of the parties and the political system. In party reform as in life, good intentions are never enough, and wishing does not make it so. It is a basic article of faith in the American creed that for every ill there is a remedy; by now experience with party reform should have taught that, at least where political institutions are concerned, for every remedy there is probably an ill.

❧   ❧

Why the New Right Lost

IN THE YEARS BETWEEN 1969 and 1975 Kevin Phillips, William A. Rusher, Patrick J. Buchanan, and Richard J. Whalen all wrote books[1] assessing the strengths, weaknesses, and prospects of the American conservative movement as they understood it and recommending strategy and tactics for 1976. These writers do not represent *the* conservative position—there is no such thing. Indeed, they are considered by some, especially among the "Old Right," not to be conservatives at all, but neopopulist pseudoconservatives. Yet because they are articulate in formulating and vocal in justifying a position which has frequently lacked defenders among American intellectuals, their views have had an important influence on the way the conservative movement is perceived by other observers of American political life.

Although there are differences in approach, style, and strategy among these writers, they share certain qualities characteristic of what has come to be called the "New Right." Many of their perspectives are common to all conservatives: preoccupation with the nation's waning self-confidence; concern over the decline of such traditional values as discipline, restraint, consensus; rejection of guilt-ridden liberalism, of judicial decision-making, of social engineering, and of burgeoning bureaucracy; commitment to patriotism and a strong national defense.

In addition, however, the New Right holds certain other beliefs which may or may not be shared by other conservatives.
Among these are the idea that there exists in the electorate a
hidden conservative majority; that the social division with the
greatest potential political significance is not that between "haves"
and "have-nots" but between the liberal elite and everybody else;
that a realignment of the parties into two ideologically homogeneous groups is both desirable and likely; that the Republican
party may not prove an effective institutional channel for the expression of truly conservative politics and should perhaps be abandoned; and that the principal obstacles to the conservative cause
are the nation's media monopolies through whose "distorting lens"
is filtered "almost every scrap of information Americans receive of
their national government, its programs, policies and personalities"
(Buchanan).

The conviction that there exists out there in the electorate a
permanent conservative majority is a basic article of faith for the
new conservative intellectuals. Yet given the fact that George Wallace succeeded in winning only 13.6 percent of the vote in 1968,
and that Barry Goldwater—the only major-party candidate to
present himself unambiguously as the leader of a conservative
coalition—was buried in Lyndon Johnson's 1964 landslide, the
case for the existence of a conservative majority is not self-evident.
It requires interpreting the notion of a conservative broadly, to
include all persons who are attached to traditional values and
conventional practices; or who are hostile to the bureaucratization
of society; or who favor a strong military establishment, an anti-
Communist foreign policy, and an aggressive defense of the national interest; or who stress liberty as against equality; or who
desire to preserve the framers' vision of the constitutional system
against transformation. Theorists of the hidden conservative majority do indeed count all such persons as conservatives. They
also take comfort from the successive public opinion polls which
have revealed that when asked whether they are liberals or conservatives, the proportion of adults who describe themselves as
conservative has increased, while the percentage of self-described

liberals has declined. Thus, though conservatives still do not constitute a majority, they are considerably more numerous than liberals. The conservative advantage is further expanded when it is (dubiously) assumed, as Rusher for example does, that persons who are "undecided" as to whether they are liberal or conservative would divide in the same manner as persons with an opinion.

The preferred data on the existence of a conservative majority are the elections of 1968 and, especially, 1972. In *The Emerging Republican Majority* (1969), Kevin Phillips described 1968 as a turning point in the American party system comparable to 1828, 1860, 1896, and 1932. He argued that in Nixon's narrow victory against Humphrey the shape of the future could be discerned. Having fallen victim to "the ideological impetus of a liberalism which had carried it beyond programs taxing the few for the benefit of the many (the New Deal) to programs taxing the many on behalf of the few (the Great Society)," the Democratic party was being deserted by blue-collar ethnics and middle-income taxpayers. The result, Phillips argued, was an emerging Republican majority based "in the heartland of the South and California against a minority Democratic party based in the Northeast and the Pacific Northwest (and encompassing Southern as well as Northern Negroes)."

Gratifying as the outcome in 1968 was to theorists of the conservative majority, their pleasure in 1968 paled beside that of 1972—not because it brought a landslide for Richard Nixon, about whom they had great doubts, but because it seemed to them to have provided the electorate with a clear choice between ideologically distinct alternatives and to have resulted in a grand coalition of "conservatives." Never mind that Nixon had already (in Rusher's words) "systematically and cynically abandoned between 1969 and 1972 most of the conservative principles that justify participation in politics"; or that, as Whalen observed, the bureaucracy, terrified in 1968, had learned by 1972 that Nixon planned no dismantling of big government; or that Nixon had, in Buchanan's view, "made a conscious decision [after 1968] to shift leftward on domestic and social policy—to appease those who

most opposed him." Despite all this, it was still possible for
Rusher to conclude that in 1972 "the conservative majority, united
at last, had won overwhelmingly," and for Buchanan to assert that
"in the 'new majority' mustered together by President Nixon remain the constituent elements of conservative victory."

But faith in the existence of a conservative majority did not
depend only on public opinion data and electoral victories. More
important, the theory rested on an interpretation of contemporary
society which postulated "objective" social factors. Thus Kevin
Phillips argued in *The Emerging Republican Majority* that while
the old political alignment reflected a community of economic interests among the largely white urban working class and the South,
the new alignment would reflect the heightened ethnic consciousness of Catholic and blue-collar voters, the greatly increased political role of blacks, and the conservative inclinations of the dramatically enlarged Sun Belt.

In the wake of the 1972 election, however, a new interpretation began taking shape which deemphasized demographic factors.
What was now stressed instead was the emergence of a new socio-
cultural class structure and with it a new class struggle. This new
class struggle—which was variously described as pitting "producers" against "nonproducers" (Rusher's formulation), or as
pitting a new liberal elite based in the "knowledge sector" against
the working and middle classes (Phillips's formulation)—drew
heavily on the theory of postindustrial society enunciated by Daniel Bell, Rolf Dahrendorft, and others. Common to all these formu-
lations was a conviction that the economic divisions which traditionally separated the "haves" from the "have-nots" (and were
reflected in the Roosevelt coalition) had been superseded by the
rise of a privileged liberal elite whose interests as a group were
said to be concealed in an ideology favorable to the transfer of more
and more power from the private to the public sector. As Buchanan wrote:

Is it not the liberals' artistic and academic friends who get the
grants from the federal endowments for arts and humanities? Is

it not journalists of their persuasion who are given the large salaries and big fees for pontificating on "public television"? Is it not their children [who are] lured by Vista and the Peace Corps, and selected for Reggie Heber Smith fellowships to work out their ideology in Legal Services? Is it not their Naderite collaborators who will wind up with the positions of authority in a new federal consumer protection agency? Has it not been the professional bureaucrats, planners, consultants, and professors whose power, prestige, and income have grown directly proportional to the growth in federal power the last decade and a half?

In a similar vein, by the time he wrote *Mediacracy* (1975), Kevin Phillips's version of a liberal establishment which served its private interests by promotion of "sociological jurisprudence, moral permissiveness, experimental residential, welfare, and educational programming, and massive federal spending" had been revised to emphasize the role of the "knowledge sector," especially "academicians, journalists, urban planners, consumer advocates, welfare workers, and related occupations."

The belief that there has appeared in American politics an intelligentsia (often called the new class) hostile to bourgeois culture and institutional practices is, of course, shared by many persons not associated with the New Right. However, Lionel Trilling, Daniel Bell, Seymour Martin Lipset, Midge Decter, Michael Novak, and other intellectuals affiliated with the Democratic party who have emphasized the rising political importance of the new class *do not identify it with the welfare state.* These Democratic intellectuals see an important distinction between traditional welfare-state politics, which aims at providing all with a minimum share of economic well-being, respect, and political power, and the so-called new politics, which aims less at the diffusion of power than its concentration in the hands of the new class.

As conceived by the New Right, in any case, the new divisions between classes are based neither on an "objective" relation to the means of production (as Marx believed them to be), nor on disposable income and resources, but on occupation and culture. While occupation does not determine culture (else Phillips,

Buchanan, Rusher, Whalen, and their allies would themselves all be members of the liberal elite), persons associated with the knowledge sector and the bureaucracy are seen as the likely carriers of postindustrial morality and elitist politics, and as hostile to the interests and values of workers, businessmen, and farmers who are still engaged in the production of material goods and the frank pursuit of material advantage.

In this clash of cultural perspectives, no group is thought to have greater importance than the "media monopolists" or "media moguls" of the Washington–New York axis in whose hands rests the power to focus attention, filter information, set the nation's agenda, and make or break politicans. By 1970 hostility to "big media" had become a basic tenet of most conservatives and was held with special intensity by the New Right. The progressive concentration of power in the major networks and wire services and the growing number of one-newspaper cities had, it was argued, given control over the formulation and dissemination of news into the hands of "a small group of men," in Agnew's famous characterization, who "decide what forty to fifty million Americans will learn of the day's events in the nation and the world." From the point of view of the New Right, the danger of such a concentration of power was rendered even greater by the liberal perspective of the media moguls, which focused on negative and problematic aspects of the society, manufactured endless "crises," and eroded confidence in the nation's institutions and leaders.

Obviously, the class divisions described by Rusher, Phillips, and Buchanan have a great deal in common with those postulated and exploited by George Wallace. There is hardly—as Wallace might have put it—a dime's worth of difference between Rusher's elite bent on busing at any price or Buchanan's man of government who wants mass transit instead of automobiles because "that would mean government, rather than individuals, would dictate how people travel in America" and George Wallace's pointy-headed bureaucrats whose spendthrift schemes squander the taxes of working people to finance unworkable programs which, instead of solving problems, compound them.

Indeed, the theorists of the New Right noted what many liberal commentators, eager to dismiss the Wallace movement as racist, ignored: that the appeal of George Wallace grew out of the same process of cultural and social polarization which fed the candidacies of Eugene McCarthy and George McGovern. Out of that process of polarization, which drew into the political arena questions of morals and of legitimacy on which there has traditionally been broad consensus, two extreme positions developed: a McGovernite Left closely associated with the counterculture, and a Wallaceite Right committed to a comprehensive defense of the traditional culture. On this spectrum, voters were not arrayed according to their views of the welfare state, but on the basis of their attitudes toward the traditional society and culture.

It was Wallace who, in 1968 and 1972, mounted the most aggressive, unembarrassed defense of nationalism, patriotism, law and order, and the work ethic, as well as of that darker underside of the traditional culture—white racism. Wallace's success in attracting portions of the white working class was surprising only to those who *assumed* that the electorate could be placed on a political spectrum dominated by economic issues. But the postulated "new" conservative majority which integrated neopopulist Wallaceites and Republican business perspectives could come into being if, and only if, the economic issues on which the traditional political cleavages were based remained less salient than the social and cultural issues of the late 1960s. Theorists of the New Right believed that the cultural cleavages were here to stay.

Here, then, was an opportunity to build a new ideologically homogeneous party uniting all those who considered themselves conservatives in a grand alliance against those who considered themselves liberals. The intellectuals of the New Right were attracted to the idea of a new party because most of them were, and are, extremely ambivalent in their feelings about the Republican party. Interested above all in an institutional vehicle for the expression of conservative principles, they were offended by the continuing presence in the Republican party of a liberal minority which, ideologically speaking, belonged on the other side, by party professionals who in their relative unconcern with ideology belonged on no side, and by upper-class devotees of the "Old Right" who had as much in common with the liberal elite as with the conservative masses. Why, asked the New Right intellectuals, should the Republican party attract the loyalty of less than a fourth of the electorate when nearly half of all adult Americans considered themselves conservatives? Why should it fail to attract new voters—even those not attracted to the Democrats? Why could it not hold the support of those Southerners and Catholics and blue-collar voters who had crossed party lines to support Dwight Eisenhower, Richard Nixon, and even, in the Deep South, Barry Goldwater?

To Phillips and Rusher, the answer was that the Republican party was contaminated—by liberals, opportunists, ideologically neutral professionals, and crooks—and was a likely candidate for extinction. Rusher advocated a "new, broadly based major party" which would be called the "Independence" party and would include the "populist" followers of George Wallace and the "conservative" Republicans. Richard J. Whalen thought that conservatives might be more comfortable in a Democratic party led by Henry Jackson. Kevin Phillips, who is sometimes described as "hating" the Republican party, expressed doubt about the capacity of either party to adapt to continuing social changes, and noted that the functions of parties were, in any case, being progressively taken over by the communications industry. Even Patrick J. Buchanan, the most "Republican" of the leading conservative intellectuals, thought it possible that "when the crunch comes in the summer of 1976" conscience might require conservatives to abandon the GOP in favor of a third party which would state the conservative case in an unambiguous and aggressive fashion. Buchanan, however, also reminded his readers of the dangers of rule-or-ruin politics, and noted that the refusal to support an inadequately conservative Republican party would probably result in the election of more liberal Democratic candidates.

New Right theorists and conservative intellectuals of activist bent approached the 1976 presidential season with plans and determination. Conservative sectarianism intensified, organizations and committees crystallized around the candidates and potential candidacies of Ronald Reagan, George Wallace, John Connally, and Gerald Ford. The American Conservative Union, the Young Americans for Freedom, and the *Human Events* and *National Review* crowd joined the Reagan campaign; most of the Republican leadership—including even Barry Goldwater, John Tower, and eventually, Mississippi's Clark Reed—supported the nomination of Gerald Ford; and Wallace loyalists rallied behind Wallace.

But the hopes for a "pure" conservative party died as George Wallace dropped out of contention, as Ronald Reagan lost his bid for the Republican nomination, and finally, as Lester Maddox and his segregationist allies captured control of the American Independent party. No new party emerged, no realignment took place, the grand coalition of white working-class Democrats and middle-class Republicans fell apart, the Sun Belt was split down the middle as the South went home to the Democrats, the conservative majority did not materialize, and even Gerald Ford was ultimately defeated. What happened constitutes, in itself, an instructive critique of the New Right theory of American politics.

This theory is mistaken, first, because it is based on an over-simplified conception of ideology in contemporary American politics; second, because it overestimates the electorate's ideological inclinations; and, third, because it misunderstands the nature of political organization. Each of these errors helps to explain why the expectations of the New Right intellectuals were disappointed in 1976 and also why their disappointment is probably a chronic condition.

It seems quite clear that at least three dimensions have been involved in American politics over the last decade: an economic dimension, which includes attitudes toward private property, the distribution of wealth, private ownership, and governmental control; a cultural dimension, which includes attitudes toward tradition, order, authority, the deferral of gratification, and the moral bases for the allocation of resources; and a foreign-policy dimension, which includes attitudes toward nationalism, defense and the use of force, the Third World, and detente and related matters.

Most of the political debate of recent decades has involved the economic dimension, which was, of course, central to the New Deal alignment. From the entry of the United States into World War II until roughly 1966, a "bipartisan" foreign policy kept most questions of foreign relations and defense out of the political sphere, much as widespread consensus on the legitimacy of government and the public order precluded serious debate on these questions outside the little magazines and the fringe press. From World War II to the collapse of the Vietnam consensus, American politics *was* virtually one-dimensional and the liberal/conservative spectrum measured the kind of more/less questions which can be compromised in such a fashion that everyone gets something of value. The result was a style of "marketplace" or "broker" politics which conformed to the expectations of the Founding Fathers and to which the system was admirably suited.

The 1960s changed all that by introducing questions of culture and of foreign policy into the electoral sphere. Popular reaction to the disorders of the late 1960s—urban rioting, student rioting, massive violent protests and demonstrations, draft evasion —made it unambiguously clear that a large majority of American adults were conservative in the sense that they were attached to the existing society and would support it against challenges to its legitimacy. Nixon's 1972 landslide surely did demonstrate the presence of such a majority, but only as against a candidate who was perceived as the spokesman for a counterculture and at a time when violent assaults were being mounted against the existing social and political order. Under other circumstances—such as obtained, for example, in 1976—whether a voter votes his "conservative" views on a particular question will depend on its salience in a given contest as compared with other issues, on the ideological clarity of the choice offered in the election, and on the pull of nonideological factors like personality, regionalism, and party.

Most of the misunderstanding concerning what it is to be a liberal or conservative today grows out of the attempt to treat this multidimensional political universe as though it all hung together.

While it is possible to find persons who take "conservative" positions on every issue (assuming one can decide what a conservative position *is* on every issue), both public opinion data and electoral behavior make it entirely clear that a great many voters support an active role for government in the economic sphere, oppose challenges to the authority of government, distrust the Soviet Union and support a strong defense posture, or adopt some other combination of "liberal" and "conservative" positions.

The New Right belief that the large majorities who support traditional values and practices would vote conservative in presidential elections if only the conservative candidate provided adequate leadership might be correct if all elections featured one candidate who identified with a sectarian attack on the traditional social order and another who came to its defense. But most elections do not and cannot be expected to gratify the New Right by offering so easy a contest.

The New Right theory of politics is not only wrong because it assumes that people who are conservative on one issue are "conservatives"; it also errs in assuming that voters are more ideological than they in fact are.

Those who believe in the conservative majority argue that it can be mobilized for the purposes of electoral victory by a leadership that articulates the "basic" disagreements separating liberals and conservatives in our time. Ronald Reagan stated this position repeatedly after the 1976 election, arguing that the Republican party can be revitalized only if its leaders commit it to a clear-cut conservative position. And Buchanan counsels: "Conservatives should seek out, not avoid, political conflict with liberals of both parties. . . . We have nothing to lose by confrontation politics."

Experience with this strategy ought to be more discouraging than it is to the advocates of ideological polarization. It is an undeniable *fact* that each party has tried out the strategy in the recent past, and that the two candidates—Goldwater and McGovern—who provided the desired kind of leadership were overwhelmingly defeated by opponents who advocated and practiced consensus politics. The "moral" of the Goldwater and McGovern

debacles is not that the American electorate is neither as "conservative" as Barry Goldwater nor as "liberal" as George Mc-
Govern, but that the voters will repudiate candidates who offer a
narrowly ideological rhetoric and a divisive appeal.

The desire for ideologically homogeneous, disciplined, cohesive parties, for campaigns which pose a clear choice between
mutually exclusive programs, for leaders who "stand for" ideas—
all this flies in the face of the voters' proclivity to choose their
leaders not simply because of the "ideas" they represent, but because of the kind of men they are or seem to be, the party labels
under which they run, and the kind of men they are running
against. Neither does it take account of the ideological complexity
of the political world and the ideological cross-pressures which
derive from the variety of roles any individual voter may play
(occupational, regional, racial, religious, etc.).

The situation is further complicated by the fact that candidates themselves are likely to have complex ideological commitments and identifications. Jimmy Carter was the prototype of such
a candidate. The ideological ambiguity which characterizes his
image to this day was a source of strength in both the primaries
and the election. In Massachusetts, likely Democratic primary voters in 1976 split almost evenly on whether Carter was a liberal (15
percent thought so), a conservative (18 percent believed this to be
the case), or a moderate (as another 18 percent thought); and
Carter's supporters were also drawn from across the political
spectrum (25 percent conservative, 24 percent liberal, 45 percent
moderate). In Florida, the pattern was similar: 19 percent of
likely Democratic primary voters thought of him as conservative,
and 22 percent as a liberal. Although the selection of Walter Mondale as his running mate, and other openings to the Left, persuaded a good many voters of Carter's liberalism, substantial un-
certainty concerning his ideological identity persisted through the
campaign. The New York Times/CBS poll revealed that, early in
the nominating contest, roughly equal portions of a nationwide
sample of voters perceived Carter as liberal or as conservative (20
percent each), while 30 percent perceived him as a moderate. As

the campaign developed, the number of people who believed him a liberal rose to 37 percent, but 28 percent and 19 percent respectively continued to see him as a moderate or a conservative. Carter's narrow electoral success obviously owed a great deal to his ability to preserve a conservative-to-moderate image among Democrats who saw themselves as moderate or conservative, while at the same time consolidating the support of Democratic liberals.

Finally, the New Right theorists misunderstand the nature of political organization. Like their counterparts on the Left, these conservative theorists seem to believe that organizations can and should be only vehicles for the expression of political ideas. But in fact, students of organizational behavior know that all political organizations have some characteristics and requirements independent of ideology, that a variety of skills and temperaments are needed to perform their functions, and that they can be maintained only as people develop attachments to the organization itself.

Research has established that the party regular is attached to politics by social as well as ideological incentives (and sometimes also by material incentives) and that such attachment encourages the virtues of the good team member: cooperation, perseverance, loyalty, service, and the will to win. The ideological perspective, in contrast, is hostile to the construction and maintenance of organizational solidarity, for several reasons: first, because persons attached to politics by ideology do not identify themselves with organizations but with a point of view, and their commitment to organizations is therefore weak, instrumental, conditional; second, because persons attracted to politics by ideological incentives tend to hold relatively extreme and intense views and to have relatively comprehensive ideological orientations which encourage them to see particular questions as part of a larger whole. This in turn means that virtually any policy or issue can be perceived as involving "fundamental" questions of conscience which cannot be compromised without a sacrifice of "principle."

The ideological perspective in politics thus breeds intolerance of diversity, impatience with compromise, and the kind of intransigence characteristic of sectarian, rule-or-ruin politics. Ideological purists encounter persistent and probably insurmountable difficulties in building institutions through which to achieve their political goals, not only because their clearly defined programs cannot attract more than a minority, but also because their inclinations and habits are the opposite of those required to maintain large, inclusive democratic political organizations.

The intellectuals of the New Right understand, at least in theory, that compromise is required if a majority coalition is to be assembled; Rusher in particular stresses this point. But the difficulties they and their followers have displayed in accepting actual compromises with Republican loyalists like Gerald Ford who share *most* of their conservative views provide little reason to suppose that hypothetical compromises with Wallaceites would prove more palatable if they ever became a concrete possibility.

There are some suggestive similarities between the theory of the New Right and the theory espoused by votaries of the new politics at the other end of the political spectrum. The hidden conservative majority has its analogue in the army of the alienated —the poor, the young, the oppressed, the idealistic, the Wallaceites, the elderly—whom McGovern expected to rally behind his banner. The New Right version of class struggle based on "producers" and "nonproducers" (or some functional equivalent) is a mirror image of the division postulated by the new politics between the comfortable and the smug on the one hand, and the alienated and their champions on the other. There is, furthermore, general agreement about the geocultural bases of these classes: both Kevin Phillips and Kirkpatrick Sale have located the Left in WASP New England and the nation's major universities and the Right in the culturally conservative, demographically ascendant Sun Belt. (Sale termed these groups the Yankees and the Cowboys.) And there is, finally, in the case of both the New Right and the new politics, an imperviousness to empirical disproof. Defeat of their position never demonstrates that the putative hidden majority does not in fact exist; it only proves that the cause was sabotaged by the media or betrayed, or at least failed, by its leaders. The belief in a hidden majority, indeed, puts an especially heavy bur-

den on leadership, while sustaining partisans in the face of repeated losses and providing a sense of solidarity with "the people."

There are also interesting parallels between the New Right in
1972–76 and the "Radical Right" associated with the late Senator
Joseph McCarthy. As analyzed by Daniel Bell, Richard Hofstadter, Nathan Glazer, Seymour Martin Lipset, and others, the
Radical Right of the 1950s was itself the product of a "new politics" which cut across partisan and ideological alignments, uniting
persons of diverse economic interests in a novel coalition based on
shared "status aspirations" and "status anxieties" against liberals,
left-wingers, intellectuals, nonconformists, and suspected and real
Communists.

While these analysts of the Radical Right sometimes sounded
embarrassingly like embattled defenders of a threatened aristocracy (the Radical Right was, they thought, a revolt by lower-
and middle-class Americans against their betters), and while at
other times they wrote as though major strains of American history were some kind of disease (there was much talk of authoritarian personalities, projection, and paranoia), they did not dismiss the new dissidents as insignificant. Instead, they saw the
Radical Right as, in Hofstadter's words, "one of the long waves of
20th-century American history and not a momentary mood."

To read such analyses today is to be reminded that the New
Right is not really new at all, but represents a strain of nativist
populism whose roots are deep in American history and which has
already played a highly important role in American politics, especially in the South and Southwest. As such, it is no more likely to
disappear from the contemporary political scene than it is to become the center of a new majority party. Its current version will fail
because of its hostility to another deeply rooted aspect of contemporary politics: the welfare state, whose benefits no majority in any
democratic country has yet forsworn. Nevertheless, in one form or
another, it will remain with us for a very long time to come.

Politics and the "New Class"

WHEN POLITICS IS a voluntary activity, as in this society, political activity depends on a "fit" between personal predispositions and skills on the one hand, and role perceptions and opportunities on the other. Various types of politics feature distinctive preoccupations and styles that are attractive to different kinds of people. A "marketplace" politics dominated by economic interests and concerned with issues more or less in the here and now is very different from a politics dominated by intellectual questions and concerned with matters of justice and injustice in history. Since half a loaf *is* better than none, compromising over material goods is relatively easy. But it is never easy to compromise the kind of moral and ideological questions preferred by political intellectuals, because compromise is tantamount to sellout and error. So people attracted to the one style of politics are likely to be bored and quite possibly offended by people attracted to the other.

In periods of rapid social change, political institutions also change, as new kinds of people perceive previously unnoticed opportunities for achieving personal and political goals. If enough of them become active in a political institution, they may "tilt" it from, say, a politics chiefly concerned with the distribution of goods to a politics concerned with morals. Such a process of institutional reorientation has been under way in American politics and government for some time, and has resulted in the increasing number and influence of "new class" representatives and the declining role of business and labor in the polity.

Unlike Marx's conception which defines class in terms of ownership of the means of production, and the "sociological" conception which identifies class with socioeconomic status, the new-class concept defines class less in economic than in functional terms. Members of the new class are defined not by what they own, but by what they do. They constitute what Harold Lasswell termed a "skill" class, trained in the manipulation of ideas, words, and meanings. Though most new-class members have relatively high levels of education and income and are found in professions requiring verbal and communications skills, the new class can be recognized not by its socioeconomic characteristics but by its relation to culture: to the meanings that constitute a culture and to the symbols through which those meanings are expressed.

The growing influence and importance of the new class has been repeatedly noted in this century. Lasswell and his collaborators described the distinctive role of theoreticians, propagandists, and other middle-class symbol specialists in the Bolshevik, Nazi, Fascist, and Chinese revolutions. James Burnham, among others, described the progressive displacement of owners by a new managerial elite. Milovan Djilas noted the rise of a new political class system in Yugoslavia, where the Communist party claimed a monopoly of social and economic power.

I believe it is demonstrable that the new class has become in the last decade or so progressively important in the American political elite and mid-elite and that its increased role has had observable consequences in government, political parties, and pressure groups.

The most important of these consequences have been the decline of consensus, the progressive involvement of broader cultural forces in politics (this was especially obvious in the presidential races of 1964, 1968, and 1972), and the ever-increasing use of government power and organizations to achieve "rationalist" goals. The rise of the new class has also had a significant impact on the style of the ruling elite and the processes through which its members are recruited and the standards by which it is judged. In sum, the growing importance of the new class is a major factor in the transformation of American political reality.

The presence of the new class in the ruling elite was signaled by the changing educational and occupational characteristics of its members. The declining numbers of farmers and self-employed businessmen and the rising numbers of teachers, clergymen, and journalists not only reflect general occupational trends within the society but also testify to the increased prestige of "symbol skills" in politics.

Today, businessmen rarely seek public office and are not inclined to take part in the great debates surrounding politics. The repeated efforts of corporations to persuade their managers and executives to "get involved" in the political arena have come to little. When a captain of industry ventures into politics, he is likely to say something inept, which is then repeated and ridiculed by the guardians of the symbolic environment, who regard their own ability to communicate effectively as the *sine qua non* for respect and power. A single verbal faux pas can wreck political prospects: the presidential campaigns of George Romney, Edmund Muskie, and Gerald Ford provide instructive examples.

It will be (and often is) said that the manner in which a candidate expresses himself is important not merely as a measure of his verbal competence but for the insights it provides into the "true" man. And there is the proverbial grain of truth in this assertion: from Romney's confession that he had been "brainwashed" about Vietnam we learned that he was given to overstatement, from Ford's remarks on Poland we learned something about his tendency to defend a mistake once it was made, and so forth. These bits of information about the men who seek to rule us are useful—about as useful as knowing whether they have ever met a payroll. But it is unlikely that these insights will be better predictors of presidential performance than Harry Truman's business failure was. (That we were so much less concerned about Carter's business record than about his Baptist convictions is just one more example of the pervasive influence of the new class on political standards.)

I do not think that intellectuals emphasize verbal skills out of a crass desire to drive up the price of their talents (though the emphasis, in fact, has that effect). Businessmen do not simply have a "vested interest" in the capacity to balance a budget, make a profit, or meet a payroll; political bosses do not only have a "vested interest" in the capacity to "deliver" a district on election day; communications specialists do not simply have a "vested interest" in the ability to analyze arguments and state propositions clearly. More important, each is most sensitive to the aspects of the environment to which his predispositions and skills are most relevant. This is why the new class values verbal skills in politicians and other new standards of fitness.

The new class has achieved increased influence in politics because many of its members conceive of public policies as relevant to their private destinies and see themselves as having the public mission of criticizing (and, more recently, defending) the dominant political culture; because they possess the skills (analyzing, criticizing, moralizing, and persuading) and other resources (the mass media and the educational institutions) needed to communicate that sense of mission; and because they have an audience today, the product of mass higher education, which is at least potentially attentive and responsive to their claims and critiques. What wealth is to the capitalist, what organization is to the old-style political boss, what manpower is to the trade unionists, words are to the new class. This is another way of saying that the new class comprises intellectuals and semi-intellectuals (other specialists in communications, like clergymen and public relations men). As Schumpeter, wrestling with similar problems of definition, observed, "Intellectuals are in fact people who wield the power of the spoken and the written word." Harold D. Lasswell called this group "symbol specialists" and emphasized that their potential functions extend to the whole symbolic environment—including the definition of reality, purpose, morality, and obligation.

In democratic politics, mass support is necessary to achieve political power. The existence of a large and continually growing educated class facilitates the rise of the new class, but is not a prerequisite to its accession to political power. The new class has recently achieved greater importance because of profound cultural dislocations, involving challenges to the most basic beliefs, assumptions, values, and standards of contemporary society. Intellectuals pose questions about these matters, and intellectuals try to answer them. In traditional societies, habit underpins authority, obedience is customary, and doctrines of legitimacy are self-evident. But in periods of rapid change, moralists and wordsmiths become indispensable to rulers who need continuous legitimation of their power. The new class specializes in questions of legitimacy.

It is almost impossible to exaggerate the importance of political culture to the conduct of government and politics. Political culture locates the individual in the political world—the ethnic, religious, regional, racial, national, and other collectivities in terms of which politics is conducted. It states expectations about what government can do and should do, about the rights and duties of rulers and citizens and the relations between the two, and about the terms and limits of acceptable behavior in the pursuit and exercise of power.

The cultural hegemony of Marxism has tended to obscure the fundamental importance of political culture to our contemporary political system. But the relation between the two was no secret to earlier ages. Plato understood well the dependence of a regime on its political culture and emphasized the creation and protection of the central myths and values of the polity. In *The Republic* he proposed a myth to link the structure of the polity to divine purpose and to reinforce the distribution of social roles and the authority of the ruling class, which was to be the product of a most careful education in a most carefully controlled symbolic environment. By the time he wrote *The Laws*, Plato was less sanguine about the possibilities of creating an ideal state, but no less certain that an appropriate political culture was required to sustain a polity. And, like Rousseau, Plato proposed the death penalty for atheists—not because he valued piety for its own sake, but because he was convinced that religion provided necessary reinforcement for the authority and legitimacy of the state. Meanwhile, in Plato's Athens, a new class was actively analyzing the bases of law and the state, demythologizing religion and authority, and debating at length the obligations and limits of citizenship. Despite the execution of Socrates, their discussions continued.

Plato, Aristotle, and the Sophists were all engaged in the political activities for which intellectuals are best suited and to which they are most attracted: the demoralization and remoralization of politics and society. Demoralization makes explicit the beliefs and loyalties that hold a society together and submits them to a comprehensive critique in the light of abstract, rationalist assumptions; remoralization provides new myths and new authorities. Both processes proceed by investing small questions with large meaning, by finding previously unsuspected moral significance in routine practices. Both offer the opportunity to define reality, to determine social stations and duties, and to reinforce personal visions and preferences with political power. The chance for all this presents itself only in times of rapid change and unusual freedom—like our own times, in places like the United States and Western Europe.

In any vital society, the initial attack on political authority (mounted by intellectuals) provokes a response and results in an intensified ideological struggle leading inexorably to the enhanced role of the new class. The greater the role of the new class in politics, the more ideological politics becomes; the more ideological politics becomes, the more important the new class becomes. Its critical skills are required to analyze the moral inadequacies of the existing society, its verbal skills to dramatize them. But other members of the new class are then needed to criticize the critics, to defend the symbols of legitimacy, to state the case for the values and beliefs embodied in the existing political culture and institutions.

As the above comments imply, *members of the new class do not necessarily share the same political views and values; they may*

be found across our multidimensional political spectrum. The
tendency to liberalism is strong, but the problems of welfare states,
command economies, and Marxist-Leninist leviathans have stimulated critiques of liberalism. And in the United States today, the
new class includes many of the nation's journalists, many of the
clergy, the professoriate, and some of the bureaucrats (especially
those at upper levels).

There will always be exceptions, but some reasonably accurate generalizations are possible. Members of the new class tend
to share some orientations that transcend their differences over
policy. The most important common characteristic is a marked
tendency to rationalistic, moralistic, and reformist approaches to
politics. Among these, the most basic is the tendency toward rationalism and the belief that reality should reflect a conception of
history. Hegel's expectation that the ideal would be realized at the
end of history lives on—not only among Marxists, who have explicitly incorporated it into their "laws of history," but among
the new class, which uses historical criteria to judge political processes and institutions. Institutions are quite literally expected to
embody ideas. Political parties, campaigns, and administrations
are expected to stand for ideas; when they turn out to be multifunctional and ideologically impure (as they always do), new-class
purists of Right and Left react with disappointment, disaffection,
and not infrequently, determination to reform them. The goal of
the new-class reformer—whether of Left or Right—is to bring the
real into conformity with the ideal (that is, with an *idea* of reality).

This goal explains the intellectual's perennial enthusiasm for
programmatic political parties, an enthusiasm found at all points
of the political spectrum. It is not enough that political parties
should have somewhat different clienteles and orientations; they
must define their identity and mission in terms of programs.
In this view, the function of candidates is to present a program and
quite literally to stand for it; the function of activists is to win the
election on behalf of the program.

The desire that parties, candidates, and governments stand

for programs not only reflects the intellectual's fascination with policy, but also manifests a broader belief that social institutions should conform to and serve abstract principles. The most serious problems with this rationalist approach were recognized by Aris totle, who criticized Plato's blueprint for the ideal state. Plato believed that an individual's moral quality derived from his membership in a just society in which everyone accepted his assigned station and duties and voluntarily and consistently subordinated personal to collective goals. Aristotle argued that his teacher overestimated human malleability and underestimated the tenacity of organic ties and human wickedness. Aristotle also argued that experience and law were better guides than reason alone to the good society and that Plato's proposal would sacrifice real goods to illusory ideals.

Roughly the same criticisms were made for the next two thousand years, to this day. As Aristotle perceived, rationalism in politics is closely associated with both extremism and utopianism. Its habit of confounding the realm of abstraction with that of experience invariably results in the oversimplification of social processes, because principles are never as complex or intractable as experience. Rationalism also tends to utopianism and extremism because it ignores the distinction between the possible and the probable and encourages optimism about the accomplishment of the highly improbable. The great danger of rationalist politics is that the complexity and multifunctionality of political institutions will be overlooked and that schemes designed to maximize one value will destroy the social tissue that supports many others.

Concentration on the manipulation of ideas and words (like concentration on the manipulation of paints or musical tones) probably induces an exaggerated notion of the world's plasticity and also of human powers, since the only limits on artistic or intellectual creation are those imposed by imagination, creativity, and skill. But even the slightest effort at manipulating the social world involves man in psychological problems and social relations of incredible and invariably unforeseen complexity. The vast complexity of actual human societies creates obstacles to realizing ideas, and the difference between abstract principles and actual social systems makes principle and ideology a poor blueprint for political action. But the contemporary American new class has a great interest in ideology and little interest in the more useful study of history. New-class members also rarely have practical experience with the institutions that are the objects of their attention. Describing the class of which he was part (as I am), Schumpeter noted, with more cogency than kindness, "One of the touches that distinguish [intellectuals] from other people who do the same [sort of things] is the absence of direct responsibility for practical affairs. This touch in general accounts for another—the absence of firsthand knowledge—which only actual experience can give."

Contemporary politics is dominated by a rhetoric of dissatisfaction born from the new-class vision of possibility. Of course, the new class's generally negative orientation toward the status quo has other roots—in the businessman's concern for the practical and the material, and his underestimation of the importance of culture and the "impractical" people who specialize in the manipulation of meaning, and perhaps in the relatively low income and status of intellectuals in capitalist, democratic societies (as compared to their much greater power in contemporary revolutionary regimes). But I suspect that the most important source of the adversary culture is the intellectual's habit of measuring institutions and practices against abstract standards: reality is invariably found unsatisfactory. It seems almost certain that the rationalist orientation creates disenchantment with concrete people, places, and practices. When today's housing, health care, or income levels are compared with those of the last decade or those of other societies, the society may look progressive and reasonably successful. But when society is measured against an abstract conception of a just order, it will be seen to have failed.

It is also easy to understand why the new class is more often liberal than conservative. The habit of measuring existing practices against abstract principles inevitably leads to discontent with the status quo, and the belief that reality can be brought into conformity with principles creates a predisposition to act to remedy unsatisfactory situations. Rationalism, optimism, and activism have been and still are the source of liberal and radical political action. They are also characteristics of the politics of the new class.

The tendency to find reality wanting is compounded by an equally marked proclivity for moralistic politics. It is not entirely clear why new-class activists of both Right and Left should invest politics with so much moral meaning, but the habit is strong. The Goldwater campaign and the antiwar movement were both propelled on waves of moral indignation. In the mid-1950s, Daniel Bell, Richard Hofstadter, and others regularly ascribed moralistic politics to the "Radical Right" and linked it to evangelical Protestantism and the search for respectability. It now appears that moralism is linked to the decline of religion, but not in the expected way. Today, the relationship between secularism and moralism is especially clear on the Left, where absence of religious affiliation and faith is frequently associated with moralistic politics. George McGovern's habit of lapsing into the fervent rhetoric of his Methodist past illustrates the affinity on the Left between religious and political revivalism. The rhetoric of the ideological Right and Left alike shows how readily political contests may be conceived as ongoing battles between the forces of light and darkness. The higher the moral content of politics, the more interested the new class becomes; predictably, the more interested the new class becomes, the more the political universe is likely to be moralized.

New-class perspectives have been a regular feature of the American political scene since World War II. Recall the response to Harry Truman's nasal twang and down-home rhetoric, the disdain for Dwight Eisenhower's convoluted syntax and Lyndon Johnson's cornpone style, and the celebration of Adlai Stevenson's eloquence and John Kennedy's verbal grace. But the new class has been decisive in only a few political events of our times: the conflict over McCarthyism, the intensification of cultural conflict in politics, and the bureaucratization of almost everything.

Even today, two and a half decades later, the set of events called McCarthyism resonates across the barriers of generation and time. The curious disproportion between the actual events and the emotions they have evoked in the political folklore of the century signifies that the controversy—like a fairy tale—raised perennial anxieties and provided a meaningful and reassuring resolution. The putative stakes in the struggle were the right of Communists and their sympathizers to hold jobs in government and in government-related enterprises. The actual prize was jurisdiction over the symbolic environment. Government was increasingly trying to reinforce with sanctions the demand for loyalty, and there was also a more generalized demand for conformity. Again and again, McCarthy and those associated with his crusade confused Communists with nonconformists, loyalty toward the regime with attitudes toward public ownership, religion, and even football. And McCarthy's foes, understanding as well as he did that the stakes were higher than stated, not only attacked his procedures and the impulse to social conformity, but also rejected the notion that government had any jurisdiction over the attitudes of its citizens.

McCarthy served then and now as a symbol of the demand that intellectuals support the values and beliefs of the society, revere what the society defines as sacred, and respect whomever the society defines as authorities and whatever it defines as authoritative. The extent to which McCarthy became a symbol for the demands of what was then termed the "Radical Right" is clear in the rhetoric and analyses contemporary with the events. Richard Hofstadter identified McCarthyism as a variant of status politics, emphasized McCarthy's demand for generalized conformity, and suggested that the "pseudoconservatives" of the Radical Right, of whom McCarthy was the prototype, had as their true targets "liberals, critics and nonconformists of various sorts, as well as Communists and suspected Communists." Garry Wills recently went even further, suggesting that McCarthyism should be equated with anti-Communism of all varieties. "It is unfortunate," he asserted in a paean to Lillian Hellman, "that McCarthyism was named teleologically for its most perfect product, rather than genetically—which would give us Trumanism."

The struggle against McCarthy, which now has the character

of an epic, quickly came to stand for the demand of the new class for autonomy in the realms of truth and values, for jurisdiction over culture. The intellectuals won, and their victory was a precondition of the rise of the counterculture in the 1960s. And the fear of McCarthyism still continues because their authority never seems as secure or as complete as it might. It is challenged from time to time by parents or elected officials demanding control over textbooks, or by a prosecutor with an indictment for conspiracy to incite draft evasion or violence. The intensity of the intellectuals' opposition to Barry Goldwater's presidential campaign was guaranteed by his offensive against their cultural dominance. The hostility of the new class toward Richard Nixon was rooted in the conviction that he was still a censor at heart, who, if the opportunity presented itself, would turn the control of culture back to the Yahoos of the Radical Right. The Hiss case, too, I suspect, has been from the beginning part of the struggle for the control of culture. The reluctance of some intellectuals to accept Hiss's guilt (for Chambers' charges) is rooted in their prior reluctance to accept the notion that a government can legitimately demand loyalty from its citizens. The legitimization of disloyalty is, after all, only the next step (the last?) in a long process of emancipating the individual from ascriptive identifications. Our national progress down this particular slippery slope is already far advanced: from Private Slovik to "fragging" in Vietnam, from vigilante justice for draft dodgers to amnesty for war resisters, from Ezra Pound's incarceration to antiwar parades featuring Viet Cong flags and U.S. senators, from the execution of spies to the prosecution of counterspies. Once the claims of the collectivity to the loyalty of its members are abandoned, and membership is made a matter of individual decision, the concept of treason is void, and rehabilitation is granted to "principled" spies.

While Joseph McCarthy symbolized the threatening demand for conformity, in the early 1950s the urbane and articulate Stevenson symbolized the promise of power to come and served as a catalyst for a new political generation. The appearance of significant numbers of college-educated, socially mobile, issue-oriented voters in urban and suburban reform clubs was noted by political observers in New York, California, Wisconsin, Missouri, and elsewhere. The new middle-class activists brought distinctive goals, standards, and styles into the political arena. Their ideal was almost invariably "reform," defined as wresting power from traditional leaders and organizations and transferring it to themselves and their political factions. Their new standards required that politics be conducted by articulate volunteers rather than political professionals who spoke like Richard Daley. The new style was issue-oriented, moralistic, and reformist.

The politics of the early 1950s provides the model for new-class concerns. McCarthy and Stevenson symbolized the issues and candidates that could mobilize large portions of the new class. The Vietnam War and the Kennedys generated similar levels of antagonism and admiration in the 1960s. Like the struggle against McCarthyism, the antiwar movement pitted relatively educated, high-status nonconformists against traditionalists. That the peace marchers were far more aggressive in their defiance of traditional taboos than had been the timid victims of Joe McCarthy reflected the distance that the cultural revolution had proceeded. That the Kennedys were able to reap larger political profits from their personal elegance than had Stevenson reflected the growing tendency to judge politics by standards previously reserved for entertainment. Both changes were at least in part a consequence of the enhanced influence of the new class in politics.

Since the struggle over McCarthyism, the involvement of basic cultural symbols in the political arena has become a regular feature of our politics. As avant-garde culture spread through rising college enrollments, the electronic media, and mass-circulation magazines, anti-bourgeois attitudes previously limited to a few became the basis of the anti-establishment politics of the 1960s—with "establishment" defined as nothing less than the entire social order. The presidential politics of 1968 and 1972 featured a full-scale challenge to the legitimacy of most of the society's major institutions—family, schools, trade unions, business, and especially government.

By 1968, significant portions of the nation's elite had responded empathetically to new-class critiques of traditional authority, obedience, discipline, law and order, and other key values of the political culture. There first began a dramatic and continued decline of popular confidence in political parties, politicians, government, courts, business, labor, and even the media, and a sharp increase in popular cynicism. Second, within the new class a backlash developed among intellectuals who found the counterculture and the new politics less compelling and more dangerous than the traditional culture (especially the traditional political culture), which in turn stimulated a challenge within the intellectual community to the political doctrine and influence of the adversary culture. (The neoconservative movement, the Coalition for a Democratic Majority, *Commentary*, the *Public Interest*, the *American Spectator*, and some of the New Right are the agents of this challenge.) Third, the intensified assault on traditional values and institutions precipitated the disintegration of traditional liberalism and conservatism. Eugene McCarthy, George McGovern, George Wallace, and Richard Nixon were both agents and beneficiaries of this process. Lyndon Johnson and Hubert Humphrey were among its principal casualties.

The election of 1972 nicely illustrated the politics of cultural polarization. In that election, issues achieved a salience unique in modern presidential politics. The issues that preempted voter attention were not the bread-and-butter questions that had structured the electorate since the New Deal, but cultural and social questions that created new cleavages and coalitions pitting supporters of traditional notions of work and welfare, war and peace, law and legitimacy, against supporters of the counterculture. Antiwar demonstrations celebrated new life-styles and articulated new demands (including the right to support an enemy with whom the nation was actually if not legally at war). Welfare policy became involved in conflicting views of the work ethic, and day-care programs with the debate over Women's Liberation. Environmental protection was enmeshed in a generalized assault on technology, and law enforcement policy entangled with broader judgments concerning the legitimacy of the social order. Cultural politics are especially intense because they involve values anchored in the ego.

The introduction of cultural conflict into American politics dramatizes the developing cleavages in the society and their social bases. It is now clear that the assault on the traditional culture was mounted by young and not-so-young representatives of the relatively privileged classes, while the basic institutions of the society were defended by less prosperous, less educated, lower-status citizens. Some of the byproducts of these developments were a redefinition of the concepts of liberalism (one version of which became the ideology of the privileged) and conservatism (a version of which is now the position of the less privileged); a partial realignment of the social bases of the two parties (with the Democrats acquiring the upper-income devotees of cultural liberalism and losing the loyalties and votes of a significant portion of the white working class); and growing distance between the political elite, which was heavily influenced by new-class liberalism, and the rank-and-file voters, who remained traditionalist in their cultural perspectives.

Cultural conflict played a much smaller role in the politics of 1976, doubtless because both parties were led by men who cultivated traditional virtues in their personal lives and avoided inflammatory rhetoric in their public lives. Since no candidate symbolized a challenge to the traditional political culture, there was only limited interest in its defense (though nearly enough to make Ronald Reagan the Republican nominee then). However, it would be premature to assume that consensus has been restored to American politics. Most of the disagreements of the previous decade remain; most of the issues of the previous decade are still debated within the new class, where arguments are ready and waiting for the candidates and issues to dramatize them.

An equally important consequence of the increased political influence of the new class on American government is the expansion of what has come to be known as the "public sector." Although the expansion of government in this century is sometimes considered a defining characteristic of modernity, it is not really clear that government growth was an inevitable consequence of industrialization or modernization.

What is certain is that government's functions have both expanded and changed as conceptions of the purposes of government have changed. Theories of government change before governments change. Adam Smith made the case for a market economy before mercantilism was dismantled; Marx made the case for state ownership before the Bolshevik Revolution; various socialists, neo-idealists, and communitarians made the case against minimal government and for expansion of government's role in the economy and society decades before governments began to assume these functions.

The New Deal brought significant numbers of intellectuals and semi-intellectuals into government for the first time, to solve pressing problems that had eluded solutions. In fact, the perceptions that poverty and joblessness were intolerable and that government could and should do something about them preceded the New Deal and shaped its programs.

Historical conceptions of problems and appropriate responses vary along with other aspects of the culture. As the contemporary culture specialists, the new class has a large and, I believe, decisive influence that in recent decades has been exercised to shift responsibility for the quality of social life from the individual, family, and other private groups to government. Two arguments were made to justify this shift: first, widely acknowledged ills were not being met satisfactorily, and second, transfers would promote social justice.

These two motives frequently lead to quite different kinds of programs, although the differences are denied or glossed over. For example, it is sometimes argued that mandated busing is "merely" a logical extension of *Brown v. Board of Education*, or that racial or sexual quotas are "only" a logical extension of outlawing discrimination, or that regulations stipulating the size of toilet seats for employees are "only" a logical extension of the same concern for work safety involved in mine inspection. But there are important differences among these uses of government that are central to the current agenda of the new class and to the debates that have developed within it.

Until sometime in the mid-1960s, reform proceeded in response to some concrete evil. Since then, more and more reforms have been stimulated by the goals of reformers, rather than the desires of the affected groups. It is almost impossible to overstate the importance of the distinction between government programs that are desired by their beneficiaries, promulgated by elected officials, and carried out with the consent of the affected communities and programs that are undertaken because of a bureaucratic or judicial conception of the good of the putative beneficiaries, promulgated by judges and bureaucrats who are not politically accountable, and imposed by force on resisting communities. The difference is nothing less than the distinction between democratic government and the revolutionary dictatorship of a coercive elite. The fundamental premise of self-government is that ordinary people are better able to judge their own interests than any ruler is. The basic premise of dictatorship is that, by virtue of its superior wisdom, a vanguard is best able to judge the interests of everyone —since almost all are too blinded by "false consciousness" to know what they need or even what they "really" want.

No universal abstract principle can mechanically distinguish between caring that sustains and caring that coerces. There are only endless specific judgments about when and where the cumbersome and coercive machinery of government will reinforce autonomy and when it will subvert it. The peculiar predilection of intellectuals to a rationalist approach which pushes principles and policies toward their "logical" conclusion makes these distinctions especially troublesome. Harold D. Lasswell noted, in his *World Revolutionary Elites*, that revolutions of the "post-bourgeois" era had brought symbol specialists to power in Fascist Italy, Nazi Germany, the Soviet Union, and China, as part of "the major transformation [of our times, which] is the decline of business and of earlier social formations and the rise of intellectuals and semi-intellectuals to effective power." Lasswell's collaborator, Daniel Lerner, described these "new men with new ideas" as "coercive ideologues" and noted that "each totalitarian regime began with its variant of 'intelligentsia' at or near the apex of the new elite." Supplementing Aristotle's observation that men do not become tyrants in order to avoid exposure to the cold, Lasswell and Lerner suggested that in our times men become tyrants because they believe they can use political power to bring society, culture, and personality into conformity with their vision of what they should be.

The political temptation of the new class lies in its believing that its members' intelligence and exemplary motives equip them to reorder the institutions, the lives, and even the characters of almost everyone—this is the totalitarian temptation. This is also the reason that a politics featuring large roles for intellectuals is especially dangerous to human liberty.

Obviously, a free society cannot eliminate the new class from politics, any more than it can eliminate businessmen or truck drivers. But a society that cherishes liberty will do well to protect itself from the excesses of the new class. As surely as a monopoly of power or wealth is dangerous to the rest of us, a new-class monopoly on meaning and purpose is incompatible with the common weal.

Regulation, Liberty, and Equality

LIKE MOST HUMAN ACTIVITIES, government regulation is usually prompted by the best of motives. Perhaps the commonest of these is the desire to aid the weak, the poor, and the downtrodden by providing a more equal distribution of money, influence, education, leisure, health care, and other comforts. To this end, the power of government is used to distribute the good things of life more evenly than unregulated interactions could. But because regulation uses the coercive power of government to alter outcomes, it diminishes individual liberty: people are persuaded by the threat of sanctions to act differently than they would otherwise prefer.

The resulting tension between liberty and equality is not only a central feature of the welfare state but is a permanent characteristic of the values themselves, and of democratic government. Although it has become commonplace in our times to hold that equality can be achieved only at the expense of liberty and that liberty can be preserved without concern for equality, liberty and equality are compatible, mutually reinforcing values which can and, in fact, must exist and grow together. The existential relations between them hold important lessons for liberals and conservatives alike, and especially for policymakers who make the rules that enhance or endanger our freedom.

Should a discussion of liberty and equality seem remote from everyday concerns, it is only necessary to call to mind the myriad of rules—now abolishing a boys choir, now busing children across Boston, now raising the minimum wage, now calling for portable toilets in cornfields—which both limit and expand our alternatives. Since governments enforce their rules with severe sanctions (such as the loss of property, freedom, or even life), government involvement in an aspect of social life always introduces powerful constraints into whatever interactions it seems to affect. Wherever government regulates, it supplants the judgment and preferences of private individuals with its own judgment, backed by its unique authority and coercive power.

Believing that liberty and the public interest were better served by leaving decisions to private individuals, classical liberalism—a doctrine associated with the names of John Locke, Jeremy Bentham, David Ricardo, and James and John Stuart Mill—emphasized individual freedom, especially freedom from government. It stressed individual rights in the political sphere and individual initiative in economic activity. It was more concerned with the production than with the distribution of goods. It did not doubt that men and societies were happier and more productive when not constrained by the "dead hand of government."

The problem with this conception of the relation between liberty and government is, of course, that government is not the only source of constraints on human freedom. By the time he wrote his essays *On Liberty* and *On the Subjection of Women*, John Stuart Mill had come to believe that social pressure and prejudice could be a greater threat to liberty than government action. Marx, Proudhon, and Goodwin (to name just three critics of classical liberalism) disagreed about many things but were one in emphasizing economic constraints on human freedom. Where, they demanded, was the freedom of a worker forced by need and subsistence wages to send his children into mines and factories, to work long hours at grueling labor until he died? A famous jingle made the point:

> The golf course is so near the mill
> That almost every day
> Little children at their work
> Can watch the men at play.

T. H. Green and his successors spelled out a notion of positive government that focused attention on the possibilities of using government to expand liberty. Government action, they argued, could increase the freedom of working children and their mothers and fathers by regulating wages, hours, and working conditions. The concomitant restrictions on employers' freedom of contract did not seem too high a price to pay. The result of this approach was welfare-state liberalism, which augments the commitment to individual liberty with an emphasis on freedom from certain types of economic hardships. This orientation (which merges imperceptibly into social democracy) promises minimum levels of economic well-being for all, expects that these can be achieved by intelligent use of government's powers, and affirms that this can be accomplished without sacrificing individual civil liberties. Welfare-state liberalism has very nearly preempted the politics of the Western democracies since World War II.

The same type of argument that spawned the welfare state is now being used to support a new expansion of government's regulatory powers. This time, social rather than economic deprivation is the target: government is called on to offset disadvantages of sex, race, and age.

With only a bit of oversimplification, it can be said that in the United States (and elsewhere) eighteenth-century liberalism gave priority to political equality as well as political freedom; that the liberalism dominant from the late nineteenth century down to roughly 1965 sought a degree of economic equality in addition to political freedom and political equality; and that beginning sometime in the late sixties American liberalism shifted its focus to incorporate a new emphasis on social equality. Universal suffrage is the most important institutional expression of political equality;

social security is a typical programmatic expression of the search for greater economic equality; busing and affirmative action are quintessential expressions of the search for greater social equality.

Some commentators explain the evolution of liberalism as a reflection of the progressive triumph of equality over liberty. Proponents of this explanation frequently cite the classical liberals as the only ones *truly* committed to liberty and see that which has come after as the progressive adulteration of this commitment by notions of equality. In fact, however, a commitment to both liberty and equality is present in classical and welfare-state liberalism and also in their characteristic institutional embodiment—the liberal or democratic state. The importance of equality to classical liberalism is often not adequately appreciated. Equality under the law—including guarantees of due process, equal protection, and a single system of courts—was an integral part of the classical liberal tradition. So was political equality. Though the utilitarians did not call for one man/one vote, they saw each man as the best judge of his own interests and called for an extended suffrage and popular sovereignty. And, of course, the principle of utility itself is thoroughly egalitarian. Policies are to be judged by their capacity to secure the greatest good for the greatest number. In this calculation, each person's happiness is equal to that of every other.

Welfare-state liberalism and social democracy incorporated the classical liberal's emphasis on individual liberty and individual rights. They did not supplant it, but added to it a further egalitarian thrust. Freedom from severe economic and social deprivation was sought for all; providing the basic elements of the good life—hot lunches, old-age pensions, education, medical and dental care—became a major goal of public policy.

In classical and welfare-state liberalism, and in the as yet unnamed contemporary counterpart, the concern for equality is identical with the commitment to the widest possible sharing of freedom.

Equality, then, is important in the American (and Western)

liberal tradition and in the liberal democratic state. But it is never all-important, and it is never sought as an absolute. Contemporary democratic welfare states—Britain, France, the German Federal Republic, the Scandinavian countries, Canada, Australia, New Zealand, the United States, and others—preserve freedom of speech, press, and religion, due process, and related limits on government's power to regulate the lives of citizens.

Because it insists on maintaining basic liberties for all at the same time that it extends the freedom of some (the hitherto disenfranchised, destitute, and despised), the contemporary democratic welfare state—sometimes known as "bourgeois democracy"—demonstrates that it is possible to use government's regulatory power to expand liberty as well as to serve egalitarian goals.

The democratic welfare state's continued emphasis on the liberty of the individual sharply distinguishes it from a related but very different ideology whose principal goal is the destruction of the capitalist system in favor of a state-owned and -controlled economy. I call this *progressiste* liberalism because it is usually associated with a linear conception of history and its adherents see movement toward their goals not merely as desirable but as "progressive."

While liberty and equality coexist as irreducible values of classical and welfare-state liberalism, *progressiste* liberalism gives clear priority to equality over liberty, economics over politics. Both classical and welfare-state liberalism postulate a necessary link between the political and economic spheres—on grounds that political liberty is integrally connected with economic freedom and that popular control of government depends on wide dispersion of economic as well as social and political power. *Progressism* affirms in theory and practice not only that economic equality can be achieved in the absence of political liberty, but that liberty may be—and often is—an impediment to the achievement of equality, which must be sacrificed or "postponed" for the sake of securing economic "democracy." This notion, that liberty and equality are or may be incompatible values, is widely held and is, of course, a familiar justification for tyranny in many new nations and so-called socialist states where the rhetoric of progress is invoked to justify the seizure of power by small groups of middle-class revolutionaries.*

The belief that liberty and equality are ultimately incompatible is familiar enough. Long before busing, affirmative action, quotas, or ERA, long before Lenin and his colleagues had decided that a free press, free assembly, and free elections endangered "the revolution," Alexis de Tocqueville and J. S. Mill (among others) had expressed their concern lest the egalitarian passions of mass democracy overwhelm individual liberties. The conviction that any effort to neutralize natural inequalities would entail stifling the opportunity for individuals (especially gifted individuals) to develop their potential and exercise their powers was elaborated in the theory of mass society whose proponents see egalitarianism as one of a number of modern social and intellectual forces that tend to level distinctions, eliminate diversity, and produce a society which breeds and tolerates only mediocrity and conformity.

Reflection and experience confirm that, pushed to their respective extremes, liberty and equality are indeed incompatible. But not only is the immoderate pursuit of liberty incompatible with preserving basic equalities, and the immoderate pursuit of equality incompatible with preserving individual liberties, the single-minded pursuit of *either* of these values results in its negation. In a society that values only individual freedom, the weak are victimized by the strong, the less bright by the more bright, the poor by the rich, the ordinary by the talented. But that is not all. As Camus has argued, the "most extreme form of freedom" is "the freedom to kill." "Pure" freedom results only in a condition of Hobbesian anarchy in which all are slaves to insecurity. The same logic of extremism governs the pursuit of equality. Pushed zealously and exclusively enough, the effort to maximize equality—to neutralize the effects of natural inequalities of brains, beauty, talent, strength, and so

* Other versions of *progressiste* politics simply redefine liberty so that, instead of denoting the capacity of individuals to make choices and act upon them, it becomes an attribute of a collectivity (for example, the proletariat) and is manifested in the power position of an elite, which acts in the name of that collectivity.

forth—results in extreme inequality. The society in which a ruthlessly determined effort is made to control the effects of natural inequality will not only be an unfree society. It will also turn out to be one governed by a maximum tyrant—a Robespierre, a Mao, a Castro—who, in addition to having more power than anyone else, will also enjoy better housing, medical care, vacations, working conditions, personal security, and so forth. As Orwell understood, when rulers are fully determined to make all animals equal, some animals turn out to be more equal than others.

The fact that liberty and equality can be maximized only through moderation explains the relationship between utopia and tyranny, between extremism and nihilism—and illuminates the irreducible importance of prudential judgment to politics and statecraft. This point may be summed up by noting that extremism in the pursuit of justice (or any other political value) *is* a vice; and moderation in the defense of liberty (or any other political value) *is* a virtue. The modern age has illustrated in blood and terror the priority of the "dull" virtues—moderation, prudence, restraint—to humane government, and confirmed thereby the insights of Aristotle, Polybius, and Montesquieu into the need for a "mixed" constitution in which no one principle or portion of society can prevail utterly.

Liberty and equality are no more incompatible, then, than liberty is incompatible with itself, or equality with itself. And the dynamics of extremism ensure that the same restraint and prudence required to pursue simultaneously the goals of liberty and equality are required to prevent the pursuit of either from ending in its own negation. Though these goals are incompatible in the abstract, in the real world it turns out that those countries which value both achieve the most of each, perhaps because their simultaneous pursuit works to ensure that neither will be pushed to its extreme. Those countries whose citizens have the least liberty are most likely to have privileged classes who get the most of whatever there is to get, along with a closed system that effectively prevents the wider sharing of wealth and power; while in those countries where citizens enjoy the widest freedom, ordinary people use collective bargaining and politics to get an increasing share of income, education, leisure, health care, and other available goods. *However bothersome in the abstract, the tensions between liberty and equality prove salutary in practice.* The institutions of "liberal" or "bourgeois" democracy embody a commitment to both. Support for these institutions is a natural expression of classical and welfare-state liberalism; *progressiste* hostility to them reflects the profound opposition between these perspectives.

The fact that liberty and equality are complementary and reinforcing values has several implications for preserving and extending them in the present context. The first and most important implication is that since liberty and equality are reinforcing values which are already embodied in our political institutions, it is reasonable for Americans to cling to both and to stubbornly refuse to choose between them. However, the delicate, sometimes subtle interactions between liberty and equality make it important that programs seeking to maximize either value be neither automatically supported nor automatically opposed, but be scrutinized for their effects on the other. Court-ordered busing and HEW edicts against boys choirs, for example, might be rejected on grounds that their cost to individual liberty is unacceptable, and policies that allocate goods without regard to the cost in human suffering or the uneven advantages of those involved may be rejected on grounds that the affront to equality is too high a price to pay for the liberties involved.

Government regulation can be used to extend liberty, but its capacity for stifling liberty is also ever-present. Universal suffrage diminishes the liberty of traditional elites to pursue whatever policies they choose and extends the freedom of everyone else. Progressive taxation restricts the liberty of those with large incomes to spend their money as they wish, but, through welfare and related payments, these funds free less prosperous citizens from extreme deprivation and insecurity. Affirmative action programs restrict the freedom of, say, contractors working for the government to hire whomever they please, but augment the freedom of others to find employment in otherwise inaccessible fields. Let us be clear, however, that government action does not necessarily enhance the liberty of the many at the expense of the few. In some cases—say, court-ordered busing—the reverse may occur.

A second implication of this analysis is that the pursuit of absolute liberty or equality must be entirely eschewed, less because it is doomed to fail than because the very effort endangers both values. Here again, the perfect is the enemy of the good, the expectation of perfection encourages the devaluation of imperfect but real goods.

The success of the liberal democracies in pursuing both liberty and equality is directly and necessarily related to the essential moderation of their goals. Political equality as conceived in liberal theory and practice does not require the destruction of leadership or the creation of a republic in which no one exercises more influence over political events than any other. It looks, instead, toward giving all adults at least a minimum voice in the decision about who should rule and to what ends. The egalitarian thrust in the economic sphere has aimed not at equal distribution of goods but at providing a minimum of income and security for all; and the current demand for wider sharing of social and cultural advantages does not aim at creating absolute equality but at ensuring some minimum social and cultural advantages for all. The liberal egalitarian thrust, in sum, has been essentially and crucially moderate. Its goal has not been anarchism but political democracy, not communism but the welfare state, not a republic of equals but one in which all are accorded a minimum of well-being, status, income, and power.

Abandonment of pursuit of the absolute faces us squarely with the prospect not only of living with, but of choosing among, imperfect institutions and relative goods. This leads, I think, to heightened appreciation of the present. As Martin Diamond emphasized, "We must learn to face the truth no matter how pleasant it may be." The pleasant truth is that relatively high levels of individual freedom and a significant degree of social and political equality already exist in this society and that these can be both enjoyed and used in further political efforts. This gives liberals as well as conservatives a vested interest in the status quo, which, like all vested interests, must be defended.

Two other aspects of the relations among liberty, equality, and government regulation should be noted. Both concern the cumulative effects of government action. Because each extension of government's activities carries with it government's coercive power, the cumulative impact of regulation may be to saturate a sphere of activity with coercion. By surrounding persons who are active in a given sphere with proscriptions, prescriptions, and threats of severe penalties, government regulation may so alter the possibilities for activity and so diminish the freedom of participants as to transform the character of the activity and the kind of person attracted to it. Another unintended consequence of government regulation is also important. Whatever its specific goal, regulation also has the effect of expanding the power of the public sector and the number of persons operating in it. The progressive transfer of power from the private to the public sector and the creation of an influential group of professionals who have a vested interest in the expansion of the public sector entail risk to both liberty and equality. It is not just that power corrupts, but that bureaucrats as well as others are corruptible. The consequences for liberty and equality of a progressive concentration of power in government are very different from the consequences of any single act of regulation.

Because their effects cannot be factored into the consideration of any single policy, these cumulative risks remind us of the limits of prescience. The use of government to secure the ordered sharing of liberties is based on the belief that such wider sharing is desirable and, also, on the belief that it is possible to foresee and control the effects of government's policies. This assumption, that it is possible to achieve desired social goals through the deliberate manipulation of incentives (such as taxes, fines, imprisonment), is the intellectual cornerstone of contemporary government regulation. But our experience, and that of such other nations as Great Britain, is filled with cautionary tales reminding us that social forecasting, like social control, remains—yes—primitive.

The pursuit of liberty, equality, and most social values is not necessarily a zero-sum game that features a fixed quantity of some indivisible good of such nature that a larger share for one results in a smaller for another. The structure of medical education in the United States and abroad, for example, suggests that the Bakke case is an unnecessary kind of social conflict based on an artificial scarcity that drives qualified young Americans (black and white) abroad to study medicine and fills our hospitals with physicians who cannot speak English. However, that case also illustrates that, *in undertaking the use of power to enhance freedom or equality, modesty and caution are surely the appropriate posture*—because, as social engineers, we have a lot to be modest and cautious about.

Sources of Stability in the
American Tradition

So LITTLE DID THE AMERICAN REVOLUTION conform to the twentieth century's conception of revolution that it has become commonplace to doubt that the term can be appropriately applied to the events of 1776–78 at all. In this century a revolution is generally taken to be a radical transformation of society, culture, and personality, as well as a change of political regime which is not merely broad in scope but radical in degree.

Of course, the expectation of radical change existed also in the eighteenth century, when it was purveyed not only by such architects of the Terror as Saint-Just and Robespierre, but also by leading philosophers of the Enlightenment whose fundamental ideas—individualism, contract, nature, reason, and progress— were present in both the French and the American revolutions.[1]

The success of the American experience, however, derived in significant part from the fact that these doctrines existed in the United States in a modified form. In North America the principles of the Enlightenment were modified by the most modest expectations of the nation's early leaders and Founding Fathers, whose expectations, in turn, were grounded in the British tradition and shaped by the American experience of tyranny. In this dual heritage, eighteenth-century optimism, rationalism, and individualism were married to the sense of community, authority, and custom characteristic of the British tradition; the result was that, before the United States came into being, its political culture featured both common law and natural law, both the rights of Englishmen and natural rights, both experience and reason, the principles of both Burke and the early Utilitarians. This mixed political culture served as the ground of that most unusual event out of which the nation was formed: a conservative revolution.

Even though it was born out of a war of independence, the establishment of the American nation involved no sharp break with the past. To be sure, the events of 1776 are called a revolution, and were a revolution in the sense that they brought about a sudden shift in the identity of the rulers and in the basis of sovereignty. Unlike leaders of the French Revolution, who proposed to replace monarchy with popular sovereignty, or of the Bolshevik Revolution, who replaced a constitutional monarchy with the dictatorship of the proletariat, revolutionary leaders in America demanded that familiar rights be respected and entrenched practices be observed. The new American government was thus grounded in the same moral and political principles as the British constitution (minus only the king), and by the late eighteenth century the legitimacy of the British constitution rested less on the claims of the monarchy than on the principles of the Bloodless Revolution.

The American leaders' demands that government protect life, liberty, and property, that there be no taxation without representation, and that the Crown respect the constitutional limits on its powers were qualitatively identical with the demands to limit royal prerogative that resulted in the Magna Carta, the Act of Settlement, and other basic underpinnings of legitimacy. These were not fundamentally disturbed, and were still available to reinforce the legitimacy of the new political order.

It is important not to exaggerate. Passion and violence, death and destruction, were present in the American Revolution. Colonists loyal to the Crown were deeply offended by the revolt against the authority of the king. But because the society's most basic principles of political association and obligation were not challenged or undermined by the revolution, American political leaders avoided creating the extremes of bitterness that would serve as the basis for future conflict, and they reinforced the new regime with the rectitude that attached to traditional principles. Thus was discouraged the development of the kind of "legitimacy gap" that afflicts so many new political systems.

Since institutions are stabilized patterns of interaction based on shared, reciprocal expectations, nothing so facilitates the establishment of new institutions as their congruity with habitual ways of thinking and acting.[2] Adopting the fundamental principles of the British tradition assured that the practices of the new American government would be consistent with the habits of the people. The absence of a sharp break with the past therefore also precluded the development of the kind of gap between constitution and character, between form and function, between formal and actual practices, that so often characterizes the political life of a new nation.

The American Revolution left the new nation firmly anchored in the English political tradition, which by the late eighteenth century included, as institutionalized expectations, these propositions: that government should be strong, but though strong, limited by the rule of law, the consent of the governed, and individual rights; and that representation is the appropriate institutional mechanism for limiting power and securing government with consent. Furthermore, it left the legal system in place, political jurisdictions unaltered, and customary behavior virtually untouched.

THE FOUNDING FATHERS' ROOTS in English history and their identification with the rights of Englishmen—rights won by specific persons at specific times and places—doubtless helped them to avoid the utopian expectations to which revolutionary movements are notoriously susceptible and to which the other great eighteenth-century revolution succumbed. The leaders of the American Revolution did not rely on abstract theories of historical development to guide them in what the future would be. Neither did they embrace romantic notions of "natural man" or "natural society." They did not expect that the United States would be exempt from the problems that had beset other nations. Instead of relying on American "exceptionalism," a doctrine whose force has probably been overemphasized, the framers of the American Constitution emphasized the relevance of history and of their own past experience to the former colonies' problems.

Nowhere are these modest expectations more clearly expressed than in the Constitution and in those remarkable essays written by three of the Constitution's most brilliant authors. Of these *Federalist Papers*, which remain the best source on the intentions of the Founding Fathers, Carl Van Doren asserted:

> To read and understand them was the next thing to having had a hand in making the Constitution. They were widely reprinted. Their immediate influence is hard to trace, for they were without the passion and prejudice which rouse quick responses. But there can be no doubt that these papers, so rigorously anonymous at the time, made their way through the most reflective minds of the time and then on into posterity.[3]

The perceptions of Hamilton, Madison, and Jay concerning the problems of constructing and preserving popular government are especially useful in illuminating the close, necessary relationship between method and findings in politics. Utopian political philosophies and expectations rest on speculation, imagination, or interpretations of history which see the past and present as preface to a *qualitatively* different future. Where they are based on history, utopian political philosophies postulate a sharp rupture between history as experienced and the future as anticipated.

As Ranney, Greenleaf, Bailyn,[4] and others have emphasized, the men who wrote the Constitution and those who defended it were empiricists who believed that experience, properly considered, could serve as guide both to the pitfalls of self-government and to their solution. Like Polybius, whom they had read, the authors of the *Federalist Papers* (who signed themselves "Publius") believed that "the study of History is in the truest sense an education and a training for political life."[5] It could teach them to avoid the mistakes of the past, suggest a method for dealing with whatever contingencies might arise, and demonstrate what effects were produced by what causes. "Experience," said Madison and Hamilton in *Federalist* No. 20, "is the oracle of truth; and when its responses are unequivocal, they ought to be conclusive and sacred";[6] and Madison remarked in No. 43, "But theoretic reason, in this as in most other cases, must be qualified by the lessons of practice";[7] and Hamilton counseled in No. 6, "Let experience, the least fallible guide of human opinions, be appealed to for an answer to these inquiries."[8]

Experience taught the *Federalist* authors that some problems are the common lot of mankind, and convinced them that wise men do not ignore the lessons which history offers concerning the interaction of institutions and human nature.

Publius rejected utterly all arguments that, because of its unique circumstances or origins, the United States would escape the afflictions suffered by other nations. In *Federalist* No. 6, for example, Hamilton asserted:

> Have we not already seen enough of the fallacy and extravagance of these idle theories which have amused us with promise of an exemption from the imperfections, weaknesses, and evils incident to society in every shape? Is it not time to awake from the deceitful dream of a golden age and to adopt as a practical maxim for the direction of our political conduct that we, as well as the other inhabitants of the globe, are yet remote from the happy empire of perfect wisdom and perfect virtue?[9]

And later, in a discussion of revenues, Hamilton again takes explicit aim at the notion that America can expect to be exempt from the normal human vicissitudes:

> Reflection of this kind [concerning revenues] may have trifling weight with men who have to see realized in America the halcyon

scenes of the poetic or fabulous age, but to those who believe we
are likely to experience a common portion of the vicissitudes and
calamities which have fallen to the lot of other nations, they must
appear entitled to serious attention.[10]

Beginning with the Lycian and Achaean leagues, examples of
confederations were combed for the lessons they provided, and
almost all discussions of political institutions are related to historical experience. Hamilton, in *Federalist* No. 16, for example, but-
tresses a point concerning confederations with reference to "the
events which have befallen all other governments of the confeder-
ate kind of which we have any account."[11]

The *Federalist* essayists went to history in search of evidence,
and its data became the basis of generalizations which, collectively, comprised what they considered a new science of politics.
Hamilton particularly expressed his confidence in the "maxims" in
ethics and politics, which "though not quite so certain as in
mathematics" were nonetheless clear and accessible to those who
sought dispassionately to learn from history.[12] Indeed, much of
his hope for the new nation derived from progress in "the science
of politics," which "like most other sciences, has received great
improvement."[13]

The *Federalist* authors did not perceive history as repeating
itself. New knowledge, they thought, developed as men applied
themselves to the study and counsels of history. The ideas of representation and separation of powers were cited as discoveries of
the recent past. Concerning the proposed Constitution itself,
Hamilton counseled that innovation should be greeted with an
open mind:

But why is the experiment of an extended republic to be rejected
merely because it may comprise what is new? Is it not the glory
of the people of America that, whilst they have paid a decent regard to the opinions of former times and other nations, they have
not suffered a blind veneration for antiquity, for custom, or for
names, to overrule the suggestions of their own good sense, the

knowledge of their own situation and the lessons of their own experience?[14]

Publius's method, which has been appropriately termed the pragmatic historical method, is very different from historicism, which also relies on the study of history. Like Aristotle, Machiavelli, Montesquieu, Tocqueville, and Burke, Publius assumes that past experience is relevant to the future because human nature will prove constant and men susceptible to the same temptations and errors. All have a sharp sense of the constraints affecting political and social arrangements. Their views stand in sharp contrast to such philosophers as Vico, Hegel, and Marx, who regard history as a *preface* to a qualitatively different future, or to Plato and Rousseau, who also deny that human limitations present in the past will necessarily persist into the future. Publius went to history to learn about the vulnerabilities that had afflicted democratic institutions in the past as part of the search for remedies that could be built into the new republic.

ONE OF THE "LESSONS" of history which seemed clearest to the *Federalist* authors was that there were no perfect solutions to political problems. With Montesquieu, whom they had studied, they doubted the existence of universal or ideal political institutions, believing that there were only approximations which would not end social and political ills but ameliorate them. The possibility of finding perfect solutions is explicitly renounced by Madison in *Federalist* No. 41: ". . . cool and candid people will at once reflect that the purest of human blessings must have a portion of alloy in them; that the choice must always be made, if not of the lesser evil, at least of the GREATER, not of the PERFECT, good."[15] There could be no perfect government because the ills of government were rooted in human nature.

Examining the problems and mishaps to which men's efforts at self-government had succumbed, Publius confronted the questions which must be faced by any serious political philosopher:

First, whether undesirable human traits such as egoism and aggrandizement are shared by all men or whether some elite or some person is exempted from them; second, whether such traits are a permanent aspect of human nature or will be or might be "cured" or transcended at some future time; third, if undesirable human traits can be "cured" whether it will be by deliberate effort or by some automatic, inexorable historical process; fourth, if undesirable human traits cannot be eliminated entirely, then by what types of institutions or policies they can best be controlled.

Publius's answers to these questions were clear. He saw the most important problems confronting a republic (or any other form of orderly government) as deriving from human nature. All men, not only some race or class or mass, have fundamentally similar moral and intellectual weaknesses. Like Aristotle, Publius believed that men prefer that which is their own and that this preference constitutes the basis of self-interest and self-interested reasoning. Reason is attached to interest and to passion, making it difficult for men to perceive and evaluate evidence dispassionately. Or, in Madison's famous formulation, "As long as the connection subsists between his reason and his self-love, his opinions and his passions will have a reciprocal influence on each other; and the former will be the objects to which the latter will attach themselves."[16]

For Plato, Marx, Mannheim, and certain other political philosophers, the belief that perception is "distorted" by passion and self-interest serves as the basis of a sociology of knowledge that indicts everyone's views except those of the philosopher himself, or some designated elite who are seen as miraculously exempted from common human failings. Moreover, even extraordinary men are tainted by self-interest and may behave in ways incompatible with the public good. Publius writes, "Ambition, avarice, personal animosity, party opposition, and many other motives not more laudable than these are apt to operate as well upon those who support as those who oppose the right side of a question."[17]

Rulers as well as masses are susceptible to the pull of self-interest; masses as well as rulers are hungry for advantage and aggrandizement. In general, the *Federalist* authors expected the people to show good judgment in their selection of representatives, but they thought that even superior men would not prove exempt from the temptations of self-interest and self-aggrandizement. No vanguard or elite was envisioned which, because of superior virtue or intelligence, would be exempt from human failings. "A nation of philosophers with a reverence for laws inculcated by reason," Madison asserts, "is as little to be expected as the philosophical kings wished for by Plato."[18]

Like Burke, Hume, Tocqueville, and others impressed by the weakness of human reason, Publius believed that reason alone cannot serve as the basis of government and law, but must be fortified by prejudice and habit. However, while a certain involvement of the passions in government is necessary to strengthen the citizen's attachment to government, if the feelings attached to politics become too intense they become a source of instability.

The attachment of reason to passion and self-interest, and the tendency of all men to maximize their desired goals (power, wealth, status, rectitude, and so forth),[19] serve in Publius's view as the basis of a republic's vulnerability to demagoguery, faction, conflict, and tyranny. Not only are the seeds of faction sown in human nature, so also are the seeds of anarchy, tyranny, and war. Rulers will arise who seek to maximize their power through demagoguery, and the people, though frequently good at judging their own interests, may succumb; or the maximizing tendencies of masses could lead to "the mischiefs of faction" which have ever been the bane of democracies. Inflamed passions, intense struggle for preferment or advantage—both of which are common in republics—disturb the civil peace. Like Montesquieu, Publius saw that governments in which there is more liberty and less coercion —that is, democratic governments—are especially susceptible to the disorder and anarchy arising from faction: "Hence it is that such democracies have ever been spectacles of turbulence and contention; have ever been found incompatible with personal security or the rights of property; and have in general been as short in their lives as they have been violent in their deaths."[20]

Dealing with the mischiefs of faction, Madison thought, is as complicated as managing human nature itself because the sources of faction are as various as the objects of human passion. Though "the various and unequal distribution of property" has been the "common and durable source of factions," other interests also serve:

> A zeal for different opinions concerning religion, concerning gov- ernment . . . as well of speculation as of practice; an attachment to different leaders ambitiously contending for pre-eminence and power; or to persons of other descriptions whose fortunes have been interesting to the human passions, have, in turn, divided mankind into parties, inflamed them with mutual animosity, and rendered them much more disposed to vex and oppress each other than to cooperate for the common good. So strong is this pro- pensity of manhood to fall into mutual animosities that where no substantial occasion presents itself the most frivolous and fanciful distinctions have been sufficient to kindle their unfriendly passions and excite their most violent conflict.[21]

This point is fundamental, and should be emphasized. If human aggression derives from economic frustration and inse- curity, then there is reasonable hope of "curing" it by increasing production and redistributing wealth. Rousseau argued in this fash- ion in the *Discourse on the Origins of Inequality*, suggesting that scarcity and property are the basis of aggressive behavior; and, of course, Marx argued that evil (read alienation) derives from the form of economic organization and can be "cured" by reorganizing the economic system. Such views stand in sharp contrast to those of Hobbes, Hume, Freud—or Publius—who believe that not only profit but also other values may become the basis of human con- flict. If attachments to religious and political values are as basic, as primary, as attachment to economic interests, then the quantity and quality of potential factional conflicts are altered and the prospects for a conflict-free society become very dim. If men are as prone to quarreling about power, status, or virtue as about the distribution of wealth, then they will quarrel forever.

The more sources of faction, the more likely it becomes that internal conflicts among competing factions will be supplemented by conflict among *nations*. Factions, then, induce war between nations as well as internal discord. And war is not only an evil in itself but also stimulates intensified passions and encourages large armies which under certain circumstances themselves become a danger to liberty. Hamilton, in *Federalist* No. 6, asserts that "to look for a continuation of harmony between a number of independent unconnected sovereignties situated in the same neighborhood would be to disregard the uniform course of human events, and to set at defiance the accumulated experiences of ages."[22]

But if the most important problems confronting a republic (or any other form of orderly government) derive from human nature, if abuse of power and anarchy are normal aspects of human experience, if the seeds of tyranny and of faction are rooted in human nature, then how can men protect their lives, liberty, and property? That was the question the Founding Fathers posed for themselves and, having posed it, found a solution that has endured two hundred years.

VARIOUS REMEDIES HAVE BEEN PROPOSED for the political defects which derive from human nature. Plato believed that by detailed control of the symbolic environment and the socialization process one could produce a new human type, and relied on education to produce virtue in the guardian class, and on the virtue of the guardians to maintain the constitution designed by the philosopher-king. Many medieval political thinkers followed Plato's example in believing that a good polity depended on the correct education of the prince. Rousseau also thought that careful socialization of a people (as in the constitution of Poland) would restore their "natural" goodness and eradicate the ill effects of society.

But like most of the men who led the American Revolution,

the *Federalist* authors denied that proper education, sound values, good character, and personal virtue could serve as an adequate base for the good polity. First, because of human fallibility, "if the impulse and the opportunity be suffered to coincide, we well know that neither moral nor religious motives can be relied on as an adequate control";[23] second, because "enlightened statesmen may not always be at the helm";[24] and third, because the effort to eliminate the causes of faction by destroying the liberty which is essential to its existence, "[or] by giving to every citizen the same opinions, the same passions, and the same interests,"[25] would be worse than the disease. But if the price of eliminating human tendencies to aggrandizement was too high, controlling them seemed more feasible. Representation, extension, and separation of powers could modify and channel the effects of human maximization. Like most of the Founding Fathers, the *Federalist* authors sought a *political* remedy—not a social, cultural, or economic remedy—to the *political* problem of how to govern the thirteen former colonies in such a manner as to preserve liberty, law, and government by consent. A properly constructed constitution would provide the answer: "The chief cause of success or the reverse in all matters is the form of a state's constitution, for springing from this, as from a fountain head, all designs and plans of action not only originate but reach their consummation."[26] Expectations of the perfectibility of man never struck root in American political culture, but the possibility of improvement and of progress is affirmed and emphasized.

Though the *Federalist* authors saw men as neither perfect nor perfectible, their view of human nature was not entirely black. To the contrary, as Kendall and Carey emphasized,[27] they and other of the Founding Fathers believed that Americans were, on balance, a relatively virtuous people. In *Federalist* No. 57, for example, Madison applauds "the genius of the whole system; the nature of just and constitutional laws; and above all, the vigilant and manly spirit which actuates the people of America—a spirit which nourishes freedom, and in return is nourished by it."[28]

The prudence and love of liberty of the American people

were considered necessary but not sufficient conditions for republican government. Though liberty and law could not be maintained without them, neither could they ensure the preservation of a republic. The virtue of the people was not adequate to the task of controlling the political effects of human weaknesses. Only a properly constructed constitution could produce that happy effect.

This combination of beliefs—that progress is possible but not inevitable, that human nature may be improved but not perfected, that people are virtuous enough to rule themselves but not virtuous enough that we should trust them (or ourselves) entirely—serves as the basis of the national attitude toward social engineering, of which the Constitution is a quintessential example.

In their discussions of the Constitution, the American founders affirmed repeatedly the possibility, not of inevitable progress toward perfection, but of real though limited progress toward specific goals. History—that is, experience—would be their guide to the pitfalls awaiting a republic, and would provide clues to how these pitfalls could be avoided.

Like Polybius, the authors of the *Federalist Papers* believed that the study of history could teach them to avoid the mistakes of the past, suggest a method for dealing with whatever contingencies might arise, and demonstrate what effects were produced by what causes. *The conviction that progress is possible, given unflagging effort and correct use of "experimental method," is another of the defining characteristics of the American political tradition.*

The mechanism for ensuring progress, for protecting the nation against tyranny and anarchy, and for securing the blessings of liberty was to have a wisely constructed constitution, which the framers conceived as a great opportunity for social engineering. Although pure democracy offered no cure for the hazards of demagoguery, faction, and war, a carefully constructed representative republic would demonstrate that "in the extent and proper structure of the Union . . . we behold a republican remedy for the diseases most incident to republican government."

The differences between pure democracy and a representative republic seemed to the *Federalist* authors to guarantee the success of the latter and failure of the former, and to deny that the proposed Union would resemble the "turbulent democracies of ancient Greece and modern Italy." While history provided no examples of democratic governments which did not succumb to faction, demagoguery, and instability, Hamilton emphasized that not all republics were short-lived. "Happily for mankind, stupendous fabrics reared on the basis of liberty, which have flourished for ages, have, in a few glorious instances, refuted their gloomy sophisms."[29]

No examples were provided, but the statement constituted an assertion of his faith that governments based on liberty, law, and majority rule were not doomed to fail. To believe otherwise was to confuse pure democracies with modern republics. Madison asserted that:

> Under the confusion of names it has been an easy task to transfer to a republic observations applicable to a democracy only.
>
> Such a fallacy may have been the less perceived, as most of the popular governments of antiquity were of the democratic species, and even in modern Europe, to which we owe the great principle of representation, no example is seen of a government wholly popular and founded at the same time wholly on that principle.[30]

The reason some believed that the proposed government would be vulnerable to the ills of democracies was that representative republics were in fact something new. There were, Publius asserted, no examples in history of the type of government proposed to the thirteen former colonies. The system of representation according to which one man stood for many, by whom he was chosen and to whom he was accountable, was widely believed to be something new under the sun. In *Federalist* No. 52 Madison commented, "The scheme of representation as a substitute for a meeting of the citizens in person being at most but very imperfectly known to ancient polity, it is in more modern times only that we are to expect instructive examples."[31] Representation made it possible to enlarge the size of the democracy, so that it embraced more people than could meet together without losing the consent and participation of the governed. Moreover, the extended republic had itself many advantages over small, homogenous political units. It could embrace more diverse people and interests, thereby making it less likely a majority could unite to tyrannize the minority. Its greater distances could be expected to diminish passion and enhance capacities for reason because, as Hamilton noted, "It is a known fact in human nature that its affections are commonly weak in proportion to the distance or diffuseness of the object."[32] Furthermore, including in the legislature representatives of many areas would enhance the reasonableness of the body because it would weaken the "strong predilection in favor of local objects which can hardly fail to mislead the decision."[33] The advantages of the extended republic over the small homogenous unit are said to be comparable in importance to the advantages of the representative republic over a pure democracy.

In his article "Majority, Tyranny, and the Extended Republic Theory of James Madison," Carey emphasized that extension was also relied on by Madison to produce a disinterested "independent force" which could judiciously seek the public good when factional interests clashed. Extension reduces the likelihood of majority tyranny (1) because the "multiplicity and diversity of interests certainly does reduce the possibilities of union through common motives"; (2) because representation "is bound to temper deliberations"; (3) because "the fragmentation of interests will preclude any action"; and (4) because "the independent force, freedom from the interest bias which clouds and distorts judgment, is more likely to resort to the accepted norms of the community in making its decision."[34]

In addition to the principles of representation and extension, Publius pointed to another constitutional provision designed to protect the republic from abuse of power: the principle of separation of powers—a device basic to the constitutional engineering of the Founding Fathers. The division of power vertically, between the states and the Union, and horizontally, between three branches of government organized on different principles, embodied the conception of mixed governments known to political philosophy since Plato and the doctrine of separation of powers which had been elaborated most persuasively by Bolingbroke and Montesquieu.

The case for separation of powers is too well known to require elaboration here. At its heart lie the conception of political man as a power maximizer and a concept of equilibrium. Its purpose is to oblige government to control itself.[35] Important as is the principle of accountability through frequent elections, Publius says that "experience has taught mankind the necessity of auxiliary precautions."[36] To defend liberty and popular government against the power-maximizing behavior of political men, "Ambition must be made to counteract ambition."[37] It was therefore necessary to so contrive "the interior structure of the government as that its several constituent parts, by their mutual relations, be the means of keeping each other in their proper places."[38] The powers of government cannot be entirely separate, but "each department should have a will of its own; and consequently should be so constituted that the numbers of each should have as little agency as possible in the appointment of the members of the other."[39] The powers of each will be limited by those of the other.

Even representation, extension, and separation of powers may not be adequate, so other arrangements are proposed to further secure the people against the abuse of power by their governors. Frequent elections will remind officeholders of their dependence on the people. Their manner of election "cannot fail to produce a temporary affection, at least for their constituents."[40] The lawmaker's dependence on his constituents will tie his interests to their well-being. Members of Congress will be ineligible for offices which are created or whose emoluments are increased during their term of office.[41] Legislators can make no law which is not fully binding on themselves, their families, and friends.[42] The size of the legislative body will be kept small enough to permit orderly deliberation, because "in all very numerous assemblies of whatever character composed, passion never fails to wrest the scepter from reason. Had every Athenian citizen been a Socrates, every Athenian assembly would still have been a mob."[43] Nor is that all. Other prudent measures will be taken to ensure that the people are bound to government by habit and prejudice as well as reason, and that their passions are not too frequently stimulated or involved in the decision process. ("The danger of disturbing public tranquility by interesting too strongly the public passions is a still more serious objection against a frequent reference of constitutional questions to the decision of the whole society.")[44]

To protect citizens against tyranny and abuse of power by their rulers, the Constitution provides for periodic popular elections which permit the governed to choose their rulers, limits the tenure and jurisdiction of those rulers, and holds rulers accountable for their exercise of power. To protect the republic against the "mischiefs of faction," the Constitution provides for extending the republic to include multiple and diverse interests organized into multiple units. To secure consent, accountability, and deliberation, the Constitution provides for a complex system of representation that fragments interests as well as reflects them—through the construction of different electorates and different terms of office—and requires concurrent as well as simple majorities for the adoption of policies. The federal system was also expected to secure responsiveness to local concerns and to provide the advantages of an extended republic.

The Constitution is a prototype, then, an instrument of government designed to permit the pursuit of opposite principles. The political culture contains other such opposite tendencies, whose interaction has so far produced a kind of ever-precarious middle way: optimism about the human capacity for enlightened self-interest and public spirit coexists with a pessimistic evaluation of human nature, distrust of government coexists with pride in the nation's political institutions, and participatory citizenship coexists with multiple restraints on its expression.

The Constitution, a carefully calculated product of the "new science of politics," was designed to secure goods frequently seen as incompatible—equality *and* liberty, majority rule *and* minority rights, strong *and* limited government, responsiveness *and* stability. The notion that passion can be controlled by countervailing passions ("ambition . . . made to counteract ambition"), common in eighteenth-century psychology, economics, and politics, was used to create a new version of the mixed constitution in which the inclusion of opposite principles created moderation. The result was a complex system of interlocking, interacting institutions designed to moderate conflict, encourage aggregation, and permit action in accordance with majority will on most subjects. The late Martin Diamond emphasized this point:

> The very essence of American democracy is precisely to be complex. The American idea of democracy takes into account both local and national considerations, and also to moderate democracy and blend it with as many other things as are necessary to the public good. That blending necessitates complexity. The Electoral College is, of course, only one example of the complexity that characterizes our entire political system. Bicameralism is complex; judicial review is complex; the suspensory executive veto is a complex arrangement; the Bill of Rights introduces a thousand complexities.[45]

Four aspects of our political tradition and culture shaped the Constitution and are reinforced by it: first, consensus concerning the bases of legitimate government, which has reinforced the authority of government; second, realism rooted in the rejection by American leaders of eighteenth-century theories of perfectibility and of the rationalism that encourages extravagant expectations about what can be accomplished through politics; third, a belief in the effectiveness of political engineering; and fourth, a determination to pursue multiple, often contradictory, goals by way of a constitution (that is, complex institutional structure).

From each of these basic principles of the American tradition important benefits have flowed. The widespread conviction that legitimate government is one which seeks and exercises power through constitutional means has saved us from wars concerning who should rule and also from efforts to achieve or exercise power by force. It has saved us from men on horseback and from presidential coups. The events we call Watergate consisted of nothing less than the illegitimate (unconstitutional) use of power by a President, of the revelation of that behavior, and of the realization by the President, his supporters, and most other people that he must leave office because he had failed to respect constitutional restraints on presidential power. The same tradition of legitimacy spares the United States efforts by military officers (or anyone else) to seize control of power by force. Not only has the United States never experienced a *golpe de estado* or an attempted *golpe* (there is not even a word for these events in English), it has had few experiences with insubordinate military officers. The last dramatic challenge to civilian supremacy occurred during the Korean War. The fact that a then unpopular President, Harry Truman, had no difficulty in firing the enormously popular General Douglas MacArthur testified to the power of this concept of legitimacy. The fact that Richard Nixon and Douglas MacArthur submitted, that neither attempted to remain at his post by force, provides the strongest evidence of the pervasive power of this conception of legitimacy.

The absence of utopianism in the Constitution, law, and traditional political culture has been similarly important in limiting expectations concerning what can be achieved by politics. The history of the last two centuries confirms what the framers of the Constitution understood: that the perfect is the enemy of the good, and that the search for unalloyed virtue in public life leads to unalloyed terror. The system of checks and balances that divides power, restrains rulers, and requires consensus as a precondition to the adoption of new policies is a direct consequence of this lack of utopianism. So too has been the traditional disinclination to expect too much of government.

The belief in political engineering, in the possibility of using reason to solve problems, has also been important throughout U.S. history. The conviction that progress is possible was the foundation of the American Revolution itself and of the determined effort to achieve a viable political union among the thirteen former colonies. A pragmatic problem-solving spirit led the founders of the American nation to try again after the first effort at confederation, embodied in the Articles of Confederation, had failed. The Constitution is a prototype of an approach to political problems that finds a middle way between the extremes of perfectibility and passivity. It was neither simply the "natural" product of the organic evolution of institutions nor simply the product of the creative intelligence of the framers; it was, instead, a prudent blend of both. It is a system which built on the foundation of existing traditions new institutions designed to achieve some quite explicit goals. As Aristotle thought to achieve a polity by blending elements of democracy and oligarchy, the Constitution and political tradition have provided balance and avoided extremes through the inclusion of values with opposite tendencies (such as liberty and equality). The resulting equilibrium (achieved by complex institutional engineering) has so far constituted a safeguard against extremism in the pursuit of any one value. But the equilibrium in which conflicting tendencies exist is always potentially unstable. Overemphasis on some one value, such as equality, may jeopardize the preservation of liberty, just as an exclusive concern with liberty will leave the weak unprotected from the strong. Similarly, too much cynicism and distrust will undermine the nation's legitimacy and make action impossible, while gullibility will prepare the way for abuse of power.

LIKE ANY POLITICAL SYSTEM, that of the United States reflects the understandings of those who occupy roles in it about what they and others should and/or must do or not do. The persistence of the system depends of course on the persistence of those understandings among the participants, and of the indulgences and deprivations that reinforce those understandings.

The political culture not only supports the institutions, but in a quite literal sense it structures and restructures these institutions by way of the understandings of each new generation. When understandings change, institutions change. Whether any given institution or system will survive is always an open question whose answer depends more on the socialization of each new generation than on wars, famines, or other disasters. Rapid change is particularly threatening to the persistence of a political system. And as everyone knows, ours is a time of cultural revolution. Certain new strains have appeared in the American political culture in the last few decades which have implications for these patterns. There is a growing tendency to believe that the legitimacy of political institutions depends on the substance of the policies and decisions adopted rather than on their conformity to constitutional requirements. There is a tendency to see government as responsible for ever larger portions of the individual's environment and destiny. There is a tendency to embrace the rationalist assumption that social reality can be made to conform to any desired pattern. And there is a tendency to equate complexity in political arrangements with "half-heartedness," and "sincerity" (say, about the principle of majority rule) with the abolition of all institutional obstacles to the direct, immediate realization of a goal.

Examples can be readily cited to demonstrate that each of these tendencies is already strong enough to have significant consequences: the urban rioting and less violent (but still illegal) activities of the civil rights movement, and the illegal demonstrations, riots, and violence of antiwar protest, justified by the belief that government policy was illegitimate because it failed to conform to the protesters' views (that is, legitimacy was seen as deriving from outcomes, not from legal processes). The continuous expansion of government's jurisdictions and functions reflects a spreading belief that government action should supersede private social initiatives (whether individual or group). Impatience with complexity can be seen in contemporary attacks on the electoral college as an offense against the principle of one man, one vote (a doctrine which itself embodies the drive to oversimplify the constitutional conception of majority rule).

Whether current tendencies will prove strong enough to overwhelm traditional understandings and institutional practices is not yet clear, but we may be certain that whenever changes in expectations and identifications occur, institutional changes will not be far behind. As usual, the shape of the future is much less certain than that of the past.

The Teaching of
Democratic Values

IF DEMOCRATIC GOVERNMENT is to survive, schools must teach democratic values. Political regimes exist through the values, beliefs, and habits of their citizens; regimes persist only as long as appropriate values, beliefs, and habits endure. Since public schools are *the* institution created and maintained by the whole society for the purpose of preparing the young for adult roles in the society, it seems inarguably clear that schools not only may but should teach democratic values. It is remarkable that the question should even be raised; nevertheless, it has been raised increasingly of late.

Constitutions, Plato emphasized, are not made of sticks and stones, but depend on the character of citizens. Conventional language invites us to forget that institutions are stable patterns of interaction between people who share an understanding concerning the character and purpose of the interaction. Democratic elections, for example, can take place only as long as all major parties agree to compete with arguments and organization rather than with violence and to settle the contest with ballots rather than bullets. An election campaign becomes a civil war any time that a significant number of participants start shooting. Note that the principal determinant of how a political conflict will be settled is not the availability of weapons—these can always be had in the modern world—but the beliefs of participants about what is desirable, acceptable, and appropriate behavior. These goals and beliefs are not innate, but are learned by each of us in the process of growing up. Character, culture, and constitution reproduce themselves as the predispositions, perspectives, and habits of each new generation are shaped to fit the roles characteristic of the regime.

Political systems embody distinctive questions and answers about the purposes and modes of communal life. They persist as long as the questions are meaningful and the answers compelling for most people in the society. From families, schools, churches, media, each new generation must learn the questions and the answers. Although the human infant is not the *tabula rasa* that John Locke suggested (since instinct, heredity, and prenatal experience also shape and limit him), the infant is very nearly a blank page in many respects most relevant to politics and government. The infant does not enter the world with views and values concerning the relations among citizens; neither does he acquire these instinctively from the experience of biological maturation.

Humans do not spontaneously organize themselves into communities after the fashion of bees into beehives, ants into anthills, deer into herds. There is no characteristically human form of social organization. On the contrary, the patterns of social organization formed in human communities display an extraordinary variety. In most times and places, governments have more closely resembled Hobbes's Leviathan than the heavenly cities of the eighteenth-century philosophers. A dispassionate look at contemporary governments makes it clear that today, as in the past, most societies are not self-governing but are ruled by one or another type of dictator; that most governments are both onerous and inefficient; that most people enjoy neither civil rights, civil liberties, nor due process. Democratic governments—defined as governments whose rulers are chosen in periodic, competitive elections that feature widespread suffrage, free speech, and free assembly—remain exceedingly rare. The reason for this is that democracy makes unusually difficult demands on both rulers and citizens. No other type of government requires so much voluntary participation in power and poses so many limits on its exercise.

Democratic government requires activists and leaders sufficiently interested in influencing policy to devote long hours to a job with relatively poor pay and no job security, a job in which they are subject to continual public scrutiny and criticism. It is not required that all citizens participate or that most be well informed about complex matters of public policy; but citizens are needed who will care enough to vote, to participate, and to obey the law without much coercion.

Unusual restraint is required of both rulers and citizens in a democratic government: rulers may not use their power to destroy critics and opponents; they may not exempt themselves from the laws imposed on others. (Herein, of course, lay the failures termed "Watergate.") While citizens must care enough about who rules and how to participate, they must also be restrained enough to channel their partisanship through prescribed institutions and limit it to legal procedures. Because they rely on consent, democratic governments have an unusually great need for supportive, allegiant citizens who have internalized habits of limited participation and competition, limited victory and defeat.

Such citizens and such rulers are not randomly distributed among the world's population, they do not spring full-blown from the womb; they are *created* by the societies in which they occur.

While there is no authoritative checklist of beliefs necessary to sustain democratic practices, political philosophy and contemporary empirical investigation alike indicate there must be widespread consensus on certain basic items in the democratic creed: a belief in political equality for all citizens; a belief that rulers should be chosen by competitive, periodic elections (and not by force or heredity); a belief that rulers and ruled are alike bound by the ordinary laws of the land and entitled to due process; a belief that all persons have certain rights—including those of life, liberty, and property—that may not be legitimately abrogated by government. In addition, democratic governments, like all others, require a degree of identification, loyalty, and diffuse support from their citizens. Some of these identifications and expectations are

acquired early and "naturally" from simply growing up in a particular family, neighborhood, town. But socialization continues past
early childhood and outside the family—reinforcing, undermining,
supplementing, contradicting the early social learning.

Schools have a crucial role in this continued learning. They
are the institutions whose raison d'être is to teach children about
the nature of things—about how the world works, what causes
what and why. Schools not only teach reading, writing, and arithmetic, they also teach children about the social world, a world that
cannot be dealt with independently of its moral aspects. Daily life
in the classroom and on the playground confronts teachers and
students with moral choices and decisions. Why should a big kid
not steal lunch money from a small one, or take his place in line,
or twist his arm until he cries? Schools "teach values" on a daily
basis as they deal with just such homely moral problems. But they
also just as regularly communicate and inculcate moral principles
when they teach literature, history, and social studies, all of which
subjects present individuals with more or less worthy purposes interacting in a more or less civilized and sympathetic fashion. History and literature can no more be purged of moral meaning than
can the "real life" relations. The question is not whether schools
should teach values but whether they should teach *democratic*
values and the beliefs and behavior patterns that sustain them, and
whether they should teach these values in a self-conscious or a
haphazard fashion.

How interesting that in our times there has arisen a question
about whether the society's principal agencies of socialization
should transmit its core values. The fact that the question is raised,
and its answer debated, is itself evidence of a certain erosion of
consensus concerning the rectitude of our basic beliefs and institutions.

In fact, the reluctance of the nation's major institutions to
take responsibility for the preservation of the society's values and
institutions is one of the striking characteristics of American life in
the last decade or so. The reluctance of churches, schools, even
government, to transmit and celebrate the basic values that inspirit

the nation's institutions and inform its traditions is rooted, I believe, in a number of rather strange doctrines that deserve more scrutiny than they usually get.

One such doctrine is a variant of cultural and moral relativism according to which no social practices can be said to be more moral than any other and a corollary notion that preference for the institutions of one's own society is *prima facie* evidence of chauvinism and ethnocentrism. Though a good many semisophisticated persons espouse cultural relativism in the abstract, very few are willing to accept its logical consequences—to agree, for example, that cannibalism is only a matter of taste, that Auschwitz reflects an alternative approach to race relations, that infanticide is a somewhat archaic but nonetheless effective mode of family planning, that slavery is an alternative view about how to get a society's work done. What teachers in what classrooms give equal time to the case for slave labor, or sweat shops, or the burning of widows, or the Hindu caste system? The cultural relativism of most people tends to evaporate when they are confronted with practices profoundly offensive to their moral principles and beliefs.

Some teachers are reluctant to transmit their moral convictions, however firmly held, because they believe that there is no rational basis for preferring one moral principle to another, that moral convictions are merely personal preferences, "biases" whose defense has no more place in the classroom than the teacher's preference for chocolate ice cream. This extreme positivist position —which holds that values have no cognitive content but are arbitrary personal tastes—has gained wide popular credence during the same period that its persuasiveness to philosophers has shrunk dramatically. Today, teachers who know no higher mathematics or sophisticated biology often feel comfortable teaching students arithmetic and health, though they cannot "prove" the relations they postulate, but feel uncomfortable presenting the case for democratic institutions because they cannot ultimately "prove" that freedom of speech has "value" for individuals or society.

Another source of discomfort for some teachers is the belief that teaching values is incompatible with being "objective." If values are biases, then an "unbiased" teacher will be value-free— or will try to be. This notion is based on the confusion between objectivity and neutrality, which Lincoln illustrated with an anecdote concerning a woman whose husband was locked in mortal combat with a grizzly bear. To see how the fight was going, Lincoln noted, it would not be necessary for the wife to be neutral, shouting alternately, "Come on, husband! Come on, bear!" Neutrality as between, say, slavery and free labor is not a prerequisite to describing these two systems and their human consequences.

Yet another inhibition to the teaching of democratic values derives from a widespread contemporary misunderstanding of pluralism, which is believed by some to require that the authoritative institutions of the society be value-free, with the society's moral content to be supplied by competing cultural groups whose demands are "processed" through the morally neutral institutions. But both reflection and history establish that pluralism does not require anything as absurd as value-free institutions. To the contrary, a value-free institution is a contradiction in terms, since it is perfectly clear that such an institution would lack any basis for coherence or common action. Pluralism provides for the possibility of association among people who share *some but not all* beliefs and values. Pluralism postulates a society made up of subcultures, each with its own identity, values, commitments, united by agreement to disagree nonviolently about matters defined as outside the jurisdiction of the government.

American pluralism has its roots in freedom of conscience, in the belief that government should not attempt to settle religious questions for its subjects. This led to a constitution that placed *most* (though never all) questions of morals and ideology outside the scope of government's power; they were to be left to churches, families, and other unofficial "voluntary" agencies. Inevitably, pluralism has important consequences for the socialization of children. It permits only minimum involvement of government in socialization of the young; it is left to the various subcultures to pass on characteristic values, beliefs, goals, practices, and styles.

Still, no society or government can entirely renounce jurisdiction over morals or socialization, because too many questions—cannibalism, marriage, incest, murder, citizenship—are simultaneously moral, social, and legal. And no society can be indifferent to children's development of respect and affection for its laws and institutions.

As understood historically, pluralism neither requires nor recommends that all the institutions of the "establishment" forgo an effort to induct rising generations into the nation's culture. Recently, however, as the assault on American culture and institutions has intensified and the dissolution of society has progressed, the process of socialization itself has come under attack as essentially conservative, in the sense that it aims at preserving the society (which, of course, is precisely its function). With society attacked as the "status quo" and institutions attacked as the "establishment," the extraordinary argument is made that it is inappropriate for established institutions—schools, churches, media—to attempt to pass on to the young their culture, either because the society and culture are corrupt and any attempt to preserve them is therefore undesirable, or because deliberate transmission of one's culture is an "indoctrination," which is conceived to be illiberal, intolerant, and a victimization of the young. All the society's major institutions have been affected by these trends. Churches have been encouraged to abandon catechism in favor of ethical culture, theology in favor of comparative religion. Enlightened parents have been encouraged to expose their offspring systematically to a wide range of values and points of view, while sensitively avoiding the effort to influence their children's choices among conflicting values and belief systems.

Closely associated with this extraordinary view of socialization as repression is an equally remarkable doctrine of radical individualism whose hero is the culturally self-made man. In our times laissez-faire attitudes, waning in economics, are applied to culture. The healthy individual, it is suggested, will create himself. Each generation, each child, will start afresh. Should he choose from among the proffered cafeteria of values and world views mistaken beliefs rather than correct ones, then reality testing will bring about an appropriate adjustment, as if some invisible hand that regulates the moral universe assures that—Adam and Eve to the contrary notwithstanding—those who choose freely, choose well. The flowering of totalitarianism in our century—in Germany, Eastern Europe, China, Jonestown—suggests that this invisible hand may be no more reliable than Adam Smith's.

Our times breed high hopes and, alas, teach hard lessons. The notion of the "natural" moral man turns out to be no more tenable than the notion that children learn best when left alone to motivate themselves, discipline themselves, teach themselves. The natural savage is no more likely to observe, to learn, or to know the rules of democracy than the rules of baseball. He is as likely to swing the bat at the umpire as at the ball, as likely to fight as to vote. Teachers, lessons, explanations, are required to produce competent players and good citizens. Concepts like truth, honor, teamwork, responsibility, rule of law, restraint in the use of power, respect for others, must be introduced, illustrated, and transformed somehow into habits. In this process the roles of the school and the teacher are not only legitimate; they are irreducible, irreplaceable.

Notes

DICTATORSHIPS AND DOUBLE
STANDARDS

1. *Time*, December 18, 1979, p. 33.

2. *The New York Times*, June 28, 1979.

3. Viron Vaky, reported in *The New York Times*, June 27, 1979.

4. *The Washington Post*, June 27, 1979.

5. John Stuart Mill, *Considerations on Representative Government* (Indianapolis, Ind.: Bobbs-Merrill Co., Inc. 1958), p. 56.

6. *The New York Times*, July 12, 1979.

7. *Ibid.*

8. Concerning Latin America, Brzezinski observed: "Latin American nationalism, more and more radical as it widens its popular base, will be directed with increasing animosity against the United States unless the United States rapidly shifts its own posture. Accordingly, it would be wise for the United States to make an explicit move to abandon the Monroe Doctrine and to concede that in the new global age geographic or hemispheric contiguity no longer need be politically decisive. Nothing could be healthier for Pan-American relations than for the United States to place them on the same level as its relations with the rest of the world, confining itself to emphasis on cultural-political affinities (as it does with Western Europe) and economic-social obligations (as it does with less-developed countries)." Zbigniew Brzezinski, *Between Two Ages: America's Role in the Technetronic Era* (New York: The Viking Press, 1970), p. 274.

9. James O'Connell, "The Concept of Modernization," in *Comparative Modernization*, Cyril E. Black, ed. (New York: The Free Press, 1976), p. 13.

10. Samuel P. Huntington, "The Change to Change: Modernization, Development and Politics," *Comparative Politics III* (April 1971), pp. 283–322.

11. *Department of State Bulletin*, March 1979, p. 21.

12. *Ibid.*, April 1979, p. 4.

13. *Ibid.*, February 1979, p. 47.

14. *Ibid.*, January 1979, p. 18.

15. *Ibid.*, February 1979, p. 19.

16. *Ibid.*, p. 20.

17. *The New York Times*, August 26, 1979.

18. *Ibid.*

19. *Department of State Bulletin*, March 1979, p. 39.

20. *Ibid.*, February 1979, p. 3.

21. *Ibid.*, March 1979, p. 64.

22. *Ibid.*, February 1979, p. 20.

23. *Ibid.*, April 1979, p. 4.

24. *Ibid.*, January 1979, p. 20.

25. *Ibid.*, May 1979, p. 66.

26. *Ibid.*, September 1979, p. 55.

27. *The Washington Post*, August 3, 1979.

28. *Ibid.*

29. *Weekly Compilation of Presidential Documents*, Monday, July 30, 1979, vol. 15, no. 30, pp. 1307–08.

30. *The New York Times*, August 10, 1979.

U.S. SECURITY AND LATIN AMERICA

1. Zbigniew Brzezinski, *Between Two Ages: America's Role in the Technetronic Era* (New York: The Viking Press, 1970).

2. *Ibid.*, p. 288.

3. *Ibid.*, p. 289.

4. *Ibid.*, p. 288.

5. *The Americas in a Changing World*, report by the Commission on United States-Latin American Relations, Center for Inter-American Relations, October 1974, p. 2.

6. *The United States and Latin America: Next Steps*, Center for Inter-American Relations, December 20, 1976.

7. *The Southern Connection: Recommendations for a New Approach to Inter-American Relations*, Ad-Hoc Working Group on Latin America, the Transnational Institute, a program of the Institute for Policy Studies, Washington, D.C., February 1977.

8. *Ibid.*, p. 3.

9. *Ibid.*, p. 4.

10. *Ibid.*, p. 5.

11. *Ibid.*, p. 6.

12. *Department of State Bulletin*, November 1979, pp. 54–55.

13. William P. Bundy, "Who Lost Patagonia? Foreign Policy in the 1980 Campaign," *Foreign Affairs*, Fall 1979, vol. 58, no. 1, p. 10.

14. *Department of State Bulletin*, April 1979, p. 61.

15. *Ibid.*, September 1978, p. 55.

16. Statement to House Subcommittee on Inter-American Affairs, May 20, 1980.

17. *U.S. Policy Toward Nicaragua*, Hearings of Subcommittee on Inter-American Affairs, June 21–26, 1979, p. 40.

18. William Bundy, *op. cit.*, p. 9.

19. *Department of State Bulletin*, April 1979, p. 58.

20. *Ibid.*, p. 62.

21. *Ibid.*, March 1980, p. 69.

22. *The Economist*, May 10, 1980, p. 22.

23. Max Weber, in *Economy and Society*, Gunther, Roth and

Wittich, eds. (New York: Bedminister Press, 1968), p. 213.

24. Jean Jacques Rousseau, *The Social Contract and Discourses*, translated with introduction by G. D. H. Cole (London: J. M. Dent & Sons, 1913), p. 188.

25. *Ibid.*

26. Plato, *The Republic* (Oxford, England: Clarendon Press, 1941).

27. Harold D. Lasswell and Daniel Lerner, eds., *World Revolutionary Elites: Studies in Coercive Ideological Movements* (Cambridge, Mass.: MIT Press, 1965).

REFLECTIONS ON TOTALITARIANISM:
I. THE COUNTERCULTURE OF
TOTALITARIANISM

1. As Giovanni Sartori points out in his brilliant book on democracy, conventional definitions are not arbitrary in the sense that they permit each individual to define words for himself. Conventional usage refers to habitual use and understanding in the society. Conventional definitions derive from *history*, not from arbitrary and idiosyncratic attribution of meaning to symbols. Giovanni Sartori, *Democratic Theory* (New York: Praeger, 1967).

2. Gabriel A. Almond and G. Bingham Powell, Jr., *Comparative Politics: A Developmental Approach*, Little, Brown Series in Developmental Politics (Boston: Little, Brown, 1966).

3. Samuel P. Huntington, *Political Order in Changing Societies* (New Haven: Yale University Press, 1968), p. 12.

4. For a discussion of types of revolutionary change, see Chalmers Johnson, *Revolutionary Change* (Boston: Little, Brown, 1966). Also Lyford P. Edwards, *The Natural History of Revolution* (Chicago: University of Chicago Press, 1927), and Crase Breaton, *A Decade of Revolution: 1789–1799* (New York: Harper Torchbooks, 1934).

5. For persuasive statements of this distinction and its importance, see R. M. MacIver, *The Web of Government* (New York: Macmillan, 1947), and *The Modern State* (London: Oxford University Press, 1926). A classic modern statement is, of course, J. S. Mill, *On Liberty* (New York: Liberal Arts Press, 1956).

6. The realization that government could serve to increase as well as to limit freedom is a landmark in the evolution of modern liberalism. See especially T. H. Green, *Lectures on the Principles of Political Obligation* (London: Longmans, Green, 1941).

7. C. J. Friedrich, "The Evolving Theory and Practice of Totalitarian Regimes," in Friedrich, Michael Curtis, and Benjamin R. Barber, *Totalitarianism in Perspective: Three Views* (New York: Praeger, 1969), p. 126. See also Huntington's description of "revolutionary one-party regimes," "Social and Institutional Dynamics of One-Party Systems," in Samuel P. Huntington and Clement H. Moore, eds., *Authoritarian Politics*

in Modern Society (New York: Basic Books, 1970), pp. 3–44. On the same subject see Raymond Aron, *Democracy and Totalitarianism: A Theory of Political Regimes* (New York: Praeger, 1968); Paul T. Mason, *Totalitarianism: Temporary Madness or Permanent Danger* (Boston: D. C. Heath, 1967); William Ebenstein, *Totalitarianism: New Perspectives* (New York: Holt, Rinehart and Winston, 1962); Carl J. Friedrich, and Zbigniew K. Brzezinski, *Totalitarian Dictatorship and Autocracy* (Cambridge, Mass.: Harvard University Press, 1956); J. L. Talmon, *The Origins of Totalitarian Democracy* (Boston: Beacon Paperbacks, 1960).

8. J. L. Talmon has emphasized the relationship between utopianism and totalitarianism in his excellent books, *Political Messianism: The Romantic Phase* (New York: Praeger, 1960), and *The Origins of Totalitarian Democracy* (New York: W. W. Norton, 1970).

9. On utopian thought, see especially Talmon, *ibid.*; George Kateb, *Utopia and Its Enemies* (New York: Schocken, 1972); Lewis Mumford, *The Story of Utopia* (New York: Viking, 1962); J. O. Hertzder, *The History of Utopian Thought* (New York: Macmillan, 1923).

10. On assumptions of perfectibility, see especially John Passmore, *The Perfectibility of Man* (New York: Charles Scribner's Sons, 1970).

11. Lenin's doctrine of the seduction of the working class in capitalist countries added a new detail to the false consciousness of the masses. V. I. Lenin, *Imperialism: The Highest Stage of Capitalism* (New York: International Publishing Company, 1969).

12. *Mein Kampf*, p. 29.

13. *Ibid.*, p. 30.

14. *Ibid.*, p. 41.

15. *Ibid.*, pp. 24–25.

16. *Ibid.*, p. 29.

17. *Ibid.*, p. 26.

18. *Ibid.*

19. *Ibid.*, pp. 32–33.

20. *Ibid.*, pp. 407–12.

21. *Ibid.*, p. 412.

22. *Ibid.*, p. 334.

23. *Ibid.*, p. 68.

24. *Ibid.*, p. 77.

25. *Ibid.*, p. 90.

26. *Ibid.*, p. 115.

27. *Ibid.*, p. 42.

28. *Ibid.*, p. 63.

29. *Ibid.*, p. 391.

30. *Ibid.*, p. 383.

31. *Ibid.*, p. 396.

32. *Ibid.*, p. 329.

33. *Ibid.*, p. 318. One finds an interesting echo of this notion that the lowest class will be the least well socialized in Sartre's comment on how Cuban revolutionaries "quickly discovered the only instrument capable of carrying them out: the people—and especially the most numerous and disinherited class: the agricultural workers." *Sartre on Cuba* (New York: Ballantine Books, 1960), p. 157. Note, too, that when Marx identified the industrial worker as the potential revolutionary, he conceived him to be alienated from law, religion,

values—in short, from his culture. He turned out to be right about the psychological characteristics of revolutionaries if not of industrial working classes. (See Herbert McClosky and Giuseppe di Palma on anomie for fascinating empirical data on the incidence and distribution of anomie in this society; Herbert McClosky and Giuseppe di Palma, "Personality and Conformity, The Learning of Political Attitudes," *American Political Science Review*, 1970, vol. 64, pp. 1054–73.) The assumption that working classes will be alienated has led to many mistakes in the calculations of revolutionaries. Today's revolutionaries understand that imperfectly socialized agents of revolution are to be found not on the assembly lines, but in the schools and universities, the prisons and halfway houses.

34. *Mein Kampf*, p. 170.

35. Several studies of revolutionary character reflect the psychological bases of revolution. See, for example, H. D. Lasswell, *Psychopathology and Politics* (Chicago: University of Chicago Press, 1930).

36. "The Single Party as Source of Legitimacy," in Huntington and Moore, *Authoritarian Politics in Modern Society*, p. 57.

37. A fifth-grade child of my acquaintance recently expressed strong disapproval of the Boston Tea Party with the comment: "I think it was terrible, dumping all that tea into the harbor. Think of the pollution it caused."

38. *Works*, quoted in Bertram

D. Wolfe, *Marxism: 100 Years of the Life of a Doctrine* (New York: Dial Press, 1964), p. 202.

39. *Writings of the Young Marx on Philosophy and Society*, Lloyd D. Easton and Kurt H. Guddat, eds. (New York: Doubleday, 1970), p. 304.

40. See John Harvey Bunzel, *Anti-Politics in America* (New York: Alfred A. Knopf, 1967), on the totalitarian's abhorrence of politics.

41. Peter L. Berger, "Sincerity and Authenticity in Modern Society," *The Public Interest*, No. 31 (Spring 1973), pp. 81–90. See also Marshall Berman, *The Politics of Authenticity* (New York: Atheneum, 1970).

42. *Mein Kampf*, p. 350. He asserted, "The future of a movement is conditioned by the fanaticism, yet, the intolerance, with which its adherents uphold it as the sole correct movement . . ."

43. *Mein Kampf*, p. 380. "Only when the ideal urge for independence gets a fighting organization in the form of military instruments of power can the pressing desire of a people be transformed into glorious reality.

"Every philosophy of life, even if it is a thousand times correct and of the highest benefit to humanity, will remain without significance for the practical shaping of a people's life, as long as its principles have not become the banner of a fighting movement which for its part in turn will be a party as long as its activity has not found completion in the victory of its ideas and its party dogmas have not become the mere state principles of a people's community."

Lenin on violence, 1917: "It is well known that in the long run the problems of social life are decided by . . . civil war." *Robocky-Soldat*, August 17, 1917 Lectures, p. 357.

44. *Mein Kampf*, p. 533.

45. Speech at the 3rd Soviet Congress, January 24, 1918, quoted in Merle Fainsod, *How Russia Is Ruled* (Cambridge, Mass.: Harvard University Press, 1963), p. 125.

46. Aristotle, *Politics*, translated by Ernest Barker (New York: Oxford University Press, 1946), pp. 50–51.

47. *Ibid.*

48. The Chinese self- and mutual criticism session is a superb example of totalitarian institution-building. It communicates new norms, new ideas, and new ways of relating the ideas and norms to behavior, and practice in doing so, at the same time that it systematically evaluates, rewards and/or punishes each participant's behavior. A fascinating embodiment of the unity of cultural revolution, personal reform, and political power, self- and mutual criticism works to conform behavior to the norms of the revolutionary ideology and to ensure internalization of the new norms. It is simultaneously an educational institution and the lowest court in the judicial system.

49. Friedrich, *op. cit.*, p. 153.

50. *Ibid.*, p. 154.
51. Wolfe, *op. cit.*, p. 359.

DISMANTLING THE PARTIES:
REFLECTIONS ON PARTY REFORM
AND PARTY DECOMPOSITION

1. McGovern-Fraser commission transcripts, November 19–20, 1969.

2. The most important contribution is probably that of the "responsible party" advocates. Important among these are: E. E. Schattschneider, *Party Government* (New York: Farrar and Reinhart, 1942); Stephen K. Bailey, *The Condition of Our National Parties* (New York: Fund for the Republic, 1959); James MacGregor Burns, *The Deadlock of Democracy* (Englewood Cliffs, N.J.: Prentice-Hall, 1963); David S. Broder, *The Party's Over: The Failure of Politics in America* (New York: Harper and Row, 1972). A comprehensive review of this debate is Evron M. Kirkpatrick, "Toward a More Responsible Two Party System: Political Science, Policy Science or Pseudo Science?" *American Political Science Review*, vol. 65 (1971), pp. 965–91; and Austin Ranney, *The Doctrine of Responsible Party Government* (Urbana, Ill.: University of Illinois Press, 1954). Recent discussions of party decomposition include: Walter Dean Burnham, *Critical Elections and the Mainspring of American Politics* (New York: W. W. Norton, 1970), and "The End of American Party Politics," *Trans-Action* (December

1969); Walter De Vries and Lance Turance, Jr., *The Ticket Splitters: A New Face in American Politics* (Grand Rapids, Mich.: Eerdmans, 1972); Samuel P. Huntington, "The Democratic Distemper," *The Public Interest*, no. 41 (Fall 1975); Everett Carll Ladd, Jr., "Reform Is Wrecking the U.S. Party System," *Fortune* (November 1977); Jeane Kirkpatrick, *The New Presidential Elite* (New York: Russell Sage Foundation and Twentieth Century Fund, 1976).

3. V. O. Key, *Public Opinion and American Democracy* (New York: Alfred A. Knopf, 1961), p. 433.

4. V. O. Key, *American State Politics: An Introduction* (New York: Alfred A. Knopf, 1956).

5. I am here using the concept of functions in its everyday sense; I do not intend thereby to imply a structure-functional framework or assumptions.

6. Austin Ranney provides a useful discussion of legal regulation of the parties in *Curing the Mischiefs of Faction* (Berkeley: University of California Press, 1975). This book is indispensable to the discussion of party reform.

7. The rising number of "amateurs" in positions of influence in American parties has been cogently discussed in Nelson Polsby and Aaron Wildavsky, *Presidential Elections: Strategies of American Electoral Politics*, 3rd ed. (New York: Charles Scribner's Sons, 1971), and documented in a large literature including Kirkpatrick, *New Presidential Elite*; Frank J. Sorauf, "Extra-Legal Political Parties in Wisconsin," *American Political Science Review*, vol. 48 (1954), pp. 692–704; James Q. Wilson, *The Amateur Democrat: Club Politics in Three Cities* (Chicago: University of Chicago Press, 1962); Francis Carney, *The Rise of Democratic Clubs in California* (New York: Holt, Rinehart and Winston, 1958); Stephen A. Mitchell, *Elm Street Politics* (New York: Oceana Publications, 1959); Robert S. Hirshfield, Bert E. Swanson, and Blanche D. Blank, "A Profile of Political Activists in Manhattan," *Western Political Quarterly*, vol. 15 (1962), pp. 489–507; Robert H. Salisbury, "The Urban Party Organization Member," *Public Opinion Quarterly*, vol. 29 (1965–66), pp. 550–64; Dennis S. Ippolito, "Motivational Reorientation and Change Among Party Activists," *Journal of Politics*, vol. 31 (1969), pp. 1098–1101; Leon D. Epstein, "Who Voted for McGovern," *The Wisconsin American Politics Quarterly*, vol. 1, no. 4 (October 1973); Leon D. Epstein, *Political Parties in Western Democracies* (New York: Frederick A. Praeger, 1967), pp. 122–26; Donald C. Blaisdell, *The Riverside Democrats*, Cases in Practical Politics, no. 18 (New Brunswick, N.J.: Eagleton Institute, 1960); C. Richard Hofstetter, "Organizational Activists: The Bases of Participation in Amateur and Professional Groups," *American Politics Quarterly*, vol. 1 (1973), pp. 244–76.

8. Ranney, *Mischiefs of Faction*, p. 196.

9. *Mandate for Reform*, Report of the Commission on Party Structure and Delegate Selection (Washington, D.C.: Democratic National Committee, 1970).

10. Richard G. Stearns, "The Presidential Nominating Process in the United States: The Constitution of the Democratic National Convention" (thesis submitted to Balliol College, Oxford University, June 1971).

11. Kirkpatrick, *New Presidential Elite*, chap. 2. See also 1972 delegate surveys done by the Washington Post and CBS.

12. Kirkpatrick, *New Presidential Elite*, especially chap. 5.

13. Washington Post delegate survey, reported July 11, 1976. Also confirmed in a delegate survey conducted by the Democratic National Committee.

14. Jeane Kirkpatrick, "Why the New Right Lost," *Commentary*, vol. 63, no. 2 (February 1977).

15. Washington Post survey, reported August 17, 1976.

16. Epstein, *Political Parties*, p. 253.

17. A useful discussion of incentives to political activity is James Q. Wilson, *Political Organizations* (New York: Basic Books, 1973). See also Wilson, *Amateur Democrat*.

18. Investigation of the class basis of the new politics is still in its early stages. A suggestive treatment is Everett Carll Ladd, Jr.,

with Charles D. Hadley, *Transformations of the American Party System* (New York: W. W. Norton, 1975). Also Kirkpatrick, *New Presidential Elite*, and Kevin Phillips, *Mediacracy* (Garden City, N.Y.: Doubleday, 1975).

19. CBS and Washington Post 1976 delegate surveys (data supplied by the Democratic National Committee's Commission on Presidential Nomination and Party Structure).

20. Kirkpatrick, *New Presidential Elite*, chap. 10; Ladd, "Reform," pp. 177–78.

21. It has repeatedly been asserted that the Watergate break-in and other "dirty tricks" would not have occurred had the Nixon reelection effort been conducted by an organization with multiple loyalties and long-range interests.

22. Epstein, *Political Parties*, p. 77.

23. For example, Philip E. Converse and George Dupeux, "Politicization of the Electorate in France and the United States," *Public Opinion Quarterly*, vol. 26, no. 1 (1962), pp. 1–23.

24. Norman H. Nie, Sidney Verba, and John R. Petrocik, *The Changing American Voter* (New York: Twentieth Century Fund, 1976), chaps. 4, 5.

25. See especially Arthur H. Miller, "Political Issues and Trust in Government: 1964–1970," *American Political Science Review*, vol. 68 (September 1974), pp. 951–72, and Jack Citrin, "Comment:

The Political Relevance of Trust in Government," in the same issue, pp. 973–88.

26. An interesting discussion is Michael J. Robinson, "Television and American Politics: 1956–1976," *The Public Interest*, vol. 48 (Summer 1977), pp. 3–39.

27. The classic work on party identification remains Angus Campbell, Philip E. Converse, Warren E. Miller, and Donald E. Stokes, *The American Voter* (New York: John Wiley & Sons, 1960). It has been confirmed and extended by a large body of literature on party and socialization.

28. For a recent consideration of socialization and party identification, see Paul Allen Beck, "A Socialization Theory of Partisan Realignment," in Richard G. Niemi and associates, *The Politics of Future Citizens* (San Francisco: Jossey-Bass, 1974), pp. 199–219.

29. Schattschneider, *Party Government*, p. 61.

30. *Ibid.*, p. 11.

31. Giovanni Sartori, *Parties and Party Systems: A Framework for Analysis* (Cambridge: Cambridge University Press, 1976), p. ix.

32. Some studies which describe these changes in America are: Wilson, *Amateur Democrat*; Robert A. Dahl, *Who Governs: Democracy and Party in an American City* (New Haven: Yale University Press, 1960); and Ladd, *Transformations*. There is a large literature on the subject of shifting elites ranging from Plato through Mosca and Pareto to Lasswell.

33. John F. Banzhaf III, "One Man, 3,312 Votes: A Mathematical Analysis of the Electoral Colleges," *Villanova Law Review*, vol. 13 (Winter 1968), pp. 304–31.

34. Wallace S. Sayre and Judith H. Parris, *Voting for President: The Electoral College and the American Political System* (Washington, D.C.: Brookings Institution, 1970), p. 19. A recent argument, brilliantly stated, against abolition is Martin Diamond, *The Electoral College and the American Idea of Democracy* (Washington, D.C.: American Enterprise Institute, 1977). There is a large literature on both sides of this issue.

35. Many black and liberal organizations and spokesmen understand this and support retention of the present system.

36. Alexander M. Bickel, *Reform and Continuity: The Electoral College, the Convention and the Party System* (New York: Harper Torchbooks, 1971).

37. *Ibid.*, p. 2.

38. Key, *State Politics*, p. 153.

39. Cultural, geographic, and economic minorities are among those whose electoral clout would be decreased.

40. Note that the French experience has illustrated the appeal of such presidential races to spokespersons for the environment and women's rights, right-to-lifers, and other such issue constituencies.

41. On primary turnout, see

Austin Ranney's monograph, *Participation in American Presidential Nominations*, 1976 (Washington, D.C.: American Enterprise Institute, 1977).

WHY THE NEW RIGHT LOST
1. *The Emerging Republican Majority* (New Rochelle, N.Y.: Arlington House, 1969) and *Mediacracy: American Parties and Politics in the Communications Age* (Garden City, N.Y.: Doubleday & Co., 1975), by Kevin Phillips; *The Making of a New Majority Party* (Ottawa: Green Hill Publishers, 1975), by William A. Rusher; *Conservative Votes, Liberal Victories: Why the Right Has Failed* (New York: Times Books, 1975), by Patrick J. Buchanan; *Catch the Falling Flag: A Republican's Challenge to His Party* (Boston: Houghton Mifflin Co., 1972) and *Taking Sides: A Personal View of America from Kennedy to Nixon* (Boston: Houghton Mifflin Co., 1974), by Richard J. Whalen.

SOURCES OF STABILITY
IN THE AMERICAN TRADITION
1. An interesting discussion of these "unit ideas" of seventeenth- and eighteenth-century rationalism and of the reaction to them is Robert Nisbet, *The Sociological Tradition* (New York: Basic Books, 1966).
2. Gabriel A. Almond and Sidney Verba, *The Civic Culture: Political Attitudes and Democracy in Five Nations* (New York: Little, Brown, 1965).
3. Carl Van Doren, *The Great Rehearsal* (New York: The Viking Press, 1948), pp. 192–93.
4. Austin Ranney, APSA Presidential Address, "The Divine Science: Political Engineering in American Culture," *American Political Science Review*, vol. 70 (March 1976), pp. 140–48; W. H. Greenleaf, *Order, Empiricism and Politics: Two Traditions of English Political Thought, 1500–1700* (London: Oxford University Press, 1964); Bernard Bailyn, *The Ideological Origins of the American Revolution* (Cambridge, Mass.: Harvard University Press, 1967).
5. Quoted in Donald Kagan, *The Great Dialogue: History of Greek Political Thought from Homer to Polybius* (New York: The Free Press, 1965), p. 256.
6. *Federalist Papers*, p. 138. This and all other quotations from the *Federalist Papers* are from the New American Library edition (New York: Mentor Books, 1961). This edition was prepared by Clinton Rossiter, who also provided an introduction and index of ideas.
7. *Ibid.*, p. 276.
8. *Ibid.*, p. 57.
9. *Ibid.*, p. 59.
10. *Ibid.*, p. 192.
11. *Ibid.*, p. 113.
12. *Ibid.*, p. 193.
13. *Ibid.*, p. 72.
14. *Ibid.*, p. 104.
15. *Ibid.*, p. 255.
16. *Ibid.*, p. 78.
17. *Ibid.*, p. 34.

18. *Ibid.*, p. 315.

19. Harold D. Lasswell's eight "representative" values provide a useful checklist of the values which have motivated men. For an explication of value institutional analysis see, e.g., Harold D. Lasswell and Abraham Kaplan, *Power and Society* (New Haven: Yale University Press, 1950).

20. *Federalist Papers*, p. 81.

21. *Ibid.*, p. 79.

22. *Ibid.*, p. 54.

23. *Ibid.*, p. 81.

24. *Ibid.*, p. 80.

25. *Ibid.*, p. 78.

26. Quoted in Kagan, *Great Dialogue*, p. 256. It should be noted, though, that Polybius and Montesquieu, both of whom emphasized the importance of a mixed constitution to a good polity, also emphasized the importance of a virtuous people as the basis of such a society.

27. Willmoore Kendall and George W. Carey, *Basic Symbols of the American Political Tradition* (Baton Rouge, La.: Louisiana State University Press, 1970). Note, however, that Greene asserts that the "most considerable departure from traditional political wisdom was the idea that, contrary to the dictum of Montesquieu, public virtue might not be requisite for a popular republican government—especially if such a government extended over a large area." Jack P. Greene, "Values and Society in Revolutionary America," *Annals*, AAPSS, no. 426 (July 1976), p. 59.

28. *Federalist Papers*, p. 353.

29. *Ibid.*, p. 72.

30. *Ibid.*, p. 100.

31. *Ibid.*, p. 327.

32. *Ibid.*, p. 119.

33. *Ibid.*, p. 112.

34. George W. Carey, "Majority Tyranny and the Extended Republic Theory of James Madison," *Modern Age*, Winter 1976, p. 50.

35. On the doctrine of separation of powers in the U.S. Constitution, see especially Montesquieu, *The Spirit of the Laws*, translated by Thomas Nugent (New York: Hafner Publishing Co., 1949), and the introduction by Franz Neumann. Also Carl J. Friedrich and Robert G. McCloskey, *From the Declaration of Independence to the Constitution: The Roots of American Constitutionalism* (Indianapolis: Bobbs-Merrill, 1954), pp. xiv–xviii. On the influence of Montesquieu on the authors of the Constitution, see especially Paul M. Spurlin, *Montesquieu in America* (Baton Rouge, La.: Louisiana State University Press, 1940).

36. *Federalist Papers*, p. 322.

37. *Ibid.*

38. *Ibid.*, p. 320.

39. *Ibid.*

40. *Ibid.*, p. 351.

41. *Ibid.*, p. 345.

42. *Ibid.*, p. 352.

43. *Ibid.*, p. 342.

44. *Ibid.*, p. 315.

45. Martin Diamond, *The Electoral College and the American Idea of Democracy* (Washington, D.C.: American Enterprise Institute, 1977), p. 14.

Index